Building the Beloved Community

Building the Beloved Community

Philadelphia's Interracial Civil Rights Organizations and Race Relations, 1930–1970

Stanley Keith Arnold

UNIVERSITY PRESS OF MISSISSIPPI
JACKSON

www.upress.state.ms.us

The University Press of Mississippi is a member of the Association of American University Presses.

Copyright © 2014 by University Press of Mississippi
All rights reserved
Manufactured in the United States of America

First printing 2014

∞

Library of Congress Cataloging-in-Publication Data

Arnold, Stanley Keith.
 Building the beloved community : Philadelphia's interracial civil rights organizations and race relations, 1930–1970 / Stanley Keith Arnold.
   pages cm
 Includes bibliographical references and index.
 ISBN 978-1-62846-002-5 (hardback) — ISBN 978-1-62846-003-2 (ebook) 1. Civil rights movements—Pennsylvania—Philadelphia—History—20th century. 2. Community life—Pennsylvania—Philadelphia—History—20th century. 3. Community activists—Pennsylvania—Philadelphia—History—20th century. 4. Fellowship House—History. 5. Philadelphia Housing Association—History. 6. Fellowship Commission (Philadelphia, Pa.)—History. 7. Education—Social aspects—Philadelphia—History—20th century. 8. Housing—Philadelphia—History—20th century. 9. Labor—Social aspects—Philadelphia—History—20th century. 10. Philadelphia (Pa.)—Race relations—History—20th century. I. Title.
 F158.9.A1A76 2014
 305.8009748'11—dc23   2013046786

British Library Cataloging-in-Publication Data available

To the memory of my mother,

Dorothy Milverne Bagby Arnold,

and first cousin, Evelyn Dolores Warrick

Contents

Acknowledgments
 ix

Abbreviations
 xi

Introduction
 3

1: By the Waters of Babylon
 The Origins of the Interracial Movement
 8

2: So That All Might Learn
 Education and the Interracial Civil Rights Movement, 1931–1946
 26

3: Education for Democracy
 The Interracial Civil Rights Movement and Intercultural and Desegregated Education, 1947–1970
 45

4: A House of Many Mansions
 Race, Housing, and the Interracial Civil Rights Community, 1930–1946
 68

5: The House We Live In
 Race and Housing in the Postwar World, 1946–1970
 86

6: Labor in the Vineyard
 The Interracial Civil Rights Movement and the Struggle for Equality in Employment
 111

Epilogue
Every Man 'neath His Vine and Fig Tree Shall Live in Peace and Unafraid
133

Notes
137

Bibliography
161

Index
171

Acknowledgments

I AM FOREVER INDEBTED TO THE FACULTY, COLLEAGUES, FRIENDS, AND family without whom this book could not have been finished, especially Kenneth Kusmer, Bettye Collier-Thomas, Wilbert Jenkins, and Randall Miller. I am deeply thankful for their patience, encouragement, and criticism. A special thanks to Gail Jacky of the NIU Writing Center, who proofread the manuscript.

As a former archivist, I realize how important these professionals are to the research process. I would like to thank the staff at the Peace Collection at Swarthmore College and the Manuscript Division at the Library of Congress. I am especially thankful to the present and former staff of the Urban Archives at Temple University: Brenda Galloway-Wright, George Brightbill, and Margaret Jerrido.

This book would not have come to fruition without the enthusiasm, participation, and vision of the many people associated with the interracial civil rights movement. I am forever indebted to Sue Angrie, Roosevelt and Virginia Barlow, Mitzi Jacoby Barnes, Cushing Dolbeare, Mohammed Latif, Louis Massiah, Gladys Rawlins, Susan Rosenbloom, Val Udell, Randolph Walker, and Aura Yores. I owe a tremendous debt to the late Helen Stark Tomkins, former director of Fellowship Farm. Helen Tomkins introduced me to many of these pioneering activists, provided me with a tour of the Farm, and offered unqualified encouragement and insight.

Northern Illinois University has been my academic home since 2002. At Northern I have been extremely fortunate to work with a distinguished and supportive cadre of historians. Special thanks to E. Taylor Atkins, Sundiata Djata, Aaron Fogleman, and Beatrix Hoffman for their insightful comments and unflagging support. A paid research leave from NIU contributed to the completion of this project.

I have been extremely fortunate to work with the University Press of Mississippi. Acquisitions editor Walter Biggins has shepherded this project from the beginning. I owe him my deepest thanks for his wisdom, guidance, and patience.

I am grateful for the support of so many friends over the years. I thank Najia Aarim-Heriot, Simon Davis, Ann Dougherty, Robert Doan, John and Mary Jureller, Andrew Moore, Andrew Newkirk, Philip Nwankwo, Eric Schlaf, Frank Sundram, Joseph and Jennifer Trachtman, and Diane Turner.

Finally, my extended family has provided both emotional and spiritual support. I would like to thank the many members of the Arnold/Drew, Bagby, and McGowan families for their unwavering encouragement. My mother, the late Dorothy Milverne Bagby Arnold, instilled in me a love for history and a passion for racial justice. Her spirit continues to influence me.

My sons Luke and Dylan McGowan-Arnold have enriched my life and inspired this work. Although I have often been preoccupied by my research, they understood the need for me to work on this project, cheerfully commenting "How's that book comin' along?" My wife, Beth Ann McGowan, has lived with this project for many years. Words cannot describe my heartfelt gratitude for her love, patience, criticism, editing, and incredible sacrifice. Any credit or praise I receive for this endeavor is shared by Beth. Without her, this project would have never been completed.

Abbreviations

AFSC	American Friends Service Committee
CAP	Community Action Program
CCCP	Citizens Council on City Planning
CCDR	Citizens Council on Democratic Rights
CCT	Committee on Community Tensions
CDH	Committee on Democracy in Housing
CEC	Citizens Emergency Committee
CEHO	Committee on Equal Housing Opportunities
CEJO	Committee on Equal Job Opportunities
CFCC	Committee for a Free City College
CHR	Committee on Human Relations
CIC	Commission on Interracial Cooperation
CPA	Colored Protective Association
CPHP	Committee on Public Housing Planning
CPUSA	Communist Party United States of America
CRR	Committee on Race Relations
CWIC	City Wide Interracial Committee
EEL	Educational Equality League
EPPC	Educational Policy and Planning Committee
FHC	Fair Housing Commission
FSH	Friends Suburban Housing
GPM	Greater Philadelphia Movement
ILD	International Labor Defense
JADC	Jewish Anti-Defamation Council
JCMH	Joint Committee on Minority Housing
JCRC	Jewish Community Relations Committee
JOY	Job Opportunities for Youth
MTW	Marine Transport Workers
NNC	National Negro Congress
OIC	Opportunities Industrialization Centers
PACH	Philadelphia Advisory Committee on Housing
PCC	Philadelphia Charter Commission
PCHR	Philadelphia Commission on Human Relations
PHA	Philadelphia Housing Association
PRTEU	Philadelphia Rapid Transit Employees Union
YPIF	Young Peoples Interracial Fellowship

Building the Beloved Community

Introduction

IN HIS BOOK *STRIDE TOWARD FREEDOM*, MARTIN LUTHER KING DESCRIBED his introduction to the theories of Mohandas Gandhi at a lecture hosted by Fellowship House, a Philadelphia-based interracial civil rights organization. In the postwar era, Fellowship House formed the core of a dynamic local movement that influenced the development of a national network of locally based interracial civil rights organizations, helped to redefine race relations in the Philadelphia area, and contributed to the growth of the modern civil rights movement. These organizations, which were founded decades before the modern civil rights movement, not only shaped the struggle but also laid the groundwork for a philosophy that later became known as multiculturalism.

This book examines Fellowship House; the Fellowship Commission; and the Philadelphia Housing Association (Housing Association of the Delaware Valley). All of these organizations were established between 1909 and 1941 and had their greatest impact on the national civil rights movement and Philadelphia from World War II to the end of the 1960s. On the local and state level, they were successful in the passage of major civil rights legislation and ameliorating racial tension. Their influence on the trajectory of the civil rights movement would have national and international implications.[1]

Since the late 1960s, scholars have studied the modern civil rights struggle. Most of the early studies examined this movement from a rather limited perspective. These embryonic works focused on the contributions of national organizations such as the NAACP. In addition, these early works tended to focus on the efforts to pass civil rights legislation. Thus, there was little attention paid to the role of local movements whose tactics and objectives were often more complex. By the early 1980s new trends in the historiography began to appear. Increasingly, scholars suggested that grassroots efforts played an important role in transforming American society.

Two other trends also emerged from the scholarship. The first emphasized the intellectual and political roots of the modern civil rights movement. Known as "The Long Civil Rights Movement," this approach moves beyond what Bayard Rustin termed the classical period of the movement. In addition to exploring the foundations of the movement, scholars representing this emerging tradition examine the impact of the civil rights struggle on the understudied struggles of the 1970s and 1980s.

In the earlier scholarship, the movement to confront racism had often been cast as solely a southern movement. Scholars began to examine civil rights campaigns in locales outside the South. By placing these local and regional efforts within a national context, these studies have redefined and broadened our notion of the civil rights movement. These include Arnold Hirsch's *Making the Second Ghetto* (1984) and James Ralph's *Northern Protest: Martin Luther King, Jr., Chicago, and the Civil Rights Movement* (1990). Ralph provides an excellent analysis of the community-based Chicago Freedom Movement and the struggle for open housing in the Windy City. My work complements this pioneering scholarship.

In addition to Chicago, race relations in other northern cities have been well documented. Martha Biondi's *To Stand and Fight: The Struggle for Civil Rights in Postwar New York City* (2003); Robert Self's *American Babylon: Race and the Struggle for Postwar Oakland* (2005); and Patrick D. Jones's *The Selma of the North: Civil Rights Insurgency in Milwaukee* (2009) all focus on specific yet understudied cities within the context of the broader civil rights movement. Thomas Sugrue's pioneering work, *Origins of the Urban Crisis: Race and Inequality in Postwar Detroit* (1997), analyzes the volatile intersection of race, housing, and labor in the Motor City. His subsequent work, *Sweet Land of Liberty* (2008), examines this movement from a comparative and national perspective. Sugrue's exploration of civil rights struggles in small cities and suburban communities indicates there is still much to be uncovered. Edited by Jeanne Theoharis and Komozi Woodard, *Freedom North: Black Freedom Struggles Outside the South, 1940–1980* (2003) covers struggles across the nation. Along with Charles Payne, Woodard and Theoharis produced an excellent collection of essays, *Groundwork: Local Black Freedom Movements in America* (2005). More recently, *African American History Since World War II* (2009), edited by Kenneth L. Kusmer and Joe W. Trotter, contributes to this rapidly evolving field.

The role of postwar civil rights in Philadelphia has been gaining more attention. Matthew Countryman's *Up South: Civil Rights and Black Power in Philadelphia* (2008) examines the growth of black militancy in the Quaker City. His work traces the increasing radicalization among community-based activists from the late 1950s through the 1970s. The simmering cauldron of race and politics is also explored in James Wolfinger's *Philadelphia Divided: Race and Politics in the City of Brotherly Love* (2009). Wolfinger focuses on how Republican leaders exploited racial fears to redefine their party as the protector of white working-class voters. This contributed to a rightward shift in the local Democratic Party in the early 1960s. One of the major areas of racial conflict involved the labor market. In Philadelphia, black employment had historically been concentrated in domestic service and temporary work. With the advent of the New Deal and the economic boom of World War II, the attainment of traditional blue-collar employment became a goal. Guian McKee's work, *The Problem of Jobs: Liberalism, Race, and Deindustrialization in Philadelphia* examines the efforts to halt economic inequality. McKee's work demonstrates that local policymakers and community activists developed innovative programs to address chronic unemployment and looming deindustrialization. Although all of these works represent important contributions to the field, none examine the crucial influence of interracial organizations.

This book enhances the existing scholarship by focusing on an influential interracial civil rights movement in a critically strategic northern city. It is not, however, solely an organizational history. Rather, my work tells the story of a series of movements linked by an evolving philosophy of nascent multiculturalism. This study utilizes these organizations as a prism through which to view changing race relations in the Philadelphia region and the nation. This work investigates the movement's activism in three distinct, yet related, areas: education (primary through higher), housing, and labor. These three issues have been flashpoints of racial conflict in twentieth-century urban America and were principal areas of interest for these activists.

Most importantly, *Building the Beloved Community* constitutes a revealing intellectual history of Philadelphia's organizations and activists. Although their roots lay in Progressivism, the Social Gospel movement, and Quakerism, they were deeply influenced by the theories of pioneering scholars such as W. E. B. Du Bois, Ruth Benedict, and Franz Boas. These scholars challenged long-held notions of racial essentialism and began a dialogue that contributed in no small way to the transformation of race relations. Philadelphia's activists adapted the theories of these scholars to real-life situations. In contrast to activists in Chicago or New York who often worked closely with academic sympathizers, these activists had few comparable supporters at the University of Pennsylvania or Temple University. Although they worked closely with Swarthmore College's Institute of Race Relations, the relative dearth of intellectual involvement from the region's most prominent research institutions allowed these activists to experiment with new approaches.

This book has been arranged both chronologically and thematically. While the first approach provides a historical timeline, the second allows the reader the ability to focus on a specific issue. The first chapter, "By the

Waters of Babylon: The Origins of the Interracial Movement," examines the social and intellectual factors that contributed to the emergence of this development in the twentieth century. Philadelphia's unique position as a center of Quaker-influenced abolitionism in the nineteenth century fostered an environment where blacks and whites had a tradition of working together on issues of race. Although Quaker activism declined in the aftermath of the Civil War, demographic, social, and political factors contributed to a new assault on racism in the early twentieth century. The Great Migration and growing black militancy coupled with Progressivism and new scholarship on race fostered a dynamic synthesis among a pioneering cohort of activists.

The second chapter, "So That All Might Learn: Education and the Interracial Civil Rights Movement, 1931–1946," focuses on the rise of the Fellowship House, an institution modeled on the settlement houses of the Progressive era, and the Fellowship Commission, a coalition of local and national civil rights agencies. I examine education both as a tool for social change and an area of public policy. Founded by a young white artist, Marjorie Penney, and a black minister, E. Luther Cunningham, Fellowship House initiated an ambitious range of educational programs. Some of these efforts were oriented toward adults while others were aimed at schoolchildren. While the Fellowship House employed a grass-roots approach, the Fellowship Commission took the lead in mobilizing support for legislative changes. Their increasing calls for desegregation would create an uneasy relationship with the city's troubled school district.

In chapter 3, "Education for Democracy: The Interracial Civil Rights Movement and Intercultural and Desegregated Education, 1947–1970," I chronicle the movement's increasing alliance with the city's Reform Democrats. Although initially non-partisan, the interracial civil rights movement aligned itself with politicians interested in supporting civil rights legislation. Fellowship House opened a farm in the 1950s that served as a training ground for a generation of civil rights activists. Efforts to desegregate Philadelphia's schools continued while the movement successfully helped to create the Community College of Philadelphia, the city's first educational institution open to all races. In addition to their public policy work, these organizations laid the groundwork for multiculturalism.

In the fourth chapter, "A House of Many Mansions: Race, Housing, and the Interracial Civil Rights Community, 1930–1946," I chronicle how the movement addressed segregated housing in Philadelphia. This chapter introduces the Housing Association (PHA), later known as the Housing

Association of the Delaware Valley. While the PHA focused initially on slum clearance, by the 1940s this organization was increasingly working closely with Fellowship House and the Fellowship Commission, which lacked the expertise that the housing reformers possessed. The wartime housing shortage heightened the debate over integrated housing. Activists believed that the war would prove to be a watershed for integrated housing efforts.

Chapter 5, "The House We Live In: Race and Housing in the Postwar World, 1946–1970," explores how this movement attempted to come to terms with rapidly changing housing patterns and a new political climate. Although they found sympathetic ears among rising Democratic politicians, there was opposition to integrated housing from many white homeowners and increasing indifference from elements of the black community. In order to focus their efforts, the movement created the Committee for Democracy in Housing. Fellowship House worked at the community level to alleviate tension. Despite opposition to integrated housing, the movement was successful in securing the passage of Philadelphia's first fair housing law. This period would also witness the growing evolution of the Housing Association, which linked housing discrimination to issues such as the Vietnam War.

The last chapter, "Labor in the Vineyard: The Interracial Civil Rights Movement and the Struggle for Equality in Employment," focuses on the efforts of these activists to address workforce discrimination. Although labor did not receive as much attention as other areas, the organizations were crucial in the passage of city and statewide fair employment legislation. Despite their public policy successes, the changing nature of the labor market presented more daunting challenges for these activists.

The contribution of these activists cannot be overstated. In the face of indifference and opposition, they envisioned a world where the contributions of all racial and ethnic groups would be celebrated. While not the entire history of multiculturalism, Philadelphia's interracial civil rights movement created innovative educational programs that are now common in American schools and workplaces. Aware that laws as well as hearts needed to be transformed, these activists formed political coalitions to agitate for legislative changes. The epilogue assesses the movement's impact on Philadelphia, the nation, and the world.

CHAPTER 1

By the Waters of Babylon

The Origins of the Interracial Movement

THE CITY OF BROTHERLY LOVE HAS NOT ALWAYS LIVED UP TO ITS NAME. Its past has witnessed brutal racial, religious, and class conflicts. Yet its history also includes those who challenged accepted prejudices and sought to bridge these chasms of ignorance and hatred. This chapter examines the origins and early development of this activist spirit in Philadelphia. The interracial civil rights movement that emerged in the 1930s was influenced by Quakerism, the Social Gospel movement, Progressivism, and new academic trends in the study of race. How did these activists weave disparate strands of thought and action into a movement?

In 1688 dissident German Quakers staged the first organized protest against slavery in British North America in Germantown (now a section of Philadelphia). Despite Quaker founder George Fox's antislavery views, many members of the Society of Friends held and traded slaves. Although Quakers debated the issue frequently, it was not until the mid-eighteenth century that an abolitionist organization emerged in Philadelphia, the Pennsylvania Abolition Society.[1]

In 1833, William Lloyd Garrison of Boston and Arthur and Lewis Tappan of New York organized the American Anti-Slavery Society (AASS) in Philadelphia. There were only three African American men among the sixty-two original members. Like the earlier Abolition Society, the AASS would accept blacks only as junior partners.[2] As Garrison and the Tappan brothers established their organization, Lucretia Mott, a Quaker abolitionist from neighboring Montgomery County, organized the Pennsylvania Female Anti-Slavery Society. Mott's organization welcomed women from the city's small black middle class. Shortly after the founding of Mott's organization, the Pennsylvania Anti-Slavery Society was established.[3] Blacks were instrumental in the establishment of the PASS, and by 1845 Robert Purvis, a black activist, would become its president. Purvis was involved in the creation of the Vigilance Committee, an interracial body formed to assist "colored persons in distress."[4]

Interracial cooperation in the abolition movement did not necessarily lead to agreement on the more complex issue of racial equality. As Frederick Douglass noted, the antislavery cause did not wholly embrace the black struggle for equality.[5] Philadelphia's blacks and whites served together on military recruitment committees, but after the end of the Civil War, abolitionist organizations evaporated. For black Philadelphians, the end of slavery represented the beginning of a long struggle for equal rights.

In addition to facing segregation in public accommodations such as streetcars and theatres, blacks had been excluded from voting since 1838. The leader of the effort to overcome this exclusion was Octavius Valentine Catto, principal of the Institute for Colored Youth. Catto argued that the recently passed Fifteenth Amendment mandated that Pennsylvania return the franchise to blacks. In October 1870 Pennsylvania ratified the Fifteenth Amendment, but tension grew between black Republicans and white Democrats in Philadelphia. On Election Day 1871, Philadelphia was rocked by rioting, as Democrats attempted to keep blacks from voting. At least three blacks, including Catto, were killed in the violence.

In the wake of the 1871 riots, there was a decline in interracial activity around political issues. However, blacks and whites continued to work together on the boards of black social institutions such as the Stephen Smith Home for Aged and Infirm Colored Persons.[6] By the 1890s interracial cooperation among clergymen had increased. Concern over the increasing number of poor people of both races could have been an issue since many churches were involved in charity work. The slowly rising immigrant population, mostly Catholic and Jewish, might have also prompted these Protestant clergymen to see that they had some common concerns.

The increase in dialogue laid the groundwork for limited activism. In the 1890s a small interracial group of clergymen expressed their outrage at the growing number of lynchings in the South. In 1894 anti-lynching crusader Ida Wells Barnett spoke to an integrated audience at the Smith Home. Barnett's Philadelphia appearance prompted many clergymen to denounce lynching from their pulpits, but they did not initiate any major protests.[7]

The relative absence of protest in this period could be attributed to several factors. First, there was a significant leadership vacuum in black Philadelphia in the late nineteenth century. Most of the leaders of the antislavery movement and the Civil War protest had died. In this period of increasing segregation, no new cadre of leaders emerged. While the community was energized by the founding of the *Philadelphia Tribune*, and even though blacks held the franchise, the voting population was in the hands of an increasingly corrupt Republican regime.

For the city's growing number of progressive reformers, local concerns took center stage. Many progressives castigated the black community for its electoral support of the city's corrupt Republican regime. They turned to a young black scholar, W. E. B. Du Bois, to undertake a study of the city's predominantly black Seventh Ward. The study, entitled *The Philadelphia Negro*, was the first major statistics-driven sociological study of an urban community. Although Du Bois saw the study as a blow against racial inequality, white Progressives hoped the study would expose "the corrupt, semi-criminal vote" of this area and ultimately lead to widespread municipal reform. Most of the reformers, however, refrained from confronting the ideology of racism that had created the problems.[8]

By 1900 Philadelphia had the second largest black population in the North after New York, and it was steadily increasing. Although it would be dwarfed by the Great Migration, the city's black population surged in the late nineteenth century. Most of these new arrivals came from the Chesapeake Bay region and nearby towns in Pennsylvania, New Jersey, and Delaware.[9]

The first decade of the twentieth century witnessed an increase in disfranchisement, segregation, and racial violence in the United States. More than one hundred blacks were lynched in the first year of the twentieth century. Savage race riots occurred with increasing regularity. In 1906 Atlanta was paralyzed by several days of rioting, which left twenty-five dead, dozens injured, and scores of black homes and institutions destroyed. Concerned about a recurrence of the Atlanta violence, a small number of white business leaders called for interracial dialogue. John White, a leading white clergyman, blamed the riot on lower-class whites and chastised "the better people" of the South for not formulating a successful race relations program. Anxious to assure the city's black elite, the white business community invited Booker T. Washington to Atlanta. In the wake of Washington's visit, the all-white Atlanta Civic Council and a black counterpart, the Colored Cooperative Civic League, were formed. The principal goal of these organizations was to prevent future race riots through cooperation between the "best men" of both races.[10]

Business leaders were not alone in their concern about the endemic pattern of racial violence. In 1905 a group of black activists organized by Du Bois met in Fort Erie, Ontario, and drafted a program of action that pledged opposition to disfranchisement, segregation, and other manifestations of racism. Over the next two years the Niagara Movement, a distinguished collection of black intellectuals, clergymen, and professionals, convened on a regular basis. In 1908 a race riot in Springfield, Illinois, served as a catalyst for stronger action. The Springfield riot was by far the most vicious racial conflict witnessed in the North since the Civil War. In the wake of the carnage, several white New York–based progressives initiated a conference on race that attracted Du Bois and other Niagara radicals. In 1910 the conference participants formed the National Association for the Advancement of Colored People. The NAACP was opposed to Washington's ideology of conciliation in political affairs and championed racial equality in all aspects of American life.[11]

Renewed interest about race among white reformers contributed to a growth in interracial organizations. In 1911 the National League on Urban Conditions Among Negroes was founded. Comprised of black and white reformers, the League assisted southern migrants with jobs, housing, and education. In addition to the NAACP and the Urban League, the first decade of the new century saw the emergence of the National League for the Protection of Colored Women, an interracial New York–based organization dedicated to assisting African American female migrants in northern cities.[12] In Philadelphia reformers established the Armstrong Association to address the growing migration. Headed by John Emlen, a Quaker philanthropist, this small interracial organization focused on the immediate concerns of the migrants such as jobs and housing. In 1914 the Armstrong Association became the local affiliate of the Urban League.[13]

Although there was an increasing interest in race relations among some elements of the city's white reformers, issues such as child welfare, municipal corruption, and housing reform took precedence. In 1909 a group of housing activists founded the Philadelphia Housing Commission (later the Philadelphia Housing Association) to address housing issues. Although their primary concern was not racial inequality, the Great Migration of the World War I era impelled the organization to address racial discrimination in housing.[14] The role of the Philadelphia Housing Association in the city's interracial civil rights movement will be addressed in forthcoming chapters.

Race and Religion

ALARMED AT THE POVERTY AND INEQUITY OF LATE-NINETEENTH-CENTUry urban America, Protestant clergymen developed a theology they hoped would address these problems. The Social Gospel movement attempted to utilize Christian doctrine in the remediation of contemporary crises. By the first decade of the twentieth century, most major Protestant denominations had established "social" ministries.[15]

Although they were instrumental in establishing missionary efforts in black communities across the nation, Social Gospel adherents were not primarily interested in improving race relations. As lynching and race riots occurred with increasing regularity, some in the Social Gospel movement called for a dialogue on race relations. These "social Christians" differed greatly in attitudes toward race. Some advocated continued segregation, while others preached messages of racial equality and integration.[16] In 1908 representatives of major Protestant denominations consolidated the Social Gospel movement by forming the Federal Council of Churches of Christ in Philadelphia. The council passed resolutions supporting the rights of workers, worker's compensation, and retirement pensions. Despite the presence of forty-five black ministers at this first meeting, there was little discussion about race. The Federal Council of Churches maintained that spiritual and moral uplift would improve the material conditions of the black community.[17]

As the Social Gospel movement debated problems between the races, changes were under way within the Quaker faith. By the early twentieth century, Quaker activism on racial issues had decreased. In Philadelphia, Quakers contributed to the administration of black schools and institutions but refrained from addressing lynching, disfranchisement, or Jim Crow legislation. In addition, Quakers also faced deep internal division. The schism that had created the Hicksite and Orthodox tendencies within Quakerism in the early 1800s became increasingly institutionalized in the post–Civil War period. However, the establishment of one of the first NAACP branches in Philadelphia helped stimulate interest in activism among Quakers. The presence of several prominent Quakers among the membership symbolized a return to race relations activism.[18]

It was not the nation's racial crisis but World War I that energized Quaker activism. Horrified by the carnage on European battlefields, Quaker activists formed the core of a small yet growing pacifist movement. In 1917 Quakers founded the American Friends Service Committee (AFSC), an organization dedicated to ending military conflict. This increase in activism was aided by the establishment of a Quaker study center, Woolman House, at Swarthmore College and a growing connection between the Hicksite and Orthodox members.[19] Although activism increased around pacifism, initiatives in the field of race relations were not forthcoming. It would take another decade and a major demographic transformation for Quakers to return to activism around race.

The Great Migration and the Dynamics of Race

BY THE BEGINNING OF WORLD WAR I, A MASSIVE DEMOGRAPHIC SHIFT IN the nation's black population had begun. Natural disasters, increasing segregation, economic depression, and an unrelenting cycle of race riots and lynching prompted hundreds of thousands of southern African Americans to flee the South. The need for cheap labor in the burgeoning manufacturing centers of the Northeast and Midwest also contributed to this migration. Although the war limited the steady flow of European immigrant labor, it also stimulated industrial production as France and England became increasingly dependent on American-made military goods.[20]

As large numbers of African Americans streamed to northern cities, private social service organizations and government agencies mobilized to handle the migration. Their principal concern was that racial friction in the workplace would affect industrial output. The Department of Labor created the Division of Negro Economics under the leadership of a young black sociologist, George Edmund Haynes, a recent Ph.D. from Columbia University. His dissertation on black labor in New York City inspired a group of reformers to form the Committee on Urban Conditions Among Negroes in New York, which in 1911 united with two other organizations to form the National Urban League. During the war Haynes attempted to upgrade working conditions among blacks in defense-related industries. In addition to improving workplaces, he initiated the formation of locally based interracial committees. The primary task of these committees was to reduce the rising level of racial tension in the manufacturing sector.[21] Somewhat limited in scope, Haynes focused his efforts on northern industries. In the South, Will Alexander, a young white Methodist minister, began to work on a similar joint YMCA–War Department project designed to lessen racial tension.[22]

In 1919 the nation experienced an unprecedented wave of racial violence. In the "Red Summer," twenty-five race riots left a scar of hatred across America. Socioeconomic conditions contributed to this outbreak of violence. In the wake of the war, an economic slowdown had emerged, thus fostering fierce competition over scarce jobs. In addition to the employment crisis, a severe housing shortage in northern cities added to the tension. These riots occurred in every region of the nation, affirming that the "race problem" was no longer an isolated regional crisis.[23]

In the wake of the Red Summer, Alexander initiated the formation of a permanent institution designed to improve race relations, the Commission on Interracial Cooperation (CIC). Headquartered in Atlanta, the CIC was an amorphous network of seven thousand individuals scattered across the South.[24] The CIC neither challenged segregation nor advocated racial equality, but concentrated on ending the endemic racial violence of the South. Although it enlisted the support of black leaders such as Robert Russa Moton of Tuskegee and John Hope of Atlanta University, the CIC was an overwhelmingly upper-class white male organization. The Commission's approach to race relations was openly paternalistic.[25] In his assessment of the CIC's local affiliates, Thomas Jesse Jones of the Phelps Stokes Fund, one of the CIC's northern funding sources, reported that "the negroes draw up a prospectus of what they think they should have in the way of aid and recognition from the whites. The white committee then meets, considers the complaints of the negroes, and devises means for bettering their condition."[26]

Like many reformers, Haynes was horrified by the violence of the Red Summer but lacked an organizational vehicle to utilize his theories. In 1921 Haynes found an outlet for his philosophy when he joined the staff of the Federal Council of Churches' new Commission on Race Relations. The Great Migration and the Red Summer had infused the Federal Council of Churches with a new sense of urgency. Prior to this period, race relations had been handled by a host of committees, but recent events had forced them to reexamine their position. Haynes's approach to the problem was to utilize the Federal Council of Churches to build a national network of interracial committees.[27]

Haynes argued that segregation was detrimental to both blacks and whites. His experience during World War I had convinced him that segregation fostered a perpetual climate of ignorance between the races. When contact between black and white communities occurred, it was often conflict-oriented, such as violence over scarce jobs. Haynes reasoned that if initial encounters between the races were positive, violent conflict could be avoided.[28] He argued that "Individual and group contacts also give pleasant emotional experiences that are the bases for friendly attitudes and cooperative habits or patterns or actions."[29] He believed that both black and white churches should play a central role. Haynes, an ordained Congregational minister, maintained that Christianity had enormous potential as a tool for social change. He envisioned a two pronged approach: 1) a barrage of literature distributed to civic groups, community organizations and churches would emphasize the need for racial brotherhood, and 2) using sympathetic churches as bases, local interracial committees would be established to disseminate the message.[30]

Shortly after the formation of the Commission on Race Relations, Haynes and Alexander began to cooperate. The two groups shared personnel and similar ideologies. In an attempt to avoid competition, a tacit yet informal agreement was struck between the two. The CIC would concentrate on the South, while the Commission on Race Relations would focus on the rest of the nation. In the wake of the Red Summer, dozens of temporary interracial race relations committees were formed across the North under the auspices of the Commission on Race Relations.[31]

In addition to initiating new committees, Haynes labored to keep existing ones active. Haynes was concerned that white activists would participate in interracial committees during a period of crisis and then depart. To keep the spirit of positive interaction alive, Haynes and his colleagues initiated "Race Relations Sunday" in 1923. The Commission on Race Relations hoped the annual event would remind white Christians about the ongoing need to address racial issues. In some localities, black and white churches exchanged ministers and choirs, while others preached sermons on the importance of racial brotherhood.[32] Although both the CIC and the CRR were hampered by internal ideological conflict and external forces, they had opened a sustained interracial dialogue around race. By the mid-1920s their tactics and theories had influenced a small group of Quakers and their allies in Philadelphia.

On the Interests of the Colored Race

LIKE MANY NORTHERN INDUSTRIAL CENTERS, PHILADELPHIA EXPERIenced a massive demographic transformation during World War I. By 1920 the city population included 134,000 African Americans, a 60 percent increase since 1910. African Americans from the South were attracted to the city's burgeoning wartime manufacturing sector. The migration placed strains on the city's overcrowded housing market for blacks.[33]

In response to racial violence, the Colored Protective Association (CPA) was formed in 1918. Founded by Rev. R. R. Wright, the CPA represented the city's small black elite popularly known as "Old Philadelphians." The organization mounted a legal defense of blacks arrested during wartime and postwar racial conflict. Although they lasted less than two years, the CPA's decisive leadership inspired the NAACP to become more proactive.[34]

The violence was also a catalyst for the city's Quaker activists. Members of the city's most prominent meetinghouses on Arch Street (Orthodox) and on Race Street (Hicksite) began to discuss race relations on an ongoing basis. In 1920, members of the Race Street Meeting formed the Committee on the Interests of the Colored Race. Shortly thereafter the Arch Street Meeting started its own Committee on Race Relations. These committees had two principal goals: 1) to raise awareness about race relations among Quakers and other potential allies and 2) to protest against lynching and local discrimination.[35]

With experienced social activists as members, the Race Street Meeting's group quickly became the more dynamic of the two. In 1922 they broadened their reach by forming the Inter-Racial Committee. Organized principally to denounce lynching, the twenty-member committee included "carefully selected men and women of both races." The black representatives included Cheyney State College president Leslie Pinckney Hill, NAACP branch president and realtor Isadore Martin, and anthropologist/educator Arthur Huff Fauset.[36]

In the mid-1920s the Committee on the Interests of the Colored Race (CICR) urged all members to join the NAACP, lobbied legislators about the federal Dyer Anti-Lynching Bill, and launched an ongoing series of lectures on race. These forums brought nationally recognized figures such as Alexander and Atlanta University professor John Hope to Philadelphia. In addition to these activities, the group campaigned against segregation at the historic Walnut Street Theatre and successfully secured downtown office space for Raymond Pace Alexander, a young African American attorney who would later become one of the city's most important civil rights leaders. Although the committee represented a new voice in race relations, their work was hampered by limited financial and personnel resources and internal disagreement. Their approach to discrimination was often inconsistent. For example, they preferred to support the construction of new separate housing for blacks rather than agitate for integrated housing.[37]

In 1926 Helen Bryan, a member of the Race Street Committee, began to criticize the group's lack of direction. Bryan had organized youth groups for the YWCA in Detroit, Pittsburgh, and Macon, Georgia; she was also assistant secretary of the American Friends Service Committee's new Interracial

Section. After she became the secretary of the CICR, Bryan argued that they needed to reach a wider audience. She also maintained that the lack of permanent black members affected the group's legitimacy in the black community.[38]

Bryan maintained that race relations efforts would be strengthened by the union of the two committees. In the late 1920s the two committees began to collaborate, and by 1930 they merged to become the joint Committee on Race Relations with Bryan as secretary.[39] In addition to bolstering the city's budding interracial movement, the union also brought the two tendencies of the Quaker faith closer.

As the two committees merged, they faced an opportunity to demonstrate their commitment to activism. In early 1930 President Herbert Hoover nominated Judge John J. Parker to fill a vacancy on the Supreme Court. Parker was opposed to black political participation, and the NAACP, led by the dynamic Walter White, launched a campaign to defeat the nominee. The national campaign was supported by the CIC, the National Association of Colored Women (NACW), and the Fellowship of Reconciliation. In Philadelphia, Alexander, president of the black National Bar Association, coordinated efforts to defeat Parker. The Committee on Race Relations assisted the drive by co-sponsoring protest rallies. Due to massive political and public pressure, Parker's nomination was rejected by the Senate.[40]

Shortly after their merger, they began to discuss racism within their own ranks. In May 1930 the Committee on Race Relations held a conference to plan future action and to examine racism within the Quaker faith. Several members complained that there were too few black Quakers. How could a Quaker committee combat racism when some Quaker meetinghouses discriminated?[41]

Racism within the faith proved to be an uncomfortable issue for the group. Although the committee remained divided on this issue, most agreed that more contact and cooperation with black civil rights organizations was needed. The presence of blacks on the Committee on Race Relations was therefore essential to building links with the black community. Since a number of black activists had been working with Quakers on race relations since the mid-1920s, finding willing experienced recruits would not be difficult.

In 1925 the AFSC was organized into four sections: Foreign, Home, Peace, and Interracial. For several years the Interracial Section had quietly sponsored several forums but had engaged in little substantial outreach. In 1927 the AFSC hired a dynamic African American activist, Crystal Bird, as a field representative for the Interracial Section. Originally from the Eastern Shore of Maryland, Bird had been a social worker for the YWCA in New York. As the field representative for the Interracial Section, Bird spoke about race relations to civic groups, churches and schools. She left the AFSC due to a funding shortage, but soon joined the new, dynamic Committee on Race Relations.[42]

Virginia Alexander, a physician and sister of attorney Raymond Pace Alexander, also joined the committee. A graduate of Women's Medical College of Pennsylvania, Alexander became an advocate for ending segregation in the city's medical community. Both Alexander and Bird were well-known members of the city's new black middle class. Their participation gave the Committee a black perspective on race relations and closer links with organizations like the NACW and the NAACP.

As the anti-lynching movement entered a new phase, cooperation with the black community increased. The NAACP had suffered several major setbacks in its struggle against lynching. The failure of Congress to pass an anti-lynching law in the 1920s had prompted the NAACP to shift its focus to redressing individual cases of injustice. These legal challenges strained the tenuous human and monetary resources of the NAACP. In 1929 the onset of the Great Depression placed additional financial hardships on the association. At this time, the Communist Party of the United States (CPUSA) launched its own anti-lynching campaign. Labeling the NAACP as "misleaders of the Negro masses," the CPUSA established its own legal unit, the International Labor Defense (ILD). In the spring of 1930, the ILD held an organizational meeting in New York to plan mass rallies, membership drives, and a propaganda campaign.[43]

In an attempt to reassert NAACP leadership, Walter White reached out to sympathetic allies such as the CIC in the South and the CRR in Philadelphia. In contrast to the Marxist approach of the CPUSA, the CRR and the NAACP shared a similar reformist perspective toward race relations. Significant social change, they believed, could occur without revolutionary changes in the nation's political and economic spheres.

Helen Bryan believed that the anti-lynching struggle had the potential to mobilize large numbers of people, and brought the CRR into close cooperation with the NAACP. She felt that the committee, although moving in the right direction, was far too small to confront the monolith of racism. Bryan became convinced that a larger mass movement needed to be forged. She clearly saw that a more substantial organization could confront a multitude of issues in a sustained manner and attract dedicated activists.

Birth of a Beloved Community

AS THE DEPRESSION WORSENED, HELEN BRYAN BELIEVED THAT A DYNAMic new institutional vehicle was needed to confront the challenges. Her calls for a more activist approach were supported by Dr. Fred Wentzel, the national youth director of the Evangelical and Reformed Church. In the 1920s Wentzel had organized church-sponsored interracial summer camps for children. In contrast to the adult-oriented focus of the CRR, Wentzel had experience working with young blacks and whites. Bryan maintained that reaching youth should be a key goal of the movement and discussed with Wentzel the feasibility of holding an interracial youth conference on race relations.[44]

The CRR targeted local Protestant churches in its effort to recruit participants. Following the theories of George Edmund Haynes and the Social Gospel movement, Wentzel believed that Christianity had enormous potential as a tool for social change. Both he and Bryan believed that churches would serve as a recruiting field for an interracial mass movement. The response to the Committee's call produced a small but enthusiastic turnout. From May 15 to 18, 1931, an interracial group of eighty teenagers and young adults met at Pendle Hill, a Quaker retreat in suburban Wallingford, Pennsylvania. The diverse group included blacks like teenager Marechal Neil Ellison and social worker Roberta Lewis and whites such as Swarthmore College student W. Wendell Clepper and suburban accountant Albert E. Kunkel. The conference program featured sessions and discussions focused on race relations. Participants struggled with the following questions: What was the role of churches in the struggle against racism? How could understanding between the races be forged?[45] The crucial element in this gathering was its interracial character. The struggle against racism was to be spearheaded by young activists of both races.

The Pendle Hill Conference cited six crucial issues in the local landscape of racial relations. They were 1) religion, 2) social, 3) educational, 4) economic and political, 5) contemporary prejudice, and 6) the historic roots of prejudice. The conferees suggested a thirteen-point program to address their concerns. Their most important proposals included the organization of interracial study groups, intercultural exchanges, and lobbying efforts designed to encourage the business community to practice "race fellowship" in the workplace.[46]

Of the major Christian denominations, the Roman Catholic Church was not represented at the conference. The exclusion of the Catholics can be attributed to several factors. Bryan, Wentzel, and the other organizers of the conference believed that there was not sufficient interest in the Catholic population because of two factors: indifference from the clergy and anger from the laity. The 1910s and the 1920s had witnessed white opposition to black advances in housing and labor, and much of this resistance emerged from working-class Irish communities. Some argued that the city's powerful archdiocese was not interested in race relations. Therefore, it is doubtful that the organizers of Pendle Hill conference made a concerted effort to reach Catholics.[47]

Several conference leaders formed an ad hoc committee to continue the dialogue on race relations. The Continuation Committee planned a series of informative supper meetings in the fall. While these integrated dinners may sound trivial, they acquired significant symbolic importance. Harkening back to the early Christian tradition of agape feast, these Fellowship Dinners, as they became known, were one of the few public opportunities for whites and blacks in Philadelphia to eat, drink, and discuss. As a result, Fellowship Dinners became one of the most important and beloved traditions of this movement.

In October the Continuation Committee changed its name to the Young People's Interracial Fellowship (YPIF). In the tradition of Quaker meetings, there were no dues, no membership requirements, and no constitution. The one major concession to structure was Bryan's election as provisional chair. The new organization sponsored trips to black theatrical productions and black artists' studios. Influenced by Haynes, the YPIF were convinced that interracial social contacts were crucial to their cause. Pleasurable excursions alone would not build a mass movement, so the fledgling YPIF held a second conference at Pendle Hill in May 1932. The second Pendle Hill conference, "Building a Christian Social Order," outlined strategies for the immediate future of the YPIF. The YPIF leadership expressed concern that the young idealists lacked sufficient knowledge of the nation's current racial situation. In addition to their lack of understanding of contemporary racial issues, they did not have an appreciation of the pioneering work of scholars such as Du Bois and Franz Boas. These scholars had challenged prevailing theories on race since the early twentieth century. One of Boas's students, Melville Herskovits, had spoken to the Committee on Race Relations in 1930. Bryan wanted the YPIF to serve as a forum where these scholars could discuss their works with members and supporters.[48]

Encouraged by the enthusiasm of the YPIF, Bryan and Fauset planned a summer school on race relations. They envisaged a program that would feature nationally known academics as instructors. Although open to the YPIF, the proposed summer school's goal was to engage potential activists from across the United States. In the summer of 1933, the first Institute on Race Relations opened at Swarthmore College with Clarence Pickett of the AFSC and sociologist Charles S. Johnson of Fisk University as directors. In addition to attracting participants from across the nation, the Institute also served as an intellectual beacon for the YPIF.[49]

Although the YPIF slowly gained new members, were they simply preaching to the converted? When the group attempted to broaden its base by appealing to churches that had not supported the initial call, they were ignored. Perhaps ministers of both races believed that promoting interracial social interaction among their respective youth was too controversial.

Undeterred by their lack of external support, the YPIF strengthened its organizational structure and plunged into new activities. An informal steering committee that had been formed in late 1931 was reorganized. Four young people filled the posts of chair, co-chair, treasurer, and secretary, while their activities were overseen by four adult advisors. A membership committee and a program committee were added in 1932 and 1933, respectively. In 1934 the Cooperative Committee, later named the Cooperative Council, was formed. The role of this committee was multifaceted; it served as a liaison with other groups and informed members about progress on specific issues.[50]

The Cooperative Council also engaged in limited direct action to test the effectiveness of the Pennsylvania Equal Rights Law (PERL), which banned discrimination in public accommodation. Blacks were routinely denied admittance to clubs, restaurants, and hotels. In order to test the effectiveness of the statute, the Co-Op Council sent interracial teams to restaurants and clubs. In a 1995 interview, Gladys Rawlins, an African American YPIF member, recalled an incident at Stouffer's, a Center City restaurant. Although Rawlins and her colleagues received prompt service, their food arrived blanketed with salt.[51] These protests were limited, yet they did raise consciousness about the need for constant vigilance. In addition, the work of these activists was being recognized by the city's black community.

The YPIF also became involved in the growing national struggle for civil rights. In addition to the anti-lynching crusade, the group became involved in the struggle of southern sharecroppers. In the spring of 1935, Howard Kester of the interracial Southern Tenant Farmers Union issued a national call for support. Despite the reforms of the New Deal, southern sharecroppers remained mired in poverty and oppression. In response to Kester's urgent appeal, the YPIF launched an ongoing fundraising campaign known as Sharecropper Suppers. At these events, southern food was served; speakers informed the audience about economic exploitation in the South and raised money for the STFU.[52]

In 1935, Wentzel launched the YPIF's most ambitious project, the Fellowship Church. The "church" was an afternoon interdenominational religious service held on the third Sunday of each month. The Fellowship Church, which convened at different churches in Center City Philadelphia, was one of the few places in the city where blacks and whites worshipped together.[53] Most importantly, it created a spiritual context for the embryonic interracial civil rights organization. The Fellowship Church with its message of racial brotherhood would be central to the struggle for racial equality. Wentzel maintained that one could not be a Christian and support segregation. He argued: "How can you be committed to the great ideas of Christianity, cooperation, brotherhood, reconciliation, the Fatherhood of God, how can you believe in these things and at the same time insist that when people differ they must live in different places?"[54]

On October 20, 1935, Howard University president Mordecai Johnson delivered the opening sermon of the Fellowship Church to an enthusiastic crowd of 1,500 at Center City's First Baptist Church. However, the Fellowship Church met opposition. Many white churches refused to allow the Fellowship Church to use their buildings. Nevertheless, the participation of nationally known black ministers such as Johnson and local leaders like Reverend Marshal Shepard of West Philadelphia's Mt. Olivet Baptist Church indicated support among the black clergy.[55] In addition to the active support of black leaders, the interracial movement was aided by a transformation in the internal dynamics of the black community.

By the mid-1930s a significant political realignment had begun in the black community. To the dismay of the city's doddering G.O.P. machine, black Republicans began voting Democratic. In 1934 Shepard, a recent migrant from North Carolina and Democratic convert, won a seat in the state legislature. In addition to the political shift, the decline of Garveyism and the onset of the Great Depression led some African Americans to examine the potential of interracial cooperation.[56]

The Depression, however, strained the resources of the city's non-profit organizations. Largely dependent on the Society of Friends, the YPIF faced a severe budget crisis in the fall of 1936. Financial difficulties were compounded by Bryan's serious illness. Although a tireless worker, her energies were stretched between the CRR, the Institute on Race Relations, and the

YPIF. Despite these hardships, the YPIF continued to expand its reach. It strengthened existing ties with Quaker meetinghouses and started a publication, the *Fellowship Call*. The publication was not only a means of keeping the steadily growing membership informed of the group's activities, but also an attempt to fashion an organizational credo.[57] By late 1936 the YPIF had not yet codified its beliefs. Some activists were concerned that an organization without a coherent ideology could be ineffective. The CIC's Will Alexander had once remarked that he had no ideology.[58] While this could be seen as advantageous in terms of attracting a broad following, such a position contributed to the often contradictory philosophy and policies of the CIC. Would the YPIF evolve into a body where members held widely divergent views on race?

In 1937 these concerns resulted in the establishment of a credo that all members would be required to support. Both old and new members would affirm the following pledge:

> We, the members of the Young People's Interracial Fellowship, believing that true religion best expresses itself through comradeship, justice, and respect for all persons, pledge ourselves:
> 1) To develop an informed membership, concerned with race as a major factor in our changing world.
> 2) Through a program of action, to help bring about a community where prejudice and discrimination give way to justice and equality for all.[59]

Although brief, the pledge was an indication that the organization wanted members who were firmly committed to the struggle against racism. One such member was Marjorie Penney, a young white artist from Philadelphia who had joined the YPIF after attending one of the early Pendle Hill conferences. Penney's dynamism propelled her role in the YPIF. Along with Bryan, she represented the YPIF at meetings of the CRR and supported Bryan's call for more activism. When Bryan fell ill in late 1936, Penney assumed many of her duties and shepherded the group through its budgetary crisis.[60]

After Bryan's return in early 1937, it was clear that her illness had not dimmed her ardor. She spearheaded the creation of a finance committee and established links with the National Negro Congress (NNC).[61] Formed by political scientist and future Nobel laureate Ralph Bunche and other black intellectuals in 1936, the NNC was dissatisfied with racism within the

New Deal and began to build a coalition that would coordinate the work of black protest organizations. In Philadelphia, Arthur Huff Fauset, former member of the Inter-Racial Committee, became one of the leading organizers of the local NNC council. In October 1937, the NNC held its second national conference at the Metropolitan Opera in Philadelphia. While most NNC chapters leaned to the left, the Philadelphia chapter adopted a more moderate stance.[62] For Bryan and her followers, however, the NNC represented a step in the right direction. Although the NNC supported the basic principles of the New Deal, it did not refrain from criticizing racism within the Roosevelt administration and linked the struggle for racial justice with economic rights.

The future of the YPIF would not include Bryan. In December 1938 she resigned from the YPIF, thanking them for "the most interesting and valuable and delightful years of my life." She stated her reason for leaving: "Because I believe that the American League for Peace and Democracy is attempting to grapple with the fundamental causes of race prejudice."[63] For Bryan race and class issues had become increasingly linked. Unable to influence the YPIF in this direction, she sought more likeminded allies. Although she remained involved in race relations, Bryan would soon immerse herself in the leading international cause of the left in the late 1930s, the Spanish Civil War.[64]

Support for the embattled Republic of Spain ran deep among American leftists, but for many the battle against fascism began at home. The late 1930s witnessed a rise in American fascist groups like the Bund and the Silver Shirts. Local supporters of American fascism distributed thousands of pamphlets that blamed Jews for the Depression and a host of other social ills. Although they also attacked blacks and immigrants, the city's large Jewish community was their principal target. They distributed pamphlets in black neighborhoods that accused Jews of retarding black progress, thus undermining any potential alliances between the two communities.[65] Penney, the new secretary of the YPIF, called a conference of youth leaders from local churches to address the rising level of anti-Semitism. After securing the support of Maurice Fagan, president of the local branch of the Anti-Defamation League of B'nai B'rith, they held a series of meetings directed primarily at the city's youth. As a result of these meetings, the Emergency Youth Assembly (EYA) was formed. The YPIF, Fagan, and the EYA pressured radio stations and newspapers to condemn anti-Semitism. The campaign was successful in decreasing tension, and in the process changed the perspective of the YPIF. The organization began to actively recruit Jewish members and the religious philosophy of the YPIF began to embrace all Judeo-Christian-based faiths.[66] The outreach to the Jewish community would broaden the YPIF, both numerically and ideologically.

The expanding YPIF was also enriched by the leadership of the dynamic E. Luther Cunningham, pastor of North Philadelphia's St. Paul's Baptist Church. Educated at Lincoln University and the University of Pennsylvania, Cunningham became the second minister at St. Paul's in 1938.[67] Cunningham's rising status in the black community contributed to the YPIF's ability to recruit a new cadre of black members.

By 1940 it had become clear that the YPIF had outgrown the tutelage of the Committee on Race Relations. With nearly two hundred active members, the YPIF was a vibrant organization engaged in an increasing number of critical issues. Penny and Cunningham were interested in experimenting with new approaches to race relations. They envisioned establishing a community-based institution modeled loosely on the settlement houses of the Progressive Era. Cunningham argued that the proposed "fellowship house" would focus on transforming race relations by hosting innovative educational programs. They began to search for a site in a neighborhood beset with racial tension. Such a community could prove to be a perfect laboratory for their ambitious social experiment. Influenced by Quaker activism, elements of Progressivism, and new theories on race, a small yet determined group of activists began to plant the seeds of a movement.

CHAPTER 2

So That All Might Learn

Education and the Interracial Civil Rights Movement, 1931–1946

FRANK SINATRA WAS PERHAPS THE MOST POPULAR MAN IN AMERICA when he walked into Fellowship House on April 4, 1945. At the behest of his manager who was acquainted with one of Fellowship's board members, the celebrated crooner spoke to over 300 students about racial tolerance, At the time, Sinatra's involvement in civil rights was growing. His Philadelphia visit was part of a speaking tour focusing on social issues. As he departed, the singer donated $600 to Fellowship House to repair a decrepit cornice.[1] The appearance of Sinatra and his small yet important symbolic gift increased the movement's profile. For Fellowship House, it was a specific boon to its educational efforts. This chapter will examine the interracial movement's attempts to reach schools and the wider public utilizing a multiplicity of techniques. Although the Philadelphia school district became increasingly receptive to "intercultural" programs, administration officials remained indifferent or opposed to integration. Navigating between these two positions would prove to be a challenge for the embryonic movement.

The education of black Philadelphia had been a controversial issue since the colonial period. The Pennsylvania Abolition Society and African American churches established schools for black children in the late eighteenth century. These institutions were relatively small and focused primarily on elementary education. In 1801 Pennsylvania mandated public education for all children, regardless of color. Philadelphia's School Committee opened separate schools for whites and blacks, thus establishing an institutional precedent for segregation. In 1854 the Commonwealth of Pennsylvania mandated the segregation of public schools. Since black voters had been disenfranchised in 1838, the community had no political leverage and thus they were forced to accept the new law. During the Civil War, the city's black leaders reached a compromise with the city's new Board of Public Education. Under this agreement, black educators would be limited to teaching black students. This arrangement secured employment for an emerging cadre of black teachers, yet it also enshrined a system of segregated education.[2]

In the wake of the Civil War, the supporters of integrated education scored a victory, albeit a conditional one. In 1882 the Public School Law of 1854 was overturned by the state legislature. Although this ruling merely limited the power of local government to segregate, many blacks viewed this as a positive development.[3] Numerically small and politically weak, many African Americans viewed accommodation of the city's political elite as their only recourse.

In the early twentieth century, the Great Migration transformed the black community and complicated questions over education and race. In the 1920s the School District of Philadelphia responded to the increasing black student population by building new segregated elementary schools to house the incoming students. The district also began a complicated program to segregate the black school population by transferring the few black children in white schools to increasingly overcrowded black schools.[4] If this segregation had occurred at an earlier time, perhaps little would have happened. By the 1920s, however, the political power of the city's black community was slowly ascending.

The 1920s witnessed the rise of new black leaders like E. Washington Rhodes, Raymond Pace Alexander, and Herbert Millen. In contrast to the old Philadelphia elite dominated by church and business-based leaders, this new ascendancy had been trained as lawyers in local institutions such as the University of Pennsylvania and Temple University. These young attorneys viewed the law as a weapon in the struggle against racism. Desegregation of the public education system became a major issue for the city's growing black middle class. Despite black protests, the school district continued to segregate black students.[5]

Mobilizing black Philadelphia around school segregation would be problematic. Although the black community had developed an independent political consciousness on some issues, most voters remained firmly in the hands of a reactionary G.O.P. machine. Many black municipal workers were dependent on the Republican Party for their jobs and thus reluctant to criticize City Hall. In addition, the Pennsylvania Association of Teachers of Colored Children (PATCC) expressed concern that black teachers would lose their jobs in a desegregated system.[6]

Until the black community sponsored rallies and mass meetings in the late 1920s, there was little discussion by the two Committees on Race Relations on the issue of education.[7] The reluctance of these activists to act suggests several explanations. The absence of a coherent program and the highly politicized nature of the issue could have influenced their decision.

In addition, the dominance of African American organizations might have dissuaded them from participating. However, the most important factor was the character of the committee members, who saw their mission as advisory. Although concerned with race relations, they did not envision themselves as policy-oriented activists.

This view was not shared by all committee members. In a project designed to enlighten white schoolchildren about African American culture, Bryan attempted to introduce the work of Harlem Renaissance writers into selected schools. She organized school visits by African American poets like Arthur Huff Fauset and Alice Dunbar Nelson, while her colleague, Rachel Davis Du Bois, initiated a program to distribute the works of black authors throughout the system.[8] Although these activities were limited, this brief foray into the emerging field of "intercultural education" demonstrated to the committee members that education was an essential tool in improving relations between the races.

The union of the two committees in 1930 allowed them to concentrate their financial and intellectual resources. In contrast to the earlier efforts, the new Committee on Race Relations devoted more time to educational issues. As they attempted to formulate a position on the city's education crisis, the school district completed the controversial 6-3-3 reorganization plan. The plan eliminated elementary schools that terminated in the eighth grade and replaced them with junior high schools. Since district policy did not allow black teachers to teach at the high school level, numerous positions would be eliminated.[9] In the midst of the Depression, the dismissal of black faculty would constitute a severe economic and psychological blow to the city's precarious black middle class. More than any other issue, the school district's action helped increase the involvement of Committee on Race Relations in the battle over education.

In the fall of 1931, the CRR sponsored a forum on public education featuring Alain Locke, author of *The New Negro*, professor of philosophy at Howard University, and one of the nation's leading black intellectuals. In February 1932 the CCR issued a statement calling for the school board to allow "competent and well-trained teachers regardless of race" to teach at all grade levels.[10] The CCR established a subcommittee to address educational matters.

The hesistance of the Committee on Race Relations also emerged within the YPIF. Although the YPIF acknowledged the disparity between black and white schools, it also saw the existing structure as a potential forum to facilitate intercultural education. Thus, the focus of the YPIF was not primarily policy-oriented but rather "an attempt to build a community of individuals who could become involved in the struggle for racial justice."[11]

The YPIF's lack of direct involvement in the public policy battle could also indicate an unwillingness to confront a complex local issue. Race relations activists in Philadelphia had been active since the early 1920s in the battle against lynching. By the 1930s the anti-lynching struggle had evolved into a broad-based national movement. In contrast to the conflict over education, the outcome of the anti-lynching movement had little direct impact on the lives of most Philadelphians. For some in the fledgling organization, battling the plague of lynching was far easier than confronting racism in education in the City of Brotherly Love. High school students who protested the policies of the Board of Education could expect reprisals from teachers and administrators.

In late 1935 Bryan praised Floyd Logan, leader of the Educational Equality League, for securing the appointment of Dr. John Turner, a prominent black physician, to the Board of Education. She also announced that the YPIF had initiated a "program of action" with a small integrated student organization known as the NAACP Youth Council. Although the Youth Council had received a charter from NAACP headquarters and enjoyed the support of the local black press, the official Philadelphia branch refused to acknowledge it.[12]

While the YPIF's activist arm, the Cooperative Council, and the NAACP Youth Council discussed confronting discrimination in public accommodations, some argued that there was an urgent need to disseminate new theories on race to the general public and its membership. Howard University emerged as one of the principal intellectual centers of this new scholarship. In 1926, theologian Mordecai Johnson became Howard's first black president. The innovative Johnson initiated an ambitious program to revitalize the university's professional schools and academic departments. He promoted a young law professor, Charles Hamilton Houston, to the post of vice-dean of the law school. Houston envisioned training a cadre of black lawyers who could utilize the law to overturn segregation.

In addition to bolstering the law school, Johnson attracted rising scholars such as Ralph Bunche, Abram Harris, and E. Franklin Frazier to Howard. Although these young intellectuals credited the work of Alain Locke, Du Bois, and Woodson, their analysis of America's "race problem" was more class-conscious than race specific. They believed that economic factors were responsible for the continuing oppression of the African American community. Like many intellectuals of the 1930s, they argued that the

Great Depression demonstrated the failure of modern capitalism. Thus, they sought solutions that would address problems of both race and class.[13]

Eager to capitalize on these emerging intellectual trends, the YPIF initiated an ongoing forum series that brought scholars like St. Clair Drake, Channing Tobias, and others to Philadelphia. In addition to providing a public forum for these scholars who were generally ignored by white academia and government, the YPIF attempted to publicize its intellectual contributions through its Speakers' Bureau. The YPIF dispatched small mixed-gender interracial teams to schools, colleges, community organizations, and churches. Although the organization's policy encouraged individual opinions, speakers' public statements had to represent the consensus of the YPIF.[14]

The Speakers' Bureau quickly became one of the YPIF's most popular programs. In the 1938–39 season, the YPIF reached over eight thousand people. In response to an increasing tide of anti-Semitism, the YPIF initiated "Tolerance Trios" in the summer of 1939. This program featured black, Jewish, and white Protestant speakers, and they made their first appearances at predominantly white summer youth camps. Although well received, they faced challenging questions from their young audiences. Children posed questions like "Wouldn't the Negroes themselves be happier segregated in communities of their own?"; "What about intermarriage between races?"; "Do you think that the Negroes are bettering themselves by joining the Communist Party?"; and "Does the discrimination that Negroes meet as children have a lasting effect on them?" Although Elizabeth Yarosh of the Speakers' Bureau reported that these questions were answered enthusiastically, she did not elaborate on the content of the answers.[15]

By the late 1930s the rapidly growing YPIF discussed establishing a community center. Within the Committee on Race Relations, questions were raised about the feasibility of such a site. Financial concerns were prominent in the discussion about the YPIF's future. How would this expansion be funded? One member of the Committee on Race Relations, James Dumpson, warned that "they could not attain the size of a snowball on the budget of a shoestring."[16]

Penney and Cunningham remained persistent. They saw this proposed facility not only as a center for the educational programs, but also the home of an independent YPIF. Although many on the CCR shared many of the same values of the YPIF, the two had evolved into separate and distinct organizations. In contrast to the cautious activism of the Committee on Race Relations, the YPIF had evolved into a multifaceted entity. It was not principally a protest organization, an educational body, nor a religious community, but attempted to fuse all of these elements into a coherent operational program.

Questions about this proposed fellowship house persisted. Where would the house be located? The YPIF wanted to establish an experimental facility in a racially and ethnically tense neighborhood. In the late 1930s Philadelphia had a number of racially polarized communities, but North Philadelphia seemed the best choice for such a site. The area was located close to Center City and had several neighborhoods seething with racial tension. Furthermore, it had a tradition of settlement houses, so the residents were accustomed to the presence of outsiders.

After encountering threats from angry white residents near Broad and Girard streets, the YPIF broadened their search. In late 1940 the YPIF located a four-story structure at 1431 Brown Street that had once served as a coffin factory and later as a firehouse. In the surrounding community, poor and working-class blacks and whites lived in close proximity but had limited interaction.[17] For the YPIF, it seemed like an ideal location. Penney described the challenging nature of the neighborhood: "Here one could observe the phenomenon of Americans living so close physically, yet so far apart in spirit. Here one might test out in the schools and the churches of the community, new methods of building brotherhood. Yes, the district was the right one."[18]

The Year of Fellowship

PURCHASED WITH FUNDS FROM YPIF MEMBERS AND SEVERAL SYMPATHETIC businessmen, the building at 1431 Brown Street was in decrepit shape. In the winter of 1940–41, an interracial group of volunteers painted, cleaned, and scrubbed the floors. Among the volunteers were two enthusiastic black firefighters from South Philadelphia, Randolph Walker and Roosevelt Barlow, who would later become board members of the new organization. Walker and Barlow had been introduced to the YPIF by Roosevelt's wife, Virginia, who was acquainted with Marjorie Penney. In the early years of the organization, many members were recruited through such informal networks.[19]

Fellowship House opened to the public in February 1941. Penney was chosen by her colleagues to serve as interim director. Her first task was to develop Fellowship House's educational mission. Penney and her supporters envisioned the House as a proving ground for their ambitious educational programs. If their new projects were successful in the immediate neighborhood, they could introduce them on a citywide scale. For the Fellowshippers, one of the most important groups to reach was young children. Arguing that racism emerged at an early age, they believed that positive interaction between black and white children could allay future racial tension.

Penney selected Gladys Rawlins, a young African American YPIF member, to direct the children's program. Although she possessed little training in pedagogy, the enthusiastic Rawlins had a background in social work and civil rights activism. She became attracted to the YPIF in the late 1930s because she believed that mainstream civil rights organizations such as the NAACP had done little to increase interracial dialogue.[20]

In an effort to reach young children, Rawlins developed the Arrows program. The first Arrows were a small racially mixed group of neighborhood children aged 4 to 12 who were taught songs and games that emphasized racial tolerance. Rawlins also administered the Fellowship House Doll Library, a collection of dolls representing historical figures such as Albert Schweitzer and Harriet Tubman. The goal of the Doll Library was to teach children about the contributions of prominent men and women of all races. Both the Doll Library and the Arrows became very popular with parents, children, and schoolteachers.[21]

By summer 1941 over six hundred people had participated in educational programs at Fellowship House. Eager to build on their momentum, the YPIF hastily arranged a summer school for neighborhood children. The students attended classes in music, clay modeling, and black history. In their continuing effort to forestall racial conflict, the YPIF taught students that "friends avoid fists" by initiating role-play exercises.[22]

It is clear that Penney, Rawlins, and the volunteer teachers considered the summer school successful. They reported close interaction between the children and increasing parental participation in summer school activities. Despite the initial success, financial problems persisted. In fall 1941 the YPIF almost lost the Fellowship House due to an inability to pay the lease.[23] YPIF activists concluded that they needed a stable source of funding and decided to leave the CRR. Such a move would allow them to access foundation support without CRR oversight.

Eager to build on the momentum, Penney began forging alliances with other race and ethnic relations organizations. In the late 1930s Maurice Fagan, executive director and founder of the Anti-Defamation Council, had approached Penney about securing the YPIF's assistance in combatting a rising tide of anti-Semitism. Their alliance evolved into a lasting partnership. Both Penney and Fagan were interested in creating more cooperation between organizations involved in ethnic and race relations.[24]

Educated at Central High and the University of Pennsylvania, Maurice Fagan was a former social studies teacher whose activism was triggered by the persecution of Jews in Nazi Germany. Fagan served as secretary of the Amity Lodge of B'nai B'rith but believed that B'nai B'rith lacked the organizational expertise to address the increasing anti-Semitism at home and abroad. In response to this threat, Fagan started the Anti-Defamation Council, a local coalition of seventeen Jewish organizations in 1938.[25]

In October 1941 Penney and Fagan met with representatives of the Committee on Race Relations and the Philadelphia chapter of the Federation of Churches' Department of Race Relations to discuss cooperation on broad issues. Out of this meeting emerged an informal network called the Tolerance Clearinghouse. The central purpose of this ad hoc committee was to coordinate action among the member organizations, but they soon realized that a more formal structure was needed. On October 11, 1941, the Tolerance Clearinghouse changed its name to the Fellowship Commission, and thus began a new chapter in race relations.[26]

The Fellowship Commission was incorporated as a non-profit, non-sectarian, and non-partisan organization. Membership in the Fellowship Commission was not open to the general public, but limited to organizations battling racial, religious, and ethnic tension.[27] Thus, in contrast to other civil rights organizations, the Fellowship Commission was organized primarily as a coordinating agency for its constituent members. The Commission described its original purpose as "to promote belief in and observance of the fundamental principles of justice and democracy and to seek to apply those principles to the relief of and solution of racial, religious, nationality and social tensions."[28]

Fagan was elected chairman of the executive staff, a board comprised of the directors of the constituent agencies, while Penney served as secretary and Dr. William Henry Welsh, former associate superintendent of the Philadelphia School District, became the chairman of the new agency. The organizational structure also included commissioners who chaired subcommittees on specific issues such as education, labor, and civic affairs.[29] These commissioners were drawn from the ranks of Philadelphia's business, government and religious communities, and would give the Fellowship Commission a higher public profile than other civil rights organizations.

Although the Fellowship Commission's mission was to improve race relations, civil rights organizations such as the NAACP and Educational Equality League (EEL) were not included in its creation. Was the exclusion of these black organizations deliberate or accidental? It appears that the reasons are far more complicated. Since Logan wanted his EEL to forge an independent path in the fight to overturn segregation in education, the EEL avoided joining permanent coalitions. In contrast to the EEL, the NAACP was generally supportive of alliances with other civil rights organizations. However, in 1941 the Philadelphia branch was undergoing a change in leadership; as a result, participation in the Fellowship Commission was slightly delayed. In early 1942 the Philadelphia NAACP became the fifth constituent agency of the Fellowship Commission.[30] Under the leadership of branch secretary Carolyn Davenport Moore, the NAACP began to increase its protests against racial discrimination in the Philadelphia area. The participation of the NAACP allowed the Fellowship Commission an entrée into the black community, while the NAACP gained allies and wider public exposure.

The original mission of the Fellowship Commission proposed the utilization of newspapers, public forums, libraries, radio, and "any and all other appropriate means" to spread the gospel of racial tolerance.[31] This concentrated effort to reach a mass audience complemented the efforts of Fellowship House and the Philadelphia Housing Association, both of which adopted a more grass-roots approach. In addition to initiating a media-centered program targeting the general public, the Fellowship Commission also called for the elimination of employment discrimination in public education and a program of intercultural education in public and private schools.[32] Although Welsh's selection as chairman gave the Fellowship Commission access to the school district, this did not mean that their proposals encountered no opposition. Many board members, schoolteachers, and administrators were skeptical of these programs. However, when racial tensions in the public schools increased, officials sought solutions.

Concerned that racial conflict in housing, labor, and public space could affect public education, the school district's new superintendent, Alexander Stoddard, encouraged the work of Fellowship House and the Fellowship Commission. For the Fellowship Commission, overcoming wartime racial conflict was essential to the Allied war effort. As America entered World War II, the new organizations linked the struggle against Japanese militarism and European fascism with the struggle against racism in the United States. The "Double V" approach proved to be an effective strategy for the duration of the conflict.[33]

In the fall of 1941, Penney initiated the formation of a Sponsors' Board that pledged to provide financial support for the fledgling organization. The eighty-odd sponsors represented a cross-section of Philadelphia's black, Jewish, and WASP upper middle class. This group included Nellie Lee Bok, a veteran social activist and wife of Judge Curtis Bok; Dorothy Biddle James of suburban Wallingford who would later assist in the evolution of a Fellowship House in Media, Pennsylvania; Frederick Massiah, a Barbados-born architect and contractor; Theodore Spaulding, president of the local NAACP branch and a prominent member of its national council; and Max Shubin, a local businessman who had provided coal and a significant portion of the initial purchase price of the facility.[34]

With the financial situation slowly improving, Penney and her colleagues severed their organizational ties with the Committee on Race Relations. In early 1942 the YPIF was officially incorporated as Fellowship House, a non-profit organization with a board of directors, officers, and members. Penney became the agency's executive director and Rawlins was chosen as assistant director. Fred Wentzel, who along with Helen Bryan had originated the YPIF, assumed the post of president. In its by-laws, Fellowship House pledged "to organize people without regard to race or religion into an agency dedicated to the promotion of brotherhood and respect for individual rights and human dignity."[35] They faced a daunting challenge; in the early 1940s Philadelphia was a simmering cauldron of racial tension.

Penney and Rawlins planned to reach schoolchildren and adults through a series of outreach and House-centered programs. Increasing numbers of schoolchildren visited Fellowship House, while volunteers were dispatched to elementary schools. In addition to focusing on children, Fellowship House wanted to recruit schoolteachers as foot soldiers in the battle against racism. Adults represented another challenge for the nascent organization. In an effort to broaden the base to adults, a new program co-sponsored with the Race Relations Department of the Federation of Churches was initiated. The goal of the Units for Unity program was twofold: 1) to enlarge the pool of articulate speakers for the increasingly popular Speakers' Bureau and 2) to train people to apply Fellowship House's concepts in their own neighborhoods. The program's first brochure issued a call to arms:

> With liberty and justice for all. Can we honestly claim that this side of America is finished? The Negro boy says as he salutes the flag. Liberty and justice for all except me. Japanese American citizens uprooted from their homes and businesses placed into relocation

centers question this high sounding statement. Race riots break across the headlines....

The America which says and means, "All men are created equal, possess certain inalienable rights"—that America is in the process of becoming. Together we can make America what we will.[36]

The initial Units for Unity course consisted of a series of four lectures taught primarily by Fellowship House staff. An integrated student body read current works on race relations, race theory, and African American studies like Ruth Benedict's *Race, Science, and Politics* (1945), James Weldon Johnson's *Negro Americans, What Now?* (YEAR), and Alain Locke's *The New Negro* (1925). The sessions covered topics from anti-Semitism to xenophobia. Students were quizzed on such questions as "What contributions have ancient and modern Africans made to civilizations?" and "How would you answer the charge that Negroes are undependable, lazy, dishonest, and criminally inclined?"[37]

Although this pioneering program received praise, it was uncertain how the "graduates" would implement the lessons in their communities. Could these activists prevent the outbreak of racial violence? Was intercultural education the best approach or would more direct incident-control methods be more practical? Influenced by the new interracial civil rights movement, the school district and Mayor Bernard Samuel took new measures to lessen rising racial tension. In July 1943 Stoddard appointed a talented black principal, Dr. Tanner Duckrey, to the post of special assistant. Duckrey's job was to alleviate racial tension in the school district. The new administrator was a member of Fellowship House and served as an advisor on educational matters to the Fellowship Commission.[38] His appointment had a sense of urgency since it came in the wake of the worst racial violence of the World War II era.

In late June a race riot in Detroit had left twenty-five blacks and nine whites dead and hundreds injured. Although the riot had evolved from a brawl at an amusement park, the underlying cause of the violence was a simmering conflict over housing and employment. Across the nation, government leaders, businessmen, and race relations activists scrambled to prevent future Detroits. Similar tensions existed in Philadelphia, and many believed that the City of Brotherly Love would explode. One of Fellowship House's sponsors, Henry Lee Willet, was an eyewitness to the Motor City race riot. In a special issue of the Fellowship House newsletter, he reported on the wanton violence in Detroit, citing unprovoked attacks on blacks and the overwhelming indifference of the police to white rioters. He also criticized the Detroit Council of Churches for refusing to open the churches to refugees of the riots. In the issue's conclusion, Penney warned that Philadelphia may be next. She advised Philadelphians of all races to mobilize against racial violence. Specifically, she called for increased police patrols, bans on weapon sales, and the cooperation of the clergy and the media in decreasing racial tension.[39]

Fellowship House was not alone in its concern. In July 1943 the Pennsylvania State Temporary Commission on the Urban Colored Population shifted its focus away from postwar planning to the problem of immediate racial tension. In August Mayor Bernard Samuel appointed forty-five prominent citizens to a new agency, the City-Wide Interracial Committee (CWIC). The purpose of CWIC was to investigate racism in employment, housing and other areas. Both the Fellowship Commission and Fellowship House were well represented in the Executive Committee and the Subcommittees of this new agency. The CWIC also included Roman Catholic activists like Anna McGarry of the Catholic Interracial Council and J. Francis Finnegan of the Crime Prevention Association.[40] Since 1936 the archdiocese had sponsored a campaign to increase interracial dialogue, but the city's Catholic community was divided on this issue. In 1941 Dennis Cardinal Dougherty, Archbishop of Philadelphia, publicly condemned racism yet did not remove popular priests who encouraged the racist sentiments of their parishioners. Although the YPIF and Fellowship House were interdenominational as well as interracial, there was little official support from the Catholic community. In an era charged with religious intolerance, many of the city's Roman Catholics clergy and laity were suspicious of an organization that they believed to be dominated by Protestants and Jews.

Through its programs Fellowship House reached elementary age schoolchildren and adults, but had no programs oriented to teenagers. In late 1943 Fellowship House began to focus on the city's teenage population. The goal of the High School Fellowship program was similar to the Units for Unity program: 1) to educate young people about their concept of racial brotherhood and 2) to enlist young people in the struggle for racial brotherhood as active participants.[41] Penney publicized the program throughout the public school system but met with little initial enthusiasm. Many white parents and teachers feared both racial conflict and miscegenation.

Despite widespread concern, the program was supported by many administrators and teachers. Since the mid-1930s, social scientists and government officials had warned of a "youth crisis." During the Depression, high unemployment rates contributed to a rise in juvenile delinquency. As wartime racial tension increased, several Philadelphia high schools had become points of conflict and Fellowshippers were concerned that many white teenagers would fall prey to hate groups.

Aided by teachers like Sylvia "Boots" Le Boutillier and Connie Rosner, a junior and senior high school Fellowship program began to take shape. By June 1944 two High School Fellowship clubs had started. Upon joining a High School Fellowship club, a student pledged "to rid my heart of prejudice, my mind of the ignorance that breeds it; my lips of the falsehoods that nurture it; my actions of the injustice that reflects it."[42]

The increasing profile of the organization raised expectations. In May 1944 several volunteers spoke to students at South Philadelphia's Barratt Junior High. Students like Malcolm Johnson voiced their support:

> We must help for our own political, economic equality today not tomorrow. I have had some prejudice against people of different races because of propaganda and what they have done to me because I'm a Negro.
>
> However, I realize to gain this equality we must work for it together, all races, all religions. I realize how important your job is and I'm 100% behind you. Keep up the good work. Gung ho!!![43]

Another student, Rita Ferrelli, was transformed by the visit. The young South Philadelphian declared that "from now on no person is going to put into my head any false ideas about Jews, Negroes, or Protestants."[44] Fellowship House hoped that students like Johnson and Ferrelli would become recruits in the war against racism. Therefore, increased emphasis was placed on supporting junior high and high school Fellowship programs. In order to attract students and teachers, Penney and a team of volunteers developed an innovative program that incorporated film, music, and art.

For example, artwork created by the students was displayed at schools, department stores, and government offices. These student activists also created a speakers' bureau and attended Units for Unity sessions. Armed with new insights on race, the students returned to their schools to preach the gospel of Fellowship House at assembly programs.[45]

Perhaps the most important yet most controversial aspect of the program was the inter-school interaction. Since most Philadelphia schools were segregated, the majority of these carefully chaperoned interracial contacts occurred at "neutral" sites like Fellowship House or Center City social service agencies. Despite lingering reservations, the program expanded rapidly. By June 1945 over eight hundred teenagers were members of nineteen High School Fellowship clubs.[46]

The other educational programs of the House were also expanding their reach. By 1945 several thousand children were visiting the Doll Library each year. Adult programs such as the Speakers' Bureau and the Units for Unity course had also grown rapidly. In 1944 and 1945, Fellowship speakers reached thousands of people while several hundred potential activists were enrolled in Units for Unity. Fellowship House's innovative approach to race relations had attracted the attention of activists and government officials from San Diego to Boston. In 1943 the annual Pendle Hill retreat featured representatives of fellowship groups from Baltimore and New York City. Although these groups were relatively small, they patterned themselves after the pioneering Philadelphians. Influenced by Fellowship House, similar organizations emerged in nearby Media and Reading and as far away as Cleveland, Ohio, and Kansas City, Missouri.[47]

In addition to its increasing influence on the national scene, Fellowship House also helped in the creation of an important school district committee. In April 1944 Stoddard formed the Committee of Thirty, made up of teachers and administrators to "study race, religious, and class tensions in the schools and recommended procedures." The superintendent realized that school personnel would need the assistance and direction of race relations professionals. In September 1944 Stoddard created the Committee on School and Community Tensions, which included Duckrey, Fagan, Penney, and Moore. The new committee advised the administration on the interrelationship of school and neighborhood tension.[48] Thus, Fellowship House and the Fellowship Commission began a process to influence district policy.

The Fellowship Commission attempted to increase its influence on the public school system by co-sponsoring the Philadelphia Childhood Project. Directed by the New York–based Bureau of Intercultural Education and the Massachusetts Institute of Technology (MIT), the objective of this long-term program was to determine the roots of racial and ethnic prejudice. The project surveyed kindergarteners' impressions of race. Released several years later, the survey determined that "race prejudice existed in the early years" and recommended that very young children needed to be taught racial tolerance.[49]

Despite the increasing involvement of the interracial civil rights movement in the Philadelphia School District, their influence had limited impact on administration policy. Prior to the war, black organizations had pushed for the integration of the secondary school faculty. In 1939 Stoddard abolished the dual eligibility list that ranked teachers by race and ability. School officials, however, continued to discriminate against black candidates for high school positions. In 1946 the school district finally approved the advancement of a black educator: Ruth Wright Hayre, an English teacher, became the first African American appointed at a senior high school.[50] Although her advancement opened the door for other black educators, school district officials were by no means committed to upgrading black professionals.

Joshua's Trumpet

DURING WORLD WAR II AN INCREASING NUMBER OF WORKS ON RACE RElations appeared. Buttressed by scientific studies refuting racial superiority, writers like Hortense Powdermaker, Charles Johnson, and Carey McWilliams focused on different aspects of the American "race problem." Like Philadelphia's activists and others across the nation, these authors drew parallels between Nazi Germans and American racists and appealed for interracial unity in the face of a war against fascism. However, the most important work of this period was the groundbreaking study by Gunnar Myrdal, *The American Dilemma*.

Although the Swedish scholar was faulted for misinterpreting many aspects of African American culture, he articulated the discrepancy between the rhetoric and reality of the American Creed. Myrdal argued that higher values such as life, liberty, equality, justice, and fair opportunity were constantly being supplanted by "other valuations," such as irrational or prejudiced tendencies. These other valuations were defended in terms of tradition, expediency, or utility. To overcome the monolith of racism, Myrdal argued, the role of education was essential. Echoing Haynes, Myrdal championed intercultural education as a means to break down barriers. For the rising advocates of racial unity in Philadelphia, Myrdal's work legitimized their struggle.[51]

Encouraged by the rise of supportive scholarship, activists discussed the best means of disseminating these new concepts. The Fellowship Commission proposed the creation of the Fellowship Library, a resource center dedicated to the emerging literature. Fagan envisioned the library as a "living memorial to the men and women of all colors who were fighting for democracy."⁵² In 1944 the Fellowship Commission embarked on an ambitious fundraising drive for the library and an office building, which they planned to use as a headquarters. Since 1941 the commission had shared office space at 1431 Brown Street. Fagan and his colleagues set an ambitious goal of $100,000 for the proposed facility. The commission appealed to foundations and the general public and initially met with limited success. After the end of the war, however, contributions poured in.⁵³

By October 1946 the commission had surpassed its goal and opened the Fellowship Center and Library at 260 S. 15th Street in Center City. In addition to its extensive library space and conference rooms, the Fellowship Building also had ample office space for other civil rights agencies. Shortly after its opening, teachers began bringing their classes to the library on a regular basis. Buoyed by the popularity of the new facility, they proposed that "fellowship corners" or areas devoted to race relations collections should be established in every public library.⁵⁴

Perhaps the most sweeping and innovative educational program of the Fellowship Commission was its utilization of local media resources. In 1942 the Fellowship Commission initiated the "Great American Teams" series in several local newspapers. This cartoon series featured stories of black, white, and Jewish servicemen fighting together against Nazism and Japanese tyranny. Captions at the end of each cartoon issued a call to arms: "In war as in peace American youths of every creed, race and nationality-background find unity the only way to victory."⁵⁵ Thus, the Fellowship Commission appealed to civilians of all races to adopt the concept of the "Double V," victory against racism at home and anti-Semitism abroad.

Attempting to broaden its base, Fagan wanted to gain access to the popular medium of radio. In the fall of 1942, the Fellowship Commission started *Valor Knows No Creed*, a radio series on station WIP. The format was similar to the "Great American Teams" series. Each week, the show dramatized the wartime experiences of a selected Philadelphia serviceman. In addition to spotlighting their heroism on the battlefield, these soldiers and sailors were also portrayed as champions of racial and religious tolerance. Each broadcast closed with the reminder that "next week's hero may be white or Negro, he may be a Protestant or a Catholic or a Jew for VALOR KNOWS NO CREED."⁵⁶

The show was well received, but Fagan and his colleagues wanted to develop radio programming with more relevance to the struggle on the home front. He initiated the formation of a Press and Radio Committee to oversee the Fellowship Commission's media relations. One of the members of this new committee was scriptwriter Caye Christian, who assisted the Commission with two new radio series.[57]

In January 1945 *Within Our Gates* premiered on radio station WFIL. This new series dramatized the lives of individuals "whose contributions have benefitted all mankind."[58] Although well-known historical figures like Benjamin Franklin were profiled, the series also covered the lives of African American figures like Benjamin Banneker, Harriet Tubman, and Frederick Douglass. Contemporary notables such as Dr. Mary McLeod Bethune and Thurgood Marshall were also included in this weekly series. The Fellowship Commission provided the scripts, while WFIL supplied the studio, cast, and radio time. Actors and actresses were screened to ensure that they were sympathetic to the ideals of the Fellowship Commission.[59]

Although they often portrayed famous African Americans, few blacks were in the cast. This omission could not be attributed to the lack of qualified black actors, since Philadelphia had been a center of black theatre since the colonial era.

There is no evidence of the commission protesting this action, and in spite of this exclusion, the show received support by the black community, who voiced enthusiasm about the portraits of black heroes and heroines. The school district utilized the program by recommending it for its extension service and made the recordings and scripts available to teachers across the area.[60]

The success of *Within Our Gates* led the Fellowship Commission to initiate another radio program. In the fall of 1945, *Hate Incorporated* debuted on station WIP. This series dramatized the battle against "public enemy number one: the twisting, lying professional peddlers of intolerance."[61] *Hate Incorporated* emerged in response to a resurgence of Klan activity and a general mood of uneasiness after the end of the war. Race relations activists were concerned that as veterans returned home, the United States might relive the nightmarish Red Summer of 1919.

In an effort to forestall postwar racial conflict, Fellowship House initiated the CommUNITY program, an adaptation of the Units for Unity course that was aimed at educating demobilized veterans about racial tolerance. It also co-sponsored, with the Jewish Community Relations Committee, a visit by Dr. Julius Schrieber, director of the National Institute of Social Relations. Schrieber's talk launched a "preventative institute" for the Speakers' Bureau.[62] In the aftermath of World War II, the goal of race relations activists was to squelch the fires of hatred before they were ignited.

Fortunately, there was no widespread outbreak of racial violence in Philadelphia, and some credit must be given to the work of race relations organizations and civil rights agencies. Despite high unemployment and competition over housing, a tense peace reigned. The end of the war raised questions for the future of Philadelphia's race relations activists. Would their educational programs continue to be supported by the school system? Without the fear of a racial explosion, would people still be interested in the Speakers Bureau? How could they adapt the wartime interest in race relations to the uncertain postwar world?

Changes and Challenges in the Postwar World

IN 1945 FELLOWSHIP HOUSE REMAINED AN ORGANIZATION WITH AN UNcertain financial foundation. Although contributions from foundations like the Julius Rosenwald Fund, the Marshall Field Foundation, Benezet Fund, and B'nai B'rith had increased, they did not keep pace with rising costs. Four years after its inception, Fellowship House's budget had increased sixfold.[63] The organization continued to receive much of its support from its individual members and sympathizers. In many cases, supporters gave the House cookware, curtains, and office furniture. Ad hoc committees like the one established by Mrs. Lonnie Wall, wife of a black West Philadelphia physician, frequently raised money for Fellowship House.[64] Such displays of support among Philadelphia's rising black middle class indicated that Fellowship House had established itself as a priority in the black community.

Despite increasing contributions, a lack of a stable funding base could have affected Fellowship House's long-term plans. In late 1946 the House's fortunes improved when Penney and Fagan shared the prestigious Philadelphia Award. In addition to acknowledging their contribution to the City of Brotherly Love, the award also carried a prize of five thousand dollars.[65]

In contrast to Fellowship House, the Fellowship Commission was in a more favorable financial position. By 1945 eight constituent agencies were members of the Commission. These organizations contributed literature and clerical assistance, which reduced financial needs. Furthermore, the Commission included members of the city's business and political elite who had access to major sources of funding. The successful fundraising campaign for the Fellowship Building also proved that the Commission could raise massive funding for a race relations project. Contributors to the building campaign became members of the new Fellowship Library. Although contributors could not join the commission, they had access to the clearinghouse's resources. As a result, public support for the drive was high.[66]

Financial issues notwithstanding, both the Fellowship Commission and Fellowship House expanded their educational programs after the war. Fagan attempted to set a postwar agenda for the Fellowship Commission by outlining numerous areas that needed more attention and closer cooperation among the constituent agencies. He cited equal opportunity in public and higher education and intercultural training for police personnel as important issues. Although Fagan was the architect of the mass education program, he wondered about its effectiveness and the ability of the commission to bring about collective action. Perhaps the movement needed to look to the political environment.

In the late 1940s a resurgent Democratic Party, led by attorney and political reformer Walter Phillips, began to challenge the city's long dominant Republican establishment. To achieve victory it was necessary to cultivate the support of the city's rapidly growing African American population. Influenced by the New Deal, blacks had supported Democratic candidates for state and national offices in the late 1930s. However, on the local level, blacks continued to vote for GOP candidates.[67]

Both the Fellowship Commission and Fellowship House had sought to remain non-partisan, but some members believed that a Democratic administration would be more supportive of their programs. In 1947 Bernard Samuel was reelected to City Hall, winning 63 percent of the vote in the city's black wards.[68] Yet the election shifted the City Council in favor of the Democrats and raised the profile of the political reform movement.

CHAPTER 3

Education for Democracy

The Interracial Civil Rights Movement and Intercultural and Desegregated Education, 1947–1970

IN 1945 THE JULIUS ROSENWALD FUND REPORTED THE EXISTENCE OF three hundred racial and ethnic relations organizations in the United States. Three years later, the fund listed over one thousand such groups.[1] In the forefront of this growing "war against bigotry" in Philadelphia were such interracial organizations as Fellowship House and the Fellowship Commission. These activists had created a wide array of educational programs ranging from radio drama to racial tolerance workshops for children. But by the late 1940s Philadelphia's interracial civil rights community had started to question its strategies. The intercultural programs had won wide acclaim and had contributed to lessening racial tension; however, some activists argued that the movement needed to engage in direct action tactics, while others believed that utilizing the legislative process represented the most effective way to address racial discrimination.

Although the activists were divided about their approach, most believed that public opinion was on their side. On both the local and national level, legislators began to argue for the passage of civil rights laws. Influenced by the work of Ruth Benedict, Franz Boas, W. E. B. Du Bois, and others, academics had started to question long-held assumptions on race. World War II had raised questions about racial superiority, and the federal government had stressed racial unity as crucial in defeating the Axis. Thus, it was conceivable to the activists that they would achieve great success in the postwar era.

This chapter examines the evolution of the interracial civil rights movement in the aftermath of World War II. Despite encouraging signs, these activists also faced an uncertain world. Would their relatively non-combative theories to soothing racial tensions remain relevant in the postwar world? On the domestic front, blacks became increasingly militant in their quest for social justice, while the Cold War and anti-colonialism reshaped

45

the international political order. This chapter looks at how interracial activists confronted this new reality and were thus able to redefine and expand on their original mission.

As historian Peter Kellogg argues, there were several responses to racism in the World War II period: 1) *The American Dilemma* response, a feeling that democratic values were undermined by racism; 2) the fear of widespread racial violence; and 3) political competition for the increasingly independent and strategic black vote.[2]

Although they supported Democratic policies such as the establishment of a Fair Employment Practice Commission (FEPC), the interracial civil rights movement remained non-partisan in local politics. In contrast to most major cities, Philadelphia's local government remained firmly in the hands of the Republicans. Official non-partisanship permitted the activists to interact freely with sympathizers of both parties.

In the late 1940s a rejuvenated Democratic Party challenged the corrupt and inefficient GOP machine. Mayor Bernard Samuels's reelection in 1947 represented a Pyrrhic victory for the embattled Republicans. Grand jury investigations and the suicides of four city officials suspected of corruption further weakened the power of the GOP. In November 1948 five Democratic congressmen were elected in the Philadelphia area and the Democratic Party carried Philadelphia for Truman.[3]

Key members of both Fellowship House and the Fellowship Commission increasingly began to gravitate toward the city's Democratic reformers. For example, Sadie Tanner Mossell Alexander, a board member of Fellowship House and a member of the Fellowship Commission's Civic Committee, served on Truman's influential Committee on Human Rights. Similarly, one of the early supporters of the YPIF was Reverend Marshal Shepard Sr., the Democratic state representative responsible for mobilizing black support for Roosevelt in the 1930s. In addition to direct involvement in Democratic politics, members and officials had strong links with the city's rising Democrats. Through his leadership of the Jewish Anti-Defamation Council (JADC) and the Jewish Council on Community Relations (JCCR), Fagan had worked closely with Albert M. Greenfield, one of the city's most prominent businessmen and a leader in the renewal of the Democratic organization. Democratic reformer Joseph Sill Clark was a personal friend of Penney and a strong supporter of Fellowship House. In 1949 the Democrats scored their first major municipal victory when Clark became city controller and Dilworth became city treasurer.[4] The election of Clark and Dilworth laid the groundwork for a Democratic assault on City Hall. Many activists were hopeful that a Democratic administration would support civil rights legislation.

As political winds shifted in the postwar period, both the Fellowship Commission and Fellowship House expanded existing programs and initiated new ones. Buoyed by increasing donations, the Fellowship House was able to enhance the popular High School Fellowship program. Although this program was successful in bringing youth of all races together and stressing racial tolerance, some teachers complained that the program needed a greater focus on direct action as opposed to social interaction. They also expressed concern that the Fellowship Clubs were not reaching enough white students, the most important target audience in the struggle for racial tolerance. Some further argued in favor of programs on the dangers of nuclear conflict and warned of a growing reactionary mood among school administrators.[5]

Adult-oriented programs stressed neighborhood activism, spirituality, and culture. In an attempt to increase the involvement of their neighbors with the organization, Fellowship House initiated the creation of the Community Council, a program designed to increase the involvement of their North Philadelphia neighborhood in the life of the organization. This grassroots approach also emerged in the formation of the Neighbors Unlimited or Neighborhood Fellowship. Six private homes, owned or leased by members, served as "little Fellowship Houses." Located across the city, they became centers where blacks and whites could meet to discuss community tensions. The Neighborhood Fellowship was placed under the auspices of a reorganized interfaith department, the Religious Fellowship.[6]

The purpose of the Religious Fellowship was to inject a more diverse spirituality into the struggle for brotherhood. In contrast to the Fellowship Church of the early 1930s, the Religious Fellowship sponsored interfaith services with the participation of rabbis. Directed by Dr. Herbert Haslam, a distinguished pioneer in interdenominational relations, the Religious Fellowship attempted to frame the movement for racial understanding within a larger ecumenical context.[7]

The inclusion of Judaism in the Fellowship movement began in the late 1930s when the YPIF and the Anti-Defamation Council, with its emphasis on combatting racism and anti-Semitism, attracted many Jewish activists. The majority of Jewish Fellowshippers came from Reform congregations such as Rodelph Shalom and Keneseth Israel. In contrast to the Orthodox and Conservative traditions, Reform theology emphasized social justice and social action. The participation of Reform Jews coincided with the growth of Reform Judaism in the Philadelphia area and the increasing involvement of second-generation immigrant Jews in secular organizations.[8]

In an effort to reach a wider audience, Penney proposed the creation of an interracial choir. An innovative cultural endeavor, the Singing City Choir was founded in 1948. Directed by Elaine Brown, a nationally known conductor, Singing City was designed to be a musical expression of racial tolerance. The choir was actually a coalition of singers from church choirs and community choruses. Penney stated that these cultural ambassadors of the growing Fellowship movement were to "sing the songs of democracy" to all who would listen. Penney hoped that Singing City would attract more members to Fellowship House.[9]

As the number of programs increased, it became apparent that the facility at 1431 Brown Street would no longer suffice. In 1948 Penney proposed that Fellowship House purchase a farm at Tanguy Homes, a small interracial Quaker housing development located in suburban Delaware County. The farm would serve several purposes: 1) to train Fellowshippers from across the nation for an extended period in the summer, 2) to train members of the Junior and Senior High School Fellowship program, 3) to provide facilities for special programs like Singing City, and 4) to create a racially tolerant environment for members and visitors to live and work. In an effort to finance this ambitious venture, Penney launched a comprehensive fundraising campaign. Although the Tanguy proposal was later rejected, the House continued to search for a suitable retreat.[10] Differences over the farm proposal surfaced at the spring 1949 retreat held at the Crozer Seminary in Chester. Board member Minor Alexander argued that financial resources should be utilized in the city. Supporters of the proposal, such as Virginia and Roosevelt Barlow, said that Fellowship House could develop a camp for neighborhood children. One of the founding members, Randolph Walker, assured detractors that refurbishing costs could be held to a minimum if House members did much of the work themselves.[11]

The debate about the proposed retreat reflected concerns over the direction of Fellowship House. By the late 1940s civil rights had begun to emerge as a national issue. One of Fellowship House's most prominent supporters and frequent visitors was Howard University Law School dean Charles Hamilton Houston. Houston and the NAACP Legal Defense Fund planned to challenge the infamous 1896 *Plessy v. Ferguson* decision by attacking legal segregation in public education.[12] Although Fellowship House was opposed to segregation, members were deeply divided over the organization's institutional identity.

At the Crozer conference, some members maintained that the organization was a laboratory for human relations that could never advance beyond the experimental stage; others argued that the House was a spiritual entity open to individual interpretation; some saw the organization as a civil rights agency that should agitate for change.[13]

The Crozer Conference resolved little about the future direction of Fellowship House. However, there was a clear consensus for expanding the House's educational programs. In 1950, the Educational Equality League reported that although the number of black faculty and staff had increased, gerrymandering by school officials had created new patterns of segregation or reinforced old ones.[14] In addition to official policy, increasing residential segregation contributed to the growth of segregated schools.

School board president Walter Biddle Saul argued that the system should move cautiously on the issue of desegregation. In response to charges that black teachers were assigned to predominantly black schools, Saul stated that administrators had to be sensitive to "community feelings" in sending black educators to white schools.[15] In addition, many activists simply did not question neighborhood schools. Fellowship House member Mitzi Barnes recalled that the majority of children attended school within a short distance of home and that most activists accepted this reality.[16] They believed that their prime objective was to facilitate dialogue with students from segregated schools.

While the activists of Fellowship House worked on a neighborhood-centered level, the Fellowship Commission supervised citywide projects. In 1946 the commission's president, the Reverend George Trowbridge, pledged that they would concentrate on "the interracial," "the interfaith," and "the international." Trowbridge also outlined three methods the commission would utilize to fulfill its mandate: mass education, community mobilization, and closer coordination with the eight constituent member agencies.[17] In 1947, the executive board of the Fellowship Commission established the Educational Policy and Planning Committee (EPPC). Chaired by Anne Wright, a public school principal, the EPPC became a medium through which intercultural educational concepts were disseminated. Although instrumental in introducing new theories to school district personnel, the EPPC was not geared to protest administration policy. Its role was primarily advisory.[18]

The major educational issue for the Fellowship Commission was not desegregation in public education but expanding higher education for minorities. Prior to World War II, education reformers had proposed a tuition-free city-supported college modeled on the city college system of New York City. In 1947 Fagan began to collaborate with the Citizens for Free College Facilities. Fagan convinced the commission that a broad-based coalition was needed. By 1949 the coalition, renamed the Citizen's Committee for a Free City College (CFCC), included over 125 groups, including organizations as diverse as the Philadelphia Esperanto Society, the United Paperworkers of America, and the Daughters of the American Revolution.[19]

The Fellowship Commission served as the base of operations for the CFCC, and Fagan assumed the strategic post of secretary. The CFCC argued that racial and religious discrimination had limited the educational aspirations of many Philadelphians and that a free city college would provide opportunities for blacks and other minorities. It would be the first college in the city to be open to all applicants regardless of race or religion. Cunningham, now a member of the commission's Committee on Religion, garnered support among black churches and civic associations. They were successful in attracting support from the business community by emphasizing the positive impact a new college would have on the local economy. Despite a groundswell of public support, detractors claimed that the proposed college would be too expensive, and legislation for the project stalled in the General Assembly. Although discouraged by this defeat, the Fellowship Commission had undergone an important transformation in the orchestration of the campaign. Although it had mobilized a large segment of the population across racial, ethnic, and class lines to support the creation of an integrated educational institution, it had not marshalled enough support among politicians to pass the required legislation. Realizing that a tactical change was required, the Fellowship Commission moderated its non-partisan stance and became more involved in the political process by lobbying and forming alliances with legislators, mostly liberal Democrats.

In 1949 revelations of municipal corruption increased and resulted in the creation of the bipartisan Philadelphia Charter Commission (PCC). The PCC believed that a revision of the 1919 charter was essential to the process of municipal reform. The PCC included some of the interracial movement's most prominent members. Attorney Abraham Freedman sat on the Fellowship Commission's important Civic Committee, while Dr. Tanner Duckrey was a member of Fellowship House's board of directors and also served on the Fellowship Commission's Education Committee. As the highest-ranking black administrator in the school district, Duckrey became the Charter

Commission's most prominent spokesman on racial matters. The pioneering educator exhorted the Charter Commission to honor Quaker traditions of tolerance and to make civil rights a cornerstone of the new charter.[20]

Within the Charter Commission, debate ensued about the future of the wartime Fair Employment Practices Commission (FEPC). In late 1950 Sadie Alexander argued passionately for a new commission on human relations. She outlined plans for an agency that would have broad powers to investigate charges of discrimination in housing, public accommodations, and labor and to enforce city ordinances.[21] In the spring of 1951, a referendum on the proposed charter was held. Through the Fellowship Commission newsletter, *Report to the Community*, Fagan consistently urged support for the new charter. Fellowship House also called for passage of the charter: "Fellowship House is particularly interested in urging its adoption because of its guarantees of equality of opportunity for all citizens regardless of race, religion or national origin."[22] They also urged their members to "discuss the Charter at any speaking engagement you may have between this date and April 17th, and further that you also discuss it with your relatives, friends, and neighbors and suggest that they vote for it."[23]

The proposed charter passed. It granted greater administrative power to the mayor and reformed the structure of City Council. Most importantly, it established the Philadelphia Commission on Human Relations (PCHR), granting it much of the power proposed by the Fellowship Commission. The victory of the "Home Rule Charter" energized the reform movement. In the fall of 1951, Joseph Clark was elected mayor, ending more than a century of Republican rule. Unlike the charter referendum, neither the Fellowship Commission nor Fellowship House formally endorsed any candidate.[24]

As Clark and his supporters savored their hard-won triumph, Fellowship House shifted some of its programs to a new rural retreat. After considerable debate, in 1951 the organization acquired a 120-acre farm in Fagleysville, Montgomery County. Located about forty miles from Philadelphia, the farm was purchased with foundation support and the contributions of members and officers. Although the farm was in decrepit shape, renovations were carried out by an enthusiastic cadre of volunteers.[25] Helen Stark Tomkins, the director of the Reading Fellowship House and a frequent visitor to the Farm, said that the neighboring farmers were initially suspicious of the integrated community. Tomkins recalled: "They thought we were Communists, until they heard the sound of hymns drifting over the valleys. Then they thought we were members of Father Divine's movement."[26] Although some members expressed concerned that the House was abandoning Philadelphia, only a few programs were relocated to the retreat, now called Fellowship Farm.

Contrary to the fears of some members, Fellowship House did not neglect city-based programs. In the fall of 1949, the Arrow Program was incorporated into the public school system. The program's expansion represented Fellowship House's first concentrated outreach into elementary education. Although the Doll Library had appeared in schools since the early 1940s, the new Arrow program was much more ambitious. Each month, ten volunteers brought the message of Fellowship House to a different school for a weeklong program. The highlight of the program was a play, staged by schoolchildren, about brown and white rabbits who build an integrated community.[27]

While the Board of Education supported intercultural programs such as the Arrow, they appeared resistant to integrated education. The reform movement that had swept through the city's political landscape had not reached the "Palace on the Parkway," the imposing gray school administration building on Benjamin Franklin Parkway. In addition, one of the major obstacles to reform was Add Anderson, secretary and business manager of the Board of Education. The powerful Anderson had maintained tight control over the district's budget since the Depression and had influenced the selection of several superintendents. More importantly, he was a staunch foe of desegregation.[28]

As the Fellowship Commission celebrated its tenth anniversary in October 1951, its Education Committee sponsored a conference on racial discrimination in Philadelphia public schools. The conference, entitled "Democracy in Education," featured representatives from predominantly black organizations like the EEL and the NAACP, members of the interracial civil rights community, and the academic community.[29] The NAACP and the EEL favored research followed by legal action on the behalf of individual plaintiffs. The Fellowship Commission supported research on specific issues but did not commit to any form of action, legal or otherwise. In its 1952 annual report, Fagan stated the commission's position on the district's increasing segregation: "The Fellowship Commission has only begun to educate itself about this multi-faceted problem which is vexing every large city in the north."[30]

In an effort to coordinate its response to racial discrimination in education, housing, and employment, they hired Reverend Walter Wynn of Providence, Rhode Island, as social action director. Wynn, a former principal of a technical school in Liberia, had acquired considerable experience in race relations as an official of the Providence Urban League.[31]

The Fellowship Commission's first major postwar battle over segregated education was not directed toward the public school system, but instead at a private institution. In the early nineteenth century, Stephen Girard, a prominent shipping magnate and financier, left over six million dollars for the establishment and maintenance of a school for the education of "poor white orphan boys." In 1848 Girard College opened in North Philadelphia. For over a century the walled campus in an increasingly black community symbolized African American exclusion from the educational life of the city.[32] Although desegregating Girard would not directly affect most black children, it would constitute an important victory in the battle for integration. If the stately walls of Girard could be breached, perhaps there would be more pressure placed upon the school district to desegregate.

As the nation awaited the outcome of the *Brown v. Board of Education* case, Raymond Pace Alexander filed a lawsuit on behalf of the EEL and the NAACP against the estate of Stephen Girard. The Fellowship Commission threw its support behind the lawsuit. The victory of the NAACP in the *Brown* case demonstrated to Philadelphia's activists that legal victories were possible. In 1958 the Supreme Court of the United States upheld the right of the Girard estate to exclude African Americans. The court's decision would not be the last salvo in this battle, but the struggle to open Girard would not resume until the 1960s.[33]

While the Fellowship Commission struggled on the policy front, Fellowship House focused on the temporal aspects of the Beloved Community. Church and community groups and individuals traveled to Fellowship Farm from across the region and the nation. For visitors and residents, the highlight of a typical farm experience was the evening pilgrimage to the Hilltop, an area that overlooked the rolling countryside of central Montgomery County. The short walk to the Hilltop was followed by an extended period of meditation.[34] For Penney, intercultural education was not limited to workshops and sessions held at the farm, but in the daily work experience that Fellowshippers shared. This interaction spanned the chasms of race, class, and faith: "[P]loughing the field and sowing winter wheat ties a city man close to the agricultural peoples of the earth; grinding that wheat into flour and kneading it into great brown loaves, which the Fellowship family eats, is a sermon to many women."[35]

Although women and men shared housekeeping duties, a gender-based division of labor existed at Fellowship Farm. Women were primarily responsible for child care and food preparation, while men handled technical chores. Despite this, women like Penney and Rawlins occupied positions of power in Fellowship House. Although their efforts served as models for other women, the primary objective of the organization was not to achieve gender equality but to create a community where racial and religious understanding would flourish.

Fellowship House increasingly focused its educational efforts on cultivating an awareness of international issues, creating family-oriented programs, and enhancing its influence in the school district. Since its formation, Fellowship House had periodically highlighted international issues in its evening forums. Although the organization did not wholly embrace anti-colonial struggles of the postwar era, it did endorse the movement for Indian independence. In contrast to the often violent struggles for self-determination, India's independence movement was led by Mohandas Gandhi, whose pacifist beliefs were attractive to Quaker activists and related institutions like Fellowship House.

In an effort to understand Gandhi's *satyagraha* campaign, Fellowship House regularly invited speakers who were connected to the struggle for Indian independence. In the late 1940s Mordecai Johnson, president of Howard University and a longtime supporter of Fellowship House, traveled to India shortly after the assassination of Gandhi. In the spring of 1950, he addressed a Sunday afternoon forum at Fellowship House. In the audience was Martin Luther King, Jr., then a senior at nearby Crozer Seminary. According to historian David Garrow, King had been introduced to the works of Gandhi at Crozer, but Johnson's address was the catalyst for his interest in satyagraha.[36]

Involvement in international affairs during the early Cold War could prove controversial. Initiated by anti-nuclear activists in Sweden in 1950, the Stockholm Peace Petition called for a total ban on nuclear weapons. Over two hundred million people around the world signed the pledge. In the United States, the Peace Information Center headed by W. E. B. Du Bois sponsored the effort. Although the appeal enjoyed wide support among unions, churches, academics, and artists, many federal officials criticized the document as pro-Soviet propaganda. The House Un-American Activities Committee (HUAC) described the petition as designed to "confuse and divide the American people," while United Nations ambassador Warren Austin referred to the petitioners as "traitors."[37]

The petition was signed by a small number of high school Fellowshippers. When Constance Clayton, a Fellowship leader at Girls High, learned of the controversy, she contacted Penney. Anxious to quell any suspicions of Communist infiltration, Penney issued a warning:

> We want to caution HIGH SCHOOL FELLOWSHIPPERS to be on their guard! Before you sign anything or join any movement, make sure you know:
> 1. WHO sponsors the organization or petition,
> 2. HOW the group is financed
> 3. WHAT are the real purposes of the movement.
> REMEMBER: FELLOWSHIP is working to help create a community where prejudice and discrimination give way to opportunity and equal rights for all.... We firmly believe that these objectives can be attained through the basic principles of our own form of government as set forth in the Declaration of Independence and the Constitution of the United States.[38]

The Peace Petition incident clearly highlighted a major contradiction of Fellowship House policy during the Red Scare. Although they voiced support for free speech, they were also quick to distance themselves from any so-called "subversive" activities.

Both Fellowship House and the Fellowship Commission were affected by the Red Scare. Fellowship House seemed like a probable target of investigation. In the 1930s the YPIF worked with the National Negro Congress (NNC), an alleged "communist front" organization. Helen Bryan, the founder of the YPIF, had delved into leftist politics after leaving Philadelphia. In the early 1950s Bryan served a brief sentence at the federal women's prison in Alderson, West Virginia, for refusing to cooperate with federal investigators. During the war, Fellowship House aligned itself with the Popular Front; its library included works like *I Want to Be Like Stalin* by Counts and Lodge.[39]

In the wake of the war, however, the organization downplayed its radical origins. Some activists, however, were openly critical of the increasing Cold War. Shortly after Churchill's famous Iron Curtain speech, Raymond Pace Alexander warned that the speech was an attempt to draw the United States into a war with the Soviet Union. Statements such as these could prompt an FBI investigation, but there is no direct evidence that Fellowship House was under surveillance.[40]

The Fellowship Commission's response to the Red Scare was nuanced. During the war, the leadership refused to accept the recommendations of

Kenneth Leslie, a textbook editor who was accused of Communist sympathies. As the Cold War intensified, however, the Fellowship Commission began to address increasing restrictions on civil liberties. In 1949 the Fellowship Commission established the Citizens Council on Democratic Rights (CCDR) to focus on issues such as police abuse and free speech. They campaigned against book seizures and legislation such as plans for a city loyalty oath and a state HUAC. Tension developed when Donald Byrd, field secretary of the NAACP, criticized the Fellowship Commission for establishing a committee that would duplicate the NAACP's work around police brutality. In 1951 the CCDR left the Fellowship Commission and became the Philadelphia chapter of the American Civil Liberties Union (ACLU).[41]

Although the Fellowship Commission expressed concern about civil liberties, they also accommodated some aspects of the Red Scare. The Fellowship Commission warned of Communist penetration in the civil rights movement and supported the Attorney General's list of subversive organizations. Yet, in 1953 the Commission criticized the school district for firing teachers with Communist sympathies, and the following year the Fellowship Commission gave the National Fellowship Award to journalist Edward R. Murrow for his exposé of Senator Joseph McCarthy.[42] Their response to the Red Scare seemed inconsistent. In some cases, they sided with the investigators, while in others they supported the persecuted. This conflicted policy suggests that the Fellowship Commission assumed an official anticommunist stance yet attempted to moderate the more outrageous manifestations of the Red Scare. Such a policy would allow them to continue their programs without official interference.

One of the Fellowship Commission's constituent agencies was under FBI surveillance. In the 1940s the FBI began wiretapping the Philadelphia branch of the NAACP. Although this practice was halted in the mid-1950s, it was soon reinstated and continued into the 1960s. Suspicious of any civil rights activity, FBI director J. Edgar Hoover maintained files on most members of Truman's Commission on Civil Rights, including Sadie Alexander. In the 1930s and 1940s, Philadelphia had a fairly large branch of the Communist Party, and the FBI argued that Communists had infiltrated the NAACP.[43] Although the surveillance of members of the Philadelphia NAACP was extensive, it paled in comparison to what activists experienced in the South. Nevertheless, the activities of the FBI in the 1940s and 1950s laid the groundwork for future operations such as COINTELPRO (Counterintelligence Program) that would be initiated in the late 1960s.

Fellowship and the Fifties

IN THE WAKE OF THE PEACE PETITION INCIDENT, FELLOWSHIP HOUSE continued to include international issues within its educational programming. As Cold War tensions increased, the State Department attempted to blunt Soviet portrayals of America as a land seething with racial hate. Anxious to highlight a "fairer side" of the United States, the State Department sent dozens of foreign visitors, the majority of them government and business leaders from countries in Latin America, Africa, and Asia, to Fellowship Farm. The international perspective transformed some of Fellowship's cultural programs. It became common to have programs that featured Latin American folk music and Indian cuisine.[44]

Not all international visitors were from the ruling classes of their respective nations. In 1957 Mohammed Latif, an Iraqi college student, arrived at the Farm. He had traveled directly from Iraq after hearing about Fellowship House from a USAID official. In contrast to most foreign visitors who departed after several months, Latif remained involved with the organization for several decades.[45] Through its foreign connections, Fellowship House broadened its message of tolerance and attempted to place its work in the context of the global struggle for freedom.

In addition to its international perspective, Fellowship House also began to encourage the participation of families. An innovative program, known as Families for Fellowship, was launched in 1955. The organization marketed the Farm as a retreat that had the ambience of a summer camp but was also spiritually enriching. Each summer the Farm reserved several weeks for family-based programs.[46] In addition to increasing interracial dialogue on an intimate level, Penney and her colleagues also hoped to convince some of these families to turn their homes into Neighborhood Fellowship Houses.

One family committed to the concept of the Beloved Community were the Massiahs of North Philadelphia, who frequented the Families for Fellowship gatherings. Frederick Massiah, a Barbadian immigrant and the city's most prominent black architect, had been a contributor and supporter of the interracial civil rights movement since the late 1920s. Although a strong supporter of black economic self-determination in the Garveyite tradition, Massiah also believed in interracial cooperation. His son, Louis, described the Families for Fellowship program as "a week filled with work, music, and play for children and adults." He recalled that the well-integrated gatherings included occasional interaction with African visitors.[47]

The Families for Fellowship program reflected the organization's attempt to reach a wider audience. By the late 1950s Penney would argue that Fellowship House needed to expand its mission to middle-class white suburbanites. While she continued to urge more black and ethnic Catholic participation in the movement, Penney realized that the Philadelphia area, like many metropolitan areas, was undergoing a massive demographic transformation. Although Philadelphia's population decline had started in the 1940s, it accelerated in the 1950s.[48] Her call for an increased emphasis on suburbanites was an attempt to adapt to changing socioeconomic conditions. In addition, Penney was also aware that the postwar baby boom had resulted in a national population increase of over twenty-three million.[49] Through its Families for Fellowship program, Penney hoped to enlist the support of this dynamic new segment of the population in the cause of racial tolerance.

In addition to its international and familial focus, Fellowship House increased its efforts in the school district. Although the Arrow program was reaching thousands of public school children annually by the mid-1950s, the High School Fellowship program had actually lost members since the late 1940s. In an effort to keep the youth movement alive, the organization drew on its past accomplishments in its publications:

> A letter from one of our great housing projects reads:
> "I was a member of your Junior High School Fellowship Club
> It gave me hope and help. Now I want my girl to belong."
>
> Suburban member Jeanne S. writes: "Who persuaded our Home and School association to study Human Relations this year? My neighbor, who says she was a High school Fellowshipper 10 years ago.[50]

Despite declining rates of participation among high school students, other school-based initiatives were developed. The most important and influential program was not directed at students but at administrators and teachers. In the early 1950s the organization developed in-service courses for school district professionals. Although the Fellowship Commission's EPPC had been conducting seminars since the late 1940s, Fellowship House's in-service courses were regularly scheduled credit classes. In 1956, the House reserved a week for teacher education at the Farm.[51] As Fellowship House became more involved with the school system, the calls for district reform increased.

In 1952 the Citizens Committee on Public Education (CCPE) was formed. Headed by Germantown activist Annette Temin and comprised of members of interracial organizations, unions, business organizations, and political groups, the CCPE criticized the district for financial mismanagement and teacher shortages. Despite its small size, the CCPE kept pressure on the Board of Education. In 1958 advocates of school reform received a needed victory when the Greenfield Report was released. Coordinated by Elizabeth "Bunny" Greenfield, the board's newest member and wife of department store magnate and power broker Albert M. Greenfield, the report demonstrated that Philadelphia's teachers were the lowest paid of the nation's largest cities and that the district had no accurate way to evaluate the educational progress of city schoolchildren because the system refused to administer nationally standardized examinations.[52] The Greenfield Report convinced many Philadelphians that school reform was extremely urgent.

Civil Rights or Race Relations?

AS THE STRUGGLE FOR SCHOOL REFORM HEATED UP, FELLOWSHIP HOUSE moved to a new location in North Philadelphia. The structure at 1431 Brown Street could no longer accommodate the increasing number of visitors. Although the social and economic bases of North Philadelphia were crumbling, Fellowship House elected to remain in the community. It located a spacious former Masonic hall at 1521 Girard Street. Under the financial stewardship of businessmen Max Shubin and Frederic Mann, the organization was able to purchase this facility in 1957.[53]

By 1959 the organization had established itself as an influential force in the world of race relations. Through its Federation of Fellowships, Fellowship House had direct influence on the ideology and activities of a dozen similar organizations across the nation. Locally, sixty-three programs ranging from Music for Fellowship to the Religious Fellowship spread the gospel of racial tolerance. As Fellowship House expanded, some members raised questions about its future direction. Were they a civil rights organization or a human relations agency? Some members believed that the term "civil rights" would limit the perspective of Fellowship House. Since Fellowship House also addressed religious intolerance and xenophobia, they reasoned, it should be defined as an experiment in human relations.[54]

When these issues had been raised a decade earlier, civil rights activists had been struggling to be heard. By the late 1950s, however, civil rights had emerged as an important national issue. The movement had scored several strategic victories such as the *Brown* decision, the Montgomery bus boycott, and the Civil Rights Act of 1957, but most activists realized that the battle was only beginning.

Influenced by the momentum of the civil rights movement, Fellowship House had engaged in direct action since the early 1950s. Under the leadership of Mitzi Jacoby Barnes, Fellowship House dispatched integrated groups of High School Fellowshippers to skating rinks, swimming pools, and other recreational facilities to gauge the effectiveness of Pennsylvania's anti-discrimination laws.[55] Although the YPIF had used similar tactics in the 1930s, the protests of the 1950s evolved in the context of a dynamic national struggle. In addition to increased activity on the national scene, Fellowship House had cultivated a growing base of support in the Philadelphia area. The time for change was now. It was apparent to many within the interracial movement that the civil rights struggle was entering a new phase. It was unclear to activists what role Philadelphia's interracial movement would play in the new phase and how the southern-based civil rights struggle would affect race relations within their northern city. Could they utilize Dr. King's methods in the City of Brotherly Love?

In Philadelphia, the school district represented a likely target of a desegregation campaign. By 1960 conditions in the school district had continued to deteriorate. Although the distressed state of the school district affected all children, African American students bore the brunt of the administration's neglect. The system was now over 50 percent black, and half of the schools had an enrollment of 90 percent or more of one race. In response to the school crisis, the Greater Philadelphia Movement (GPM), a business-based urban reform group, recruited a team of researchers from Stanford to conduct the first independent survey of the district since 1938.[56] At last it seemed as though change might come to the once impregnable school district.

The passage of the Pennsylvania Fair Educational Opportunities Act in July 1961 encouraged advocates of desegregation. Three months later, Philadelphia's civil rights activists were also inspired by the brief visit of Dr. Martin Luther King Jr. to the City of Brotherly Love. Invited by Fellowship House, King's four-day visit focused on the role of youth in the civil rights struggle. Penney viewed his appearance as an opportunity to link the work of the SCLC with the work of Philadelphia activists. In his remarks, King reminded his enthusiastic audiences that racial segregation was a national problem and that they must "destroy the things that make brotherhood impossible."[57]

One of those obstacles in the road to brotherhood was the de facto segregation of the school system. By 1962, however, the pace of change in the school district was accelerated by a number of factors. They proposed a new method for selecting board members, closer school and community relations, and most importantly, educational home rule. Educational home rule was modeled on a provision in the Pennsylvania Constitution that granted greater political power to citizens in boroughs and towns. If Philadelphia had educational home rule, the public would have a greater say in school funding issues. Utilized by Clark and Dilworth in their triumph over the Republicans, the GPM hoped to use the home rule provision in an attempt to transform the district. The death of Add Anderson later that year also increased the pace of reform.[58]

Although the coalition included representatives of the NAACP, voices in the black community were concerned that the forces of reform would not adequately address racial discrimination in the district. The EEL and the NAACP filed a suit on behalf of a black parent, Terry Chisholm, who complained that his child was assigned to a distant, overcrowded black school rather than a nearby predominantly white school. The school district responded to the legal challenge by proposing a limited plan of integration. Despite the transfer of some black students and a few black teachers to white schools, the system remained only 16 percent integrated. The action by the EEL and the NAACP constituted a limited, yet symbolic, victory in the battle for school desegregation.[59]

The Chisholm case also reflected the African American community's concern about segregation and the willingness of some African American organizations to take decisive action. In 1962 the president of the Fellowship Commission, Thomas McBride, characterized the commission's approach as "paternalism, tokenism, and gradualism." McBride also maintained that the commission had ignored the problems of the black poor.[60] His statements were a response to an increasing concern about the viability of interracial organizations in Philadelphia.

As the Fellowship Commission questioned its role, it also markedly increased its direct action in the early 1960s, and much of this action was related to the national civil rights movement. Fellowship House became a hub of activity for protesters involved in demonstrations in support of SNCC and SCLC protests in the South. The organization coordinated several demonstrations in Philadelphia, suburban areas, and the border states of Delaware and Maryland. The expansion of its educational mission became increasingly oriented to the needs of the civil rights struggle. Fellowship

House began to train representatives of CORE and SNCC heading for the South to participate in demonstrations. Mohammed Latif recalled that the training included extensive role-playing exercises with an emphasis on teaching the volunteers how to protect themselves from violent police officers and segregationists.[61]

In addition to training civil rights activists, Fellowship House also adapted its intercultural educational programs to train some of the nation's first Peace Corps volunteers. Shortly after its founding in 1961, Peace Corps members arrived at the House and the Farm. Utilizing members from Asia, Latin America, and Africa, Fellowship House provided firsthand knowledge about life in the post-colonial Third World.[62]

As Fellowship House expanded into new areas and the Fellowship Commission continued to concentrate on higher education, the character of local civil rights began to change. In December 1962 the Philadelphia branch of the NAACP elected a well-known attorney, Cecil B. Moore, as president. In contrast to previous leaders of the branch, Moore envisioned building a broad-based local movement that would utilize direct action. Although the NAACP had been the city's leading civil rights organization, it had fought discrimination through petitions and lawsuits, not sit-ins and demonstrations. Moreover, the Philadelphia NAACP had drawn most of its members from the ranks of the black middle class. The new president encouraged participation by the black working class.[63]

Although Moore supported the integration of the school system, he attempted to link education with other issues in the black community, especially unemployment. In May 1963 Moore led a protest at an elementary school construction site at 31st and Susquehanna in North Philadelphia. Although the proposed school was located in a black neighborhood, there were no black workers on site. Violence broke out when police clubbed protesters, injuring several. The protest resulted in the hiring of a few black workers, but the level of violence worried some leaders of the interracial civil rights movement.[64]

As Moore and his followers took to the streets, the Fellowship Commission joined the growing call for educational home rule. This shift in policy reflected the influence of educational reform leaders like Bunny Greenfield, Richardson Dilworth, and William Wilcox of the GPM, who had become officers in the Fellowship Commission. Educational home rule would not specifically address issues such as segregation, but many reformers believed that the decentralization of power would foster a climate that would facilitate integration.

In August 1963 the Pennsylvania General Assembly approved an education home rule law for Philadelphia and established a commission whose central purpose was to fashion a constitution for a restructured school system. The Fellowship Commission contributed to this legislative victory by assisting in publicizing the importance of educational home rule. The passage of legislation did not mean the battle was over; the Educational Home Rule Commission had to hold public hearings, finalize details of the proposed constitution, and ultimately submit it to the voters.[65]

In addition to the home rule legislation, the passage of Act 484 represented an important victory for the Fellowship Commission. The law established the Community College of Philadelphia, an independent two-year institution with its own board of trustees, administration, and faculty.[66] Although the original goal of a tuition-free four-year college had not been realized, the new institution would be open to all Philadelphians regardless of race or religion. The establishment of the Community College was the culmination of an eighteen-year campaign that transformed the activism of the interracial movement. After securing allies in City Hall and Harrisburg, Fagan, Ullman, McBride, and Cunningham conducted an intensive lobbying campaign. Could the Fellowship Commission continue to build coalitions and influence educational policy in the increasingly volatile atmosphere of the 1960s?

Although Fellowship House supported school reform, it continued to focus on intercultural education and community outreach. The organization initiated a black history program for neighborhood children and, in an attempt to reach an increasingly alienated black community, established the Little Fellowship House in 1963. Located in a storefront at 1710 North 27th Street, Little Fellowship House was directed by two young African American women, Prathia Hall and Diana King. Their principal purpose was to establish small-scale educational programs for children and adults in the immediate community. Hall was a battle-tested veteran of the southern civil rights movement, having been wounded by police during demonstrations led by Dr. King in Albany, Georgia.[67]

By the early 1960s North Philadelphia housed an increasing percentage of the city's black poor. The area was plagued by inadequate housing, inferior schools, and high unemployment. Ignored by the city's political leadership, African Americans complained of frequent police brutality and price gouging by the area's predominantly white-owned retail establishments. On August 28, 1964, years of tension exploded when an altercation between several policemen and a black couple on North Philadelphia's Columbia

Avenue erupted into a major uprising. Several days of violence left three people dead, hundreds injured and arrested, and dozens of businesses looted and burned. Although Fellowship House members had been on the scene as early as the morning of August 29, they did not succeed in convincing large numbers of rioters to cease.[68]

The violence on Columbia Avenue would have a profound impact on the interracial civil rights movement. First, it strained the relationship between inner-city blacks and the Jewish community. Many of the small businesses were owned by Jews, and these bore the brunt of the violence. In addition, some Fellowship House members felt an increasing sense of isolation in North Philadelphia. They pondered whether their strategies had any relevance in the increasingly volatile environment. "We were kind of an integrated island of tolerance," recalled Mohammed Latif.[69] The reaction from the Fellowship Commission was more ominous. Fagan viewed the uprising as a warning. In late 1964, he wrote: "The essence of the Negro social revolution is the fact that the so-called power structure must now reckon with the moral, economic, and political power of 20 million Negroes who can no longer be ignored, intimidated, awed, owned, or taken for granted by white or Negro leaders."[70]

But would the majority of black Philadelphians continue to support the tactics of the Fellowship Commission and Fellowship House? Despite their contribution to interracial dialogue, discrimination remained rampant in labor, housing, and education. There was cautious optimism that educational home rule would address the segregation in the school system. In an effort to garner public support for the bill, the Fellowship Commission marshalled its media resources and launched a brief but extensive campaign. On May 18, 1965, Philadelphians narrowly approved the Educational Home Rule Charter. The main provision of the charter mandated the selection of board members by a citizens' nominating committee rather than Common Pleas Court judges. The charter also gave voters power to approve school funding bills.[71]

Civil rights activists questioned how the new charter would affect integration. Under the new leadership of former mayor Richardson Dilworth, the school board began to emphasize "quality public education." They insisted that the district's major problem was low academic performance, not segregation. The school board soon faced a barrage of criticism from the Fellowship Commission, the NAACP, and other civil rights agencies who charged school officials with sidestepping the issue of integration. Citywide desegregation would involve busing or redistricting, but there was little support for either plan among politicians, board members, faculty, and the predominantly white Home and School Association. Moreover, many working-class whites vowed massive resistance.[72]

In the midst of the school debate, Fellowship House received an additional $10,000 a year from the school district to increase programs. The new superintendent, Dr. Mark Shedd, became one of the organization's strongest supporters. Dr. Shedd had spearheaded the desegregation of the Englewood, New Jersey, school district and believed that he could have similar success in Philadelphia. With the cooperation of Dr. Shedd, city officials, and community organizations, Fellowship House launched the largest program in its history in the summer of 1967.[73]

Operation Green Grass grew out of an emergency mass meeting held at Fellowship House on July 27, 1967. Community members, activists, and government officials believed that Philadelphia would experience uprisings like Detroit and Newark. Shortly after the meeting, Fellowship House issued a statement, "An Appeal to Reason," which delineated six critical issues, such as housing and employment, and suggested solutions. While most of these issues required long-term solutions, the most immediate concern was the alleviation of tension in the inner city. Fellowship House and the school district agreed that exposure to nature would provide a temporary fix. School buses provided transportation, while the city's Department of Recreation and business community contributed over 61,000 box lunches. Administered jointly by the school district and Fellowship House, Operation Green Grass transported 70,000 children and adults to city parks, state recreation areas, and historic sites.[74] Although levels of tension remained high throughout that summer, Philadelphia experienced none of the violence suffered by other cities.

The tension on the streets was reflected within the city's civil rights community. By the late 1960s Moore's leadership faced criticism by local and national civil rights leaders. In August 1965 Moore questioned Dr. King's brief visit to Philadelphia, which was sponsored by Fellowship House. The branch president stated that Dr. King's nonviolent methods would not work in the City of Brotherly Love. Although Dr. King appeared at the ongoing NAACP protest at Girard College and attempted to make peace with Moore, many of Dr. King's supporters remained angry with the branch president's intransigence.[75]

In defense of his leadership, Moore declared: "I run a grass roots group, not a cocktail party, tea-sipping fashion-show attending group of exhibitionists."[76] Prior to Moore, the Fellowship Commission and Fellowship

House had worked closely with the NAACP. Increasingly, Moore's political militancy and flamboyant style alienated Penney, Fagan, and other leaders of the interracial civil rights community. In the summer of 1967, the Fellowship Commission denounced Cecil B. Moore for advocating violence against white business owners and moderate blacks. Later that year, the Commission legally evicted Moore and the NAACP from the Fellowship Commission offices. Fagan accused Moore, an independent mayoral candidate, of using the NAACP office facilities for his campaign. By early 1968 Moore had been suspended by the national office of the NAACP, and the city's NAACP had been divided into several chapters.[77]

Many of Moore's followers joined more militant organizations such as the Nation of Islam and the Black Panthers. This new grass-roots militancy was also reflected among high school students. On November 17, 1967, thousands of black students staged a walkout and assembled at the Board of Education building. The students demanded the right to wear African garb, the implementation of black history classes, and the renaming of several predominantly black high schools to honor black leaders. As their leaders met with school officials inside, students were brutally attacked by police led by Police Commissioner Frank Rizzo.[78]

Both the Fellowship Commission and Fellowship House criticized the action of the police. Fagan placed the police riot in the context of the sputtering campaign for integration. He castigated the inaction of the school board: "to allow discrimination to continue in open violation of anti-discrimination laws is a standing invitation to disorder and possible riots. Law and order cannot be maintained where there is widespread injustice and inequality. Violence begets violence."[79]

The Fellowship Commission was clearly concerned that continuing inequality in education would raise the level of racial tension in Philadelphia. Although they criticized the school board's support of quality education as a substitute for integrated education, the Fellowship Commission nevertheless embraced the district's new proposals. Rather than confront segregation through busing or redistricting, school officials planned to create educational parks. The proposed educational parks would consist of classrooms, recreational facilities, and laboratories. Students from racially isolated public and parochial schools would spend a specified term each year at these facilities. The high cost of the educational parks, and the notion that this project represented a detour from the goal of desegregated schools, spelled its doom.[80]

Although the interracial movement had contributed to the growth of racial tolerance through a multitude of programs, they had scarcely cracked the wall of school segregation. By the late 1960s, however, the protests leveled against school segregation were beginning to influence policymakers in Harrisburg. In 1968 the Pennsylvania Human Relations Commission and the state Department of Education published two influential reports, "Desegregation Guidelines for Public Schools" and "Recommended Elements of a School Desegregation Plan."[81]

The dilemma over school desegregation reflected the limitations of the interracial civil rights movement. Utilizing educational tactics, these activists had introduced concepts of racial tolerance to tens of thousands of people in the Philadelphia area. Their work had been emulated by similar organizations across the nation, and the establishment of Community College of Philadelphia constituted a major victory. Yet by the late 1960s it was increasingly clear that some of the movement's tactics and goals were viewed as irrelevant by a new generation of activists. Influenced by the black power and antiwar movements, this rising cadre of activists employed militant strategies and were critical of liberal notions of integration. In this way, Philadelphia's interracial civil rights movement experienced many of the same internal conflicts that had been emerging within the national civil rights struggle.

Such tensions redefined the struggle for desegregated education. Historian Thomas Sugrue argues that supporters of integrated schools began to shift their objectives by the mid-1960s.[82] White resistance to desegregated education had convinced many African Americans that creating alternatives such as community-controlled schools and Afrocentric curricula would provide their children with quality education. Since the majority of Philadelphia's schoolchildren attended neighborhood schools, the integration of public education was linked inexorably to integrated housing. The movement's efforts to desegregate housing will be discussed in the next chapter.

CHAPTER 4

A House of Many Mansions

Race, Housing, and the Interracial Civil Rights Community, 1930–1946

THE 2010 CENSUS REPORTED THAT PHILADELPHIA'S RESIDENTIAL SEGRE-gation rate was one of the highest among the nation's largest cities.[1] Although housing discrimination has been a facet of life in the "City of Homes" for decades, the patterns of spatial segregation underwent significant changes in the first fifty years of the twentieth century. This chapter traces the formation of racial housing patterns in Philadelphia and the growing involvement of interracial civil rights organizations in the struggle for integrated housing.

In the late nineteenth century, many black Philadelphians occupied dwellings behind the townhouses of their white employers. This housing pattern had its roots in the colonial era and resembled those of southern cities such as Richmond and Charleston. By the 1880s, however, a significant concentration of blacks had developed in an area south of Center City known as the Seventh Ward. The Seventh Ward became the principal laboratory for W. E. B. Du Bois's pioneering study, *The Philadelphia Negro* (1899). This seminal sociological work portrayed a community beset by poor sanitation and overcrowding. Du Bois argued that these conditions were a result of racial discrimination in housing: "The Negro who ventures away from the mass of his people and their organized life, finds himself alone, shunned and taunted, stared at and made uncomfortable; he can make few new friends, for his neighbors however well-disposed would shrink to add a Negro to their list of acquaintances."[2]

Like other cities, Philadelphia's Progressive reformers mobilized to address the crisis. In 1896 the Octavia Hill Association was formed. Named for the famed British housing reformer, the goal of the organization was to alleviate inadequate housing utilizing the private sector. The OHA purchased its first properties in the Seventh Ward, rehabilitated them, and leased the housing to indigent families. The leading proponents of this new endeavor were Hannah Fox and Helen Parrish, both of whom were affiliated with the OHA. Dr. Joseph Neff, the city's public health director, supported their efforts and agreed to sponsor a meeting for activists interested in housing reform. In September 1909 representatives of sixty local social welfare and philanthropic organizations met in Neff's office.[3] The conferees formed the Philadelphia Housing Commission (PHC) and declared their purpose: "to improve the housing conditions in Philadelphia, by making studies of the conditions that affect housing, advocating adequate housing and by securing features of town planning."[4] The conferees chose Neff as president and housing activist Gustavus Weber as executive secretary. The PHC organized committees on legislation, publicity, investigation, and finance and designed a "statistical card" to document housing complaints.[5] This flurry of activity, however, ignored racial aspects of the housing crisis. The membership of the PHC was white and drawn primarily from the ranks of the city's middle and upper classes. There is no evidence that the PHC courted black participation, although blacks occupied much of the worst housing in the city.

The PHC floundered, but finally, after several years of being unable to influence housing policy on any level, the organization shifted direction. Pledging to attack the housing problem on the "broadest possible front," the PHC hired Bernard Newman, a Unitarian minister, as executive secretary. Newman's vision was broader than the PHC's had been; he believed that a combination of scientific methodology, educational programs, and legislation could eliminate decrepit housing. As a "sanitarian," Newman echoed Progressive theories that poor housing bred contagious diseases that threatened society as a whole.

Newman's leadership was dynamic. Shortly after his arrival, he initiated an educational outreach program and successfully lobbied City Hall and Harrisburg for housing codes and zoning laws. Housing surveys conducted under Newman's direction revealed that many of the city's slaughterhouses were located in residential areas, especially the Seventh Ward.[6] The PHC's surveys were marred, as were many of its legislative efforts, by the lack of attention it paid to racial matters. For example, the PHC's Seventh Ward survey reflected none of Du Bois's penetrating analysis and had virtually no input from the black community. This disregard for race was fast becoming a serious liability for the PHC. For even as the organization pushed for legislative changes, the racial demographics of Philadelphia were on the verge of enormous change.

Early in the twentieth century, southern blacks eager to escape racial violence, poverty, and other manifestations of oppression had headed to the industrial centers of the North. In Philadelphia, the black population witnessed a nearly 60 percent increase between 1910 and 1920. Between 1916 and 1920, an estimated 35,000 to 40,000 migrants arrived in the city. The migration placed an unbearable strain on Philadelphia's limited and deteriorating housing stock.[7] The new arrivals encountered a desperate situation. Unable to find housing, thousands turned to organizations such as the Philadelphia Association for the Protection of Colored Women, South Philadelphia's Christian Street YMCA, and black churches like Rev. Charles Albert Tindley's Mt. Calvary Methodist Episcopal Church. Eager to help newcomers and interested in earning some extra cash, many African Americans families with extra space took in lodgers.[8]

In an effort to capitalize on scarce housing and immediate need, landlords and speculators hastily converted single-family homes into apartments and made rudimentary repairs on abandoned dwellings. New tenants were often at the mercy of landlords who raised rents without warning. Otto Eidlitz, a New York builder and housing reformer recruited by the federal government to investigate the situation, characterized Philadelphia as one of the worst centers of rent profiteering in the nation.[9]

The migration of tens of thousands of southern blacks drew the reluctant attention of the renamed Philadelphia Housing Association (PHA). Although race relations were not included in the organization's original mission, the members of the organization could no longer ignore the rapidly expanding African American community. The organization's first reckoning with race emerged in 1917. In that year, housing reformer John Ihlder, interim director of PHA while Newman worked on the war effort in Washington, formed the Negro Migration Committee to launch a major study of the impact of migration on the tight housing market. The team assembled to work on the 1917–18 study included prominent blacks such as realtor and NAACP leader Isadore Martin; J. Max Barber, the black publisher who had fled Atlanta in the wake of the 1906 riot; and Mrs. S. W. Layten of the Philadelphia Association for the Protection of Colored Women. The black participants' activities were not limited to an analysis of the housing situation; the Negro Migration Committee was actively involved in locating housing for migrant families, some of whom had been evicted shortly after their arrival.[10] Members of the Negro Migration Committee argued that racism was behind overcrowding: "While there are many vacant houses in Kensington, they are not available for Negro tenants . . . the districts inhabited by Negroes are filled to overflowing."[11]

The Housing Association called on the local real estate board to "secure for negro occupancy houses not previously rented to Negroes."[12] While this call resulted in an expansion of the black housing market, the expansion did not encourage integration. The association reported that they had "succeeded in having the negro districts considerably enlarged and so relieved the situation."[13] The enlargement was due to two factors: increased advocacy by housing activists and white flight. As blacks moved into white neighborhoods in West, North, and Northwest Philadelphia, whites began to move into outlying districts. Although residential segregation increased during the war, nearly 20 percent of black Philadelphians had white neighbors.[14]

When blacks attempted to challenge segregation by moving into certain white communities, they faced potential violence. The danger of integrating housing became painfully evident in the sweltering summer of 1918. In late July of that year rioting erupted when a black probation officer, Mrs. Adella Bonds, moved onto the 2900 block of Ellsworth Street in Grays Ferry, a predominantly white neighborhood in South Philadelphia. Shortly after moving into her new home, a white mob formed in front of her house throwing rocks and bottles at her windows. In response, Mrs. Bond fired on the mob. For several days the area was a racial battleground as blacks and whites fought for contested terrain. Three whites and one black died, hundreds were injured, and dozens of black homes lay ruined. The race riot of 1918 demonstrated how volatile the issue of integrated housing was in the City of Brotherly Love. In the future, both black and white activists would approach this issue with extreme caution.[15]

The experience of the riot changed the Housing Association; the organization could never again completely ignore the issue of race. Unfortunately, its attitude was often condescending. Newman returned to Philadelphia after World War I and resumed his leadership of the association. In Harrisburg, concern about racial violence led Governor Gifford Pinchot to authorize the creation of a statewide committee. Spurred by the governor, the association established a "committee of special representatives of the Colored Race." The sixteen-member committee included eleven clergymen and represented the city's traditional black elite. The committee requested that the Housing Association hire a black housing inspector who would also serve as a troubleshooter on race issues. Newman categorically refused this request and informed the committee that its role would be strictly educational.[16]

In 1923, as migration increased, the Housing Association embarked on a series of new studies on the impact of the recent demographic phenomenon. In contrast to the reports of the war years, the surveys of 1923 and 1924 concluded that the municipal government should get more involved in alleviating black housing conditions.[17] In the years following the war, the city's endemic housing shortage was somewhat eased by an increase in residential construction. Although over 20,000 new dwellings were constructed in the period between 1923 and 1925, only fifty went to black buyers, who were at a disadvantage on two fronts.[18] Most new housing ranged between four and five thousand dollars, well beyond the economic reach of most African Americans. In addition, most of the new housing included restrictive covenants prohibiting the purchase of lease of the property by specific racial or religious minorities. The combination of these two factors severely limited African Americans' housing choices.

The Housing Association's strategy to meet the needs of both the newly arriving southern blacks and native-born population was to promote the construction of private housing for African Americans. This strategy was in keeping with Newman's special interest in the private sector. He was one of the nation's leading proponents of the Better Homes Movement. Formed in 1922 by Mrs. William Brown Meloney, this national organization advocated the construction of low-cost housing by private builders because it held that private property instilled responsibility.[19] Newman and his colleagues hoped that support for the private sector would blunt the calls from some housing reformers for federal government intervention.

Housing and the Interracial Movement

FOR THE FIRST DECADES OF THE TWENTIETH CENTURY, THE HOUSING ASsociation dominated the housing reform movement in Philadelphia. The association successfully campaigned for the establishment of several city housing codes, and received increasing national attention for its work. By the mid-1920s, however, the pioneers of the interracial civil rights movement had become interested in housing issues. Although these embryonic activists did not challenge the PHA's dominance or its philosophy, they did attempt to connect racial discrimination with the housing shortage. Like the PHA, many Quaker activists held middle-class values and did not oppose segregated housing. In 1926 Rachel Davis Du Bois of the Quaker Committee on Race Relations argued that "there must be an attempt to provide decent homes for decent Negroes."[20] Du Bois and her colleagues had an earnest desire to ameliorate the conditions of the black community, but her comments about "decent Negroes" illustrate the strong class bias found within the organization. The support the Quaker activists expressed for construction of new, segregated housing indicated they were not aware of black leaders' concern about increasing segregation.[21]

Newman was eager to cultivate new avenues of support for his policies and began to collaborate with the Quakers. The two Quaker race relations committees worked with Newman on a local housing conference, a neighborhood survey, and a major study of black housing conditions. They hired Thomas Woofter Jr., who wrote a report entitled *Negro Housing in Philadelphia* (1927), one of the first studies to document the new spatial segregation emerging in the city and the serious inadequacies in housing for blacks.[22]

The relationship between the interracial civil rights movement and the PHA was tenuous at best. Although Newman had broadened his reach and the race relations committees had learned more about housing, there were substantial differences between the two. The late 1920s saw new Quaker activists such as Helen Bryan attempt to examine the link between racism and housing discrimination. In contrast, Newman and the PHA continued to downplay the significance of race in housing.

Within the housing reform movement, Newman and his colleagues faced new challenges. By the late 1920s new activists such as Catherine Bauer and Lewis Mumford began to criticize the traditional approach to housing reform. In contrast to sanitarians like Newman, communitarians argued that housing reform meant more than building codes, the destruction of slums, and the construction of individual homes. Their transcendent approach to housing envisioned decrepit neighborhoods being transformed into well-planned communities with parks, schools, and recreational facilities. Moreover, they castigated the role of the private sector in the housing market and called for the intervention of the federal government.[23]

The onset of the Depression brought radical changes to the housing reform movement. Although Philadelphia's economy had been stagnant since the mid-1920s, the Depression worsened an already precarious situation. The economic downturn devastated the city's black community; during the early Depression years, black unemployment in the city hovered at 48 percent.[24]

The Depression had a catastrophic effect on black housing in Philadelphia. In 1930, at the outset of the crash, Philadelphia had the highest number of black homeowners among northern cities. The growth of black-owned savings and loans and other financial institutions had contributed to this increase, as did the movement of middle-class whites out of city neighborhoods to the suburbs. The Depression disrupted this stability; many of the mortgages of black homeowners were now in danger of foreclosure.

The majority of the city's black population, however, consisted of renters, and they were equally vulnerable. By 1932, just a few years into the Great Depression, half of the city's black tenants faced eviction. This situation was exacerbated by an increasing shortage of housing stock as thousands of substandard dwellings were condemned and demolished in the early 1930s, very little new housing was constructed.[25] Black Philadelphia faced one of its greatest crises.

Race, Housing, and the Depression

AS THE DEPRESSION DEEPENED, A NEW FORCE IN RACE RELATIONS emerged. In May 1931 the organization that would later become the Young Peoples Interracial Fellowship (YPIF) held its first meeting at Pendle Hill in suburban Wallingford. In a summary of the first conference, the YPIF expressed concern about racial discrimination in housing. It cited the exorbitant rents paid by blacks and the exclusion of blacks from many white neighborhoods, but it did not propose any course of action.[26] The initial focus of the YPIF was to raise the awareness of whites about certain issues and to engage both races in meaningful dialogue, not to launch policy-oriented protest.

Although enthusiastic and dedicated, Bryan, Wentzel, and the YPIF lacked the political and organizational sophistication of established activists. As the YPIF began to plan, the NAACP, the *Philadelphia Tribune,* and the Armstrong Association, the local affiliate of the National Urban League, began to mobilize the black community around discrimination in housing. As John Bauman argues, northern middle-class black activists were often critical of southern migrants. Like white reformers, they believed that improved housing would remove the manifestations of vice and ignorance. For example, the *Tribune* maintained that infamous black criminal groups such as North Philadelphia's "Forty Thieves" and "Party Girl" gangs were the products of massive overcrowding in their neighborhoods.[27] What set black activists apart from white reformers was that black activists saw the overcrowding, and therefore the crime, as the product of centuries of racial discrimination.

The character of black activism was changing and becoming more militant. As a result of the Great Migration, many of the city's new influential black voices were southern-born and possessed a sense of race pride and community uplift, not always evident among many "Old Philadelphians."

This new elite was also willing to utilize legal, intellectual, and legislative resources to address racism.[28] Although this transformation of the city's black leadership would take decades to shape the political environment, this rising force began to make its mark in the 1930s.

Several members of the new black elite, such as Rev. Marshall Shepard and social worker Crystal Bird Fauset, were strong supporters of New Deal policies. The impact of the nation's economic crisis on housing had clearly demonstrated the urgent need for some form of government intervention. Even Newman, traditionally one of the harshest critics of public housing, cautiously supported the role of the federal government. In the fall of 1934, Newman joined several others on the Philadelphia Advisory Committee on Housing (PACH), a committee he would eventually direct. The Public Works Administration (PWA) was instrumental in establishing the PACH, which was to monitor housing concerns. Although the PWA pledged to uphold principles of racial equality, it included no black representatives on the PACH.[29]

By the spring of 1935, government agencies had done little to address the crisis in black housing. In response to the inertia, two of the city's black newspapers, the *Philadelphia Tribune* and the *Independent*, published a series of articles on black housing conditions. The NAACP established a slum clearance committee, while a group of black ministers formed the Committee of One Hundred to press for action. Similarly, grass-roots community organizations shifted their focus from other issues of economic discrimination to housing. For example, the North Philadelphia Civic Club, a community-based council that was involved in the "Don't Buy Where You Can't Work" campaign, began to organize around housing.[30]

As a result of pressure from the black community, the PACH appointed two prominent black leaders, Crystal Bird Fauset and Major R. R. Wright Jr. Despite their inclusion, the committee did little to address black housing concerns. To the chagrin of many blacks, Newman supported the creation of a "Harlem section" for Philadelphia. He argued, "We are seeking to promote a separate slum clearance in a Negro district, the new housing which will be for Negroes."[31] Although black housing activists in Philadelphia supported the destruction of decrepit black homes, like black housing activists nationwide, they pushed for the integration of any new housing.

The champions of this new national push for integration were the members of the National Negro Congress (NNC). Founded by Howard University social scientists at the home of political scientist Ralph Bunche in 1936, the NNC functioned as a coordinating body for dozens of African

American organizations, such as tenants' leagues and unemployment councils. Their militant manifesto called for equal opportunity in education and labor, opposition to fascism, and gender equality.[32]

Under the leadership of the dynamic Arthur Huff Fauset, anthropologist and principal of the Paul Laurence Dunbar School, the Philadelphia chapter of the NNC became the city's leading force for black housing in the late 1930s. Soon after the formation of the Philadelphia chapter, a housing disaster reminded Philadelphians about the desperate need for action. In late December 1936 a ramshackle bandbox tenement on South Street collapsed, killing seven blacks, including four children. In the wake of the tragedy, Mayor S. Davis Wilson took some limited actions on unsafe housing, but the black community was not mollified. Shortly after the disaster, neighbors of the seven victims began to discuss possible courses of action. In June 1937, they formed the Tenants League of Philadelphia.[33]

The original purpose of the Tenants League was to provide decent housing for those evicted after the South Street disaster, but soon the League began to work with the NNC on more comprehensive policy issues. The new organization formed the vanguard of a new radical housing reform movement. Although it cooperated with the PHA and older agencies on some projects, the Tenants League and its allies utilized militant tactics to press for new demands. In addition to calling for stronger enforcement of the 1915 housing code in the black community, they demanded an end to all segregated housing and the blacklisting of tenants on public relief. Instead of the quiet persuasion used by earlier reformers, these new activists employed street protests and rent strikes. Many tenants were inspired by the new mood of militancy. By early 1938 there were twelve tenants' rights organizations across the city.[34]

The militancy among housing activists was representative of a national trend. In New York City, tenant councils, dominated by the Communist Party, had engaged in a series of massive rent strikes in the early 1930s.[35] Although Philadelphia's radicals adopted many of the tactics of the New York City activists, Philadelphia's tenant struggle included, but was not dominated by, the Communist Party. In the late 1930s Communists served on tenant councils and cooperated with liberal activists. Although there is no evidence of conflict with the YPIF, some members of the Committee on Race Relations were ambivalent about working with Communists. Some black leaders, however, were more vocal in their criticism of the Communist Party. E. Washington Rhodes, editor of the *Tribune*, gave Communist activities minimal coverage. When the *Tribune* mentioned Communists, it usually focused on negative developments, such as their conflict with the NAACP over the Scottsboro case.[36] Throughout the 1930s, he was adamant in his condemnation of Communism, saying: "Thoughtful Negroes may reason that the philosophy and economic theories of Communism are unsound and will not obtain for them a more equitable distribution of the products of their labor or a larger degree of justice."[37]

In contrast to Rhodes and some Quaker activists, Helen Bryan moved to the left. She sought to involve the fledgling YPIF in this struggle. Recognizing the potential of the NNC, she courted its support shortly after its formation. The NNC presented its program of action to the YPIF, but before the two could coordinate activities, Bryan left the YPIF and became involved in organizing support for the embattled Spanish Republic.[38] In the wake of her departure, the YPIF worked with the NNC but assumed only a supporting role in protest activities, far from the leadership role envisioned by Bryan.

As Bryan departed in late 1938, the city's housing situation was undergoing a massive transformation. On the federal level, the passage of the Wagner-Steagall Act signified a new national emphasis on housing. The law provided for the creation of local housing authorities to oversee the development of publicly funded housing.[39] The advent of public housing drew support from many quarters, but the reasons for that support varied. Many housing radicals, both black and white, believed that public housing represented the best hope for the poor, especially the black poor, to obtain decent housing. Moderate white housing reformers, however, had different views of this much heralded development: they understood public housing as a means to contain the growing black population and as a means to limit the spread of slums. Elements of the black middle class differed from both of these positions, believing in the transformative power of public housing. Many thought that the disciplined surroundings of public housing would introduce the black poor, especially southern-born migrants, to middle-class values.

These factions within the housing movement clashed over the location of one of the first public housing projects. Despite the protests of the NNC, the NAACP, and the YPIF, a site at Twenty-Fifth and Norris Streets in North Philadelphia was selected as the location for the first predominantly black housing project. In October 1941 the James Weldon Johnson Homes project opened. Eighteen hundred people, over 95 percent black, became the first tenants of the new project.[40] For reformers like Newman, construction of the Johnson Homes represented a successful containment of the burgeoning black community, while the supporters of integrated public housing continued to protest. They had failed to marshal support for desegregated public housing. This failure was due in part to the increasing fragmentation within the NNC, which weakened the effectiveness of its campaign in the Johnson Homes struggle.

Race, Housing, and World War II

IN THE LATE 1930S THE YPIF REFRAINED FROM DIRECT INVOLVEMENT IN the housing movement. While it addressed discrimination through outreach programs such as the Speakers' Bureau and support of the NNC, it had not initiated any action on housing. It would take political maturity, organizational stability, and the onset of World War II for the slowly emerging interracial civil rights movement to become more involved in housing issues.

On February 16, 1940, the YPIF sponsored a special community meeting on housing. The meeting featured members of the Tenants League, and discussion focused on the looming housing shortage and the legal rights of renters. The warm reception accorded the Tenants League contrasted sharply to earlier interactions between the two groups. In late 1939 the YPIF was still strongly influenced by its moderate parent group, the Committee on Race Relations, and was concerned that the Tenants League was a radical group.[41] By early 1940 the YPIF had become increasingly independent of the CCR and more militant. YPIF leaders, like Penney and Cunningham, believed in forging alliances with different activist groups around specific issues.

As YPIF evolved, Philadelphians faced a new housing dilemma. As World War II erupted across Europe, the defense industry began to provide Britain with war material and to resupply America's lagging armed forces. The city's stagnant manufacturing sector was reawakened by a rapid increase in defense production. As the need for industrial labor increased, tens of thousands of job-hungry workers moved to Philadelphia. This population influx concerned housing reformers and race relations activists. Between 1940 and 1944, an estimated 30,000 African Americans moved to the Quaker City, nearly as many as had moved to Philadelphia during the 1930s.[42] Members of the housing movement, the media, and other activist groups feared that racial violence would erupt as black and white industrial workers competed for scarce housing.

As dangerous as the situation was, Philadelphia was in a better position than it had been during World War I. The city had committed race relations activists dedicated to reducing the possibility of racial violence. In addition, public housing could provide homes for workers and thus alleviate racial tension. New questions arose about public housing. Where would new housing developments be located? Would new projects be open to all, regardless of race? All of these issues came to the forefront during the construction of the Richard Allen Homes project.

Although the construction of the Richard Allen Homes had displaced an impoverished black community in North Philadelphia, the Philadelphia Housing Authority wanted to reserve the facility for white war workers because the housing was new and considered the best in the city. The Richard Allen Homes issue became one of the first projects of the recently formed Fellowship House. Black activists argued that the new project had to be integrated and would not settle for a compromise.[43] In early 1941, Fellowship House and the NAACP held an emergency meeting on the project.

As the battle for the Richard Allen Homes raged, Bernard Newman died. His death left a vacuum in the city's housing reform movement. For three decades, Newman had dominated the agenda for housing reform in Philadelphia. His official replacement at PHA was Edmund Bacon, a young architect and city planner. Unlike Newman, Bacon was not from the sanitarian tradition of housing reform; he represented a new kind of reformer who viewed housing reform as an essential component of urban redevelopment. Before Newman's death, Bacon, Walter Phillips, and several other politically active young professionals formed the Joint Committee on City Planning. This small but influential group brought together reformers who wanted to change the city's political and physical landscapes.[44]

Richard Allen Homes opened in early 1942. The protests of organizations such as the NAACP and Fellowship House convinced the Philadelphia Housing Authority that the new project should be open to residents of all races. Although Philadelphia was suffering a critical housing shortage, few white families moved into the project. Some whites complained that the facility was too far from major defense industries.[45] For others, the prospect of integrated living seemed too daunting. The new project was soon approximately 90 percent black, heralding a trend that would emerge across the nation. While Fellowship House, the Fellowship Commission, the NAACP, and other organizations hailed this official integration as a victory, the de facto segregation of the Homes helped to maintain segregation within the city's public housing network.[46]

In the wake of the Allen Homes affair, the Fellowship Commission tried to capitalize on wartime patriotism, calling for "the elimination of racial discrimination and segregation in the field of housing and thus aid America in the winning of the war and in gaining her rightful place as a real and great democratic nation."[47]

Both Fellowship House and the Fellowship Commission attempted to place racial discrimination in a broader context by suggesting that the battle against racial discrimination in housing mirrored the fight against Nazi and Japanese aggression.

Recognizing that the struggle to integrate housing could not be accomplished without the aid of housing reformers, they reached out to the Housing Association. Fagan and Cunningham invited the PHA to become a constituent member of the Fellowship Commission. The venerable housing reformers, however, refrained from joining the new coalition. While some individual members of the PHA were receptive to joining a coalition around race, others believed that such a partnership was not within the association's original mission. Despite the lack of official ties, the war years fostered close cooperation between civil rights activists and housing reformers. Bacon joined the Pennsylvania State Temporary Commission of the Conditions of the Urban Colored Population. Founded in 1939 by the Pennsylvania General Assembly, this small agency's purpose was to investigate economic problems in black communities in the state's largest cities. The commission soon began examining the connection between housing and economic disparities. Encouraged by E. Washington Rhodes, a member of the state commission, Bacon became more involved in interracial activities. Bacon subsequently joined the Citywide Interracial Committee (CWIC) a municipal agency when it formed in 1943. His membership in the CWIC brought him into close contact with Cunningham, Alexander, Penney, and others connected with Fellowship House and the Fellowship Commission.[48]

The felicity of the alliance between interracial civil rights groups and the housing reform movement became apparent when conflict emerged over the opening of a new housing project in semi-rural Northeast Philadelphia. The Tacony Creek project was earmarked to be an integrated facility, but white tenants and neighbors protested. The tense, yet short-lived, situation was defused by interracial organizations, the CWIC, and the Housing Authority. Spearheaded by Fellowship House, the activists organized a series of meetings among the residents of the neighborhood. Eventually, several black families moved into the project. Tension was high, but the massive rioting that occurred over the Sojourner Truth project in Detroit did not take place in Philadelphia.[49] The early involvement of these interracial organizations and the lack of a well-organized white resistance contributed to a peaceful resolution. This incident demonstrated the efficacy of this movement in preventing the racial violence witnessed in other cities.

Despite the Tacony settlement, the Housing Authority did not embrace integrated public housing. Five new housing projects (Passyunk, Oxford Circle, Abbottsford, Bartram, and Pennypacker) were reserved for white tenants. City housing officials stated that their decision was to "follow the racial pattern of the neighborhoods which are 100 per cent white."[50]

Shortly after the Tacony affair, Bacon's involvement with the emerging interracial movement ended when he joined the Navy in 1943. His successor was Dorothy Schoell, a former researcher for the Philadelphia Housing Authority and a graduate of the University of London and the University of Pennsylvania. Schoell had worked with Newman at the Housing Association, but she also had worked with the Federal Housing Administration (FHA) and the National Housing Agency (NHA). In contrast to Newman, Schoell's experience with the FHA and the NHA convinced her that government had a crucial role to play in the nation's housing. Soon after assuming the leadership of the Housing Association, she replaced Bacon on the CWIC. Fagan welcomed Schoell's enthusiasm.[51] He realized that his organization lacked expertise in a major, perhaps the most controversial, area of race relations. If the Housing Association affiliated with the Fellowship Commission, it would give the nascent coalition broader scope and influence.

By 1944 the Housing Authority had opened several "experimental" integrated housing projects. Although the integration of a facility was regarded as a success by the interracial movement, the integration of projects did not necessarily imply equal conditions within the project. For example, several members of the Housing Committee of the CWIC conducted a tour of black housing at the integrated Shipyard Homes in South Philadelphia. They discovered that blacks were housed in inferior units and that recreational and day-care facilities were segregated.[52] The situation at the Shipyard Homes presented yet another challenge for interracial civil rights activists. The Fellowship Commission and Fellowship House continued to emphasize the impact of racism on housing. In its public forums, Fellowship House stressed the high rents and poor conditions faced by most of the city's African American population. In the Fellowship House course Units for Unity, housing issues emerged in role-play training skits:

CHAIRMAN: I think we ought to get this meeting started; most of us are assembled. George, what is it you have on your mind?
GEORGE: It's very simple. Mary, I think the time has come when we have to take action about the housing in our town. Just two nights ago, another riot broke out; windows broken, bricks thrown, yelling and carrying on. Something has got to be done.[53]

Skits aside, however, not all housing was treated equally by the interracial movement. Because Fellowship House concentrated its efforts in public housing, the integration of private housing received a lower priority. Restrictive covenants and racial violence continued to limit where blacks lived. Fellowship House did not address these problems.

Although most black families' attempts to integrate occurred in white working-class neighborhoods, resistance to black homeowners also occurred in the city's more affluent sections. In 1944 Common Pleas Court Judge Curtis Bok, husband of Fellowship House board member Nellie Bok, presided over a dispute between Dr. Henry L. Gowens and his neighbors. Gowens, a well-known black physician, had purchased a Rittenhouse Square–area townhouse. His white neighbors claimed that Gowens's presence constituted a "common nuisance" and sought to force him to reconvey the property to the seller. Gowens refused and his neighbors brought suit against him. Bok ruled in Gowens's favor.[54] Despite continuing harassment of black families, neither the Fellowship Commission nor Fellowship House had developed a clear plan of action to address this form of discrimination. The lack of concrete action contributed to tension within the Fellowship Commission. Members of the NAACP were increasingly critical of the leadership of the Commission, while Fagan complained of NAACP indifference toward the coalition.[55]

As the Allies gained the upper hand in Europe and the Pacific, urban reformers drew plans for the development of postwar Philadelphia. During the war urban planners, housing activists, and businessmen had pressed for a comprehensive approach to urban renewal. The Republican city government reluctantly approved the creation of the Planning Commission, a consultative body with little legislative power. In an effort to keep the pressure for reform on City Hall, the Citizens Council on City Planning (CCCP) was formed in 1943. Eager to expand the focus of the Housing Association, Schoell became active in the rapidly expanding field of urban renewal. In 1945 Schoell began to work with the CCCP and the Housing Division of the Pennsylvania Postwar Planning Commission. She also helped Fellowship

Commission official and attorney Abraham Freedman draft the law that created the Philadelphia Redevelopment Authority, the city agency responsible for urban renewal projects.[56]

Like these city agencies, the Fellowship Commission was also planning for the postwar era, and housing emerged as a key element of its plan. In 1945 Fagan cited his organization's weakness in the field of housing and argued for definition and expansion of the housing issue: "What are the actual housing needs from the viewpoint of the so-called minority groups, and what is the best way to arouse public opinion and to what specific ends? (Housing should include residential areas, commercial and office buildings, hotel practices, etc.)"[57] At Fagan's urging, Schoell became the head of the Fellowship Commission's Housing Committee. The Housing Association became a cooperating organization of the Fellowship Commission, while contributing no funding to the commission. Although Schoell could not unilaterally bring her agency into the Fellowship Commission, she agreed to consult and cooperate on housing matters.[58]

Postwar housing presented new challenges for interracial civil rights activists. Returning veterans wanted homes, as did families whose housing choices had been limited by years of Depression and war. The Housing Association estimated that twenty thousand veterans needed homes in the Philadelphia area.[59] Once again, housing reformers and civil rights activists were concerned that racial violence would erupt over scarce housing, and they struggled to articulate a response to this new crisis.

In addition to a new housing shortage, the intimate nature of the private housing market made integration an extremely volatile issue. Homeowners could determine to whom they wanted to sell and, through a growing number of homeowner associations, could dictate who lived in their neighborhood. Integrated housing, especially in Philadelphia's crowded and close-knit communities, placed blacks and whites in daily contact with each other. For decades, many whites saw black neighbors as harbingers of crime, low property values, and miscegenation. Therefore, if interracial organizations were to succeed, they would have to transform white attitudes and not simply propose new legislation.

The situation for blacks was increasingly critical. Although new housing was being constructed in Philadelphia and the rapidly growing suburbs, most of this new housing was not open to black ownership. In 1947 the Housing Association reported that private homebuilders had constructed less than one hundred homes for blacks in Philadelphia. The situation was complicated by the thousands of black veterans searching for decent housing. The report concluded that public housing could not absorb these numbers, but it did not call for an increase in construction by private builders.[60]

In an attempt to address discrimination in private housing, the Fellowship Commission criticized the use of restrictive covenants and newspapers that published discriminatory real estate advertisements. In a brochure distributed to members of constituent agencies, the Fellowship Commission urged them to report such advertisements: "If you see real estate ads in newspapers, direct mail or leaflets which discriminate against or show a preference for particular groups . . . We are as near as the nearest phone."[61] The Fellowship Commission kept weekly surveys of both positive and negative news stories and advertisements. It focused on both major dailies, the *Evening Bulletin* and the *Daily News*. It was common for major newspapers to publish segregated help wanted and real estate advertisements. A typical weekly survey of the *Bulletin* found the following:

Apartments and Real Estate for Rent:

Christian - 4
Christian clientele - 1
Colored - 24
Gentile - 5
Jewish - 6
Jewish clientele - 3
Protestant - 1
White - 4[62]

Fellowship House continued to raise awareness of housing discrimination through its educational programs. High School Fellowshippers visited the Richard Allen Homes to examine the effect of the Housing Authority's support of segregation. In addition to its educational programs for children and adults, Fellowship House hoped that its Neighborhood Fellowship program could alleviate racial tension around housing. With the slogan "Every House a Fellowship House," Penney planned to spread the message of racial harmony throughout the city. Supporters of Fellowship House hosted informal discussions on race relations in six houses scattered across the city. These islands of tolerance also served as headquarters for community-level incident control activities. The Neighborhood Fellowship program, however, was unable to gain much support in the neighborhoods it attempted to serve.⁶³ Although programs like Units for Unity helped calm tensions, a more comprehensive approach to integrating housing was needed.

By the late 1940s the housing situation in the Philadelphia area was rapidly changing. Blacks remained locked in certain sections of the city, but the white population was spreading into the Northeast and the suburbs. Philadelphia's growing suburban population mirrored a growing national tendency. Increasing numbers of Americans were moving to the suburbs.⁶⁴

During the war, government-supported research contributed to new innovations in construction, such as stressed-skin plywood panels, gypsum-board ceilings, and welded steel roof trusses. William Levitt, a Long Island–based builder and former Seabee, utilized these methods to create Levittown, which became the model for thousands of suburban developments across the nation. However, Levitt's new developments and other similar suburban communities were not open to blacks. As the black population of the central cities grew, increasing numbers of white homeowners fled to the suburbs. Their transition was aided by low mortgages provided by the GI Bill and the 1947 pledge by the new Republican Congress to support a "free market" in residential construction and real estate. Conservative businessmen and their political supporters argued that if allowed to function with few controls, the private sector would end the nation's endemic housing shortage.

The rising suburban exodus represented a new dilemma for the race relations community. By the mid-1940s housing in the city of Philadelphia was more segregated than in the nineteenth century. With opposition to integration in both public and private housing, what strategies could activists employ to overcome segregation? What would be the role of the Philadelphia Housing Association in the struggle for equal housing? Although the association had started to recognize discrimination in the early 1940s, it did not embrace integration. In addition, unlike Fellowship House and the Fellowship Commission, the PHA had relatively few black members and staff persons, thus lacking credibility in the city's African American community.

Despite these challenges, the postwar period would witness massive changes in the struggle over integrated housing. Political developments on the local and national level would help transform both the civil rights struggle and the housing movement. Within the interracial community, new initiatives would be developed to challenge racism in housing.

CHAPTER 5

The House We Live In

Race and Housing in the Postwar World, 1946–1970

IN LATE 1947 HUNDREDS OF THOUSANDS OF PHILADELPHIANS FLOCKED to view the "Better Philadelphia Exhibition" at Gimbels department store at Eighth and Market Streets. Designed by renowned architect and Housing Association board member Oscar Stonorov, the exhibit portrayed the end of urban blight. In the exhibit, giant hands removed slum areas and replaced them with new residential, recreational, and commercial developments. Ironically, half of the exhibit's funding came from the city's faltering Republican machine, which had done little to stem urban blight. The Republicans hoped the exhibit and its implied policies would help their mayoral candidate, Bernard Samuels, retain City Hall in the November election. Although Samuels won, it would be the last mayoral victory for the GOP in Philadelphia.[1]

The popular exhibit neglected to examine the role of race in the city's proposed postwar housing design. Many civil rights activists realized that the exhibit's giant hands would remove homes of the city's black poor without clarifying where these relocated residents would be housed. In postwar Philadelphia blatant discrimination in housing, both private and public, increased the level of racial tension. This chapter examines how Fellowship House, the Fellowship Commission, and the Philadelphia Housing Association developed new strategies to confront the seemingly intractable dilemma of segregated housing.

The growing cooperation between the Housing Association and the Fellowship Commission represented the potential for substantial change. In addition to the working relationship of Fagan and the recently married Dorothy Schoell Montgomery, an increasing number of the coalition's board of commissioners became affiliated with the Housing Association. Abraham Freedman served as the PHA's treasurer; Theodore Spaulding, of the NAACP, and commissioners Frederick Gruenberg and Nochem Winnet sat on the board of directors. Despite the growing connection between the two organizations, serious differences divided the Fellowship Commission from the Housing Association.

In late 1947 the Fellowship Commission discussed a report on housing availability prepared by the Housing Association: "Do we approve the Philadelphia Housing Association's contention that fair real estate practices wait upon and can be best corrected by working for more public and private housing? How will the establishment of additional housing eliminate discrimination against those who are unable to compete for such additional housing?"[2] The members of Fellowship Commission valued the PHA's expertise in housing but were skeptical of the association's commitment to integration. They recognized that although Montgomery and her colleagues did not disregard racism completely, they downplayed its influence in housing. Some in the PHA proposed increasing the supply of housing to eradicate segregation. This response to housing segregation harkened back to the 1920s, when some race relations activists believed that increasing the supply of housing could solve a very complicated issue. But while activists had come to understand this was an insufficient response, the members of the Housing Association had not.

Despite these differences, the two organizations continued to cooperate. The Housing Association supplied the Fellowship Commission with research, information, and advice, and the commission attempted to integrate this information in their race relations work. In 1949 Montgomery participated with Fagan on a radio forum on integrated housing. The Fellowship Commission utilized its media sources to illustrate the social repercussions of segregated housing. Fagan and his colleagues knew, however, that media was not enough; they knew that housing needed to be addressed from a public-policy standpoint.[3]

For some activists, the late 1940s seemed an advantageous period for policy-oriented work. On the federal level, there were encouraging signs. In the 1948 *Kramer* decision, the Supreme Court ruled that restrictive covenants were illegal, thus removing one of the great legal barriers to open housing. Although financing remained a major problem, the Veterans Administration's mortgage-loan guaranty program allowed an increasing number of black families access to the housing market. The passage of the Housing Act in 1949, the declared objective of which was "a decent home and suitable living environment for every American family," also encouraged activists.[4]

The Housing Association's Montgomery collaborated with public housing advocates Catherine Bauer and Lee Johnson to secure passage of federal legislation on urban redevelopment. After a difficult four-year battle, the Wagner-Ellender-Taft bill was signed into law in 1949. The bill supported public housing and urban redevelopment.[5] Despite positive legislative and judicial developments, the FHA continued to support segregation, until 1950 refusing to underwrite houses in areas threatened by "Negro invasion" but continuing to write mortgages in restricted areas. The federal government's "red-lining" of black and changing neighborhoods discouraged lending by banks and savings and loans. Moreover, while some funding under the Housing Act went to urban housing, the bulk was earmarked to help suburban developers.[6]

Interested in coordinating housing policy for the commission, Fagan envisioned building an action-oriented committee. Formed in 1947, the Council on Equal Housing Opportunity (CEHO) was loosely modeled on the Council on Equal Job Opportunity (CEJO), a small constituent agency of the Fellowship Commission, which will be discussed in the next chapter. CEHO represented a host of groups interested in the intersection of race and housing. Although CEHO functioned primarily as an advisory body, it also attempted to coordinate activities among concerned organizations.[7] What housing needed, however, was a research and lobbying arm with dynamic leadership.

To fill this need, Reverend Dr. William Gray Jr. formed the Committee on Democracy on Housing (CDH) in early 1950. Gray, the former president of Florida A&M College, was at that time pastor of North Philadelphia's Bright Hope Baptist Church and one of the city's leading black ministers. His leadership in the CDH ensured a significant level of support from the black community. In addition to Gray, the CDH included Anna McGarry, one of the leaders of the Catholic Interracial Council; Theodore Spaulding, president of the Philadelphia branch of the NAACP; and Reverend George Trowbridge, pastor of St. Martin's Episcopal Church and member of the Fellowship Commission's Board of Commissioners. The CDH's ambitious goal was the integration of both public and private housing. Montgomery pledged to support the committee's efforts through advice and research.[8]

The CDH faced a formidable challenge. In 1950 Philadelphia's black population stood at 26 percent and was concentrated in three sections of the city: West, North, and South Philadelphia. The average black resident lived in a census tract that was 56 percent black. Although more houses were built in 1949 than any other postwar year, few were available for black occupancy. Most of Philadelphia's 40,000 substandard dwellings were occupied by blacks. Moreover, new construction in the city was outpaced by suburban growth. For every new house built in the city of Philadelphia, two were constructed in the city's suburbs.[9] With increasing segregation in the city coinciding with white flight, any approach to housing would also have to consider regional dynamics.

Yet, even as regional dynamics became increasingly important, the city of Philadelphia's new charter offered the possibility of substantial change in housing issues related to race. As the CDH mobilized its resources, representatives of the Fellowship Commission and the Housing Association lobbied the Charter Commission for stronger civil rights and housing codes. The Fellowship Commission and the Housing Association fought for the establishment of a department of housing, but the Housing Authority opposed the proposal. The Housing Authority prevailed, and the establishment of a department of housing was rejected by the Charter Commission.[10] Nevertheless, the CDH, Fellowship Commission, and the Housing Association were successful in assisting the Charter Commission in the creation of the Commission on Human Relations (CHR). The activists believed that the new municipal agency would provide crucial support in housing desegregation and other civil rights issues.

Integrating public and private housing presented the CDH with two very different challenges. Although effective legislation could outlaw de jure discrimination, white homeowners still resisted, objecting to black neighbors or black residents in nearby public housing developments. As Charles Abrams outlines in *Forbidden Neighbors*, many whites believed that blacks lowered property values, endangered their social status, and would eventually dominate neighborhoods if allowed to settle in them.[11] Assessing this situation, the CDH came to believe that a two-pronged approach would be needed to integrate housing: to lobby for new legislation, and to confront and transform white attitudes.

While CDH took on both of these challenges in their housing crusade, Fellowship House in the postwar era struggled to define itself as an organization. Although there was considerable debate over its future, it was increasingly clear that Fellowship House's educational programs were effective in reducing racial tension and, therefore, must be continued. The members of Fellowship House decided that their grass-roots approach to fighting racism could successfully complement the policy-oriented work of the Fellowship Commission. The major children's program, the Arrow program, was popular among elementary school pupils and educators. It addressed desegregation through a play in which different colored rabbits built an integrated community.[12]

Adult-oriented programs also focused on housing. The activists were concerned that racial violence around housing could erupt in Philadelphia.

Fellowship House also published and distributed "A Primer on Housing." The document urged cautious whites, especially housewives, to befriend their new black neighbors: "If you are like most of us you cannot work for justice in the abstract. It will help immensely if you know the household, meet the children and the parents. Do more. Take the mother shopping. Introduce her to your market, your milkman and breadman, and the neighbors you can count on to help."[13] The primer also counseled whites on how to handle the most delicate race relations questions: "One small woman, when faced with the 'marry your daughter' business, answers, 'She can always say "no" if she's asked.' (A plug for our Incident Control Course)."[14] The brochure concluded saying: "If you really want interracial, interfaith understanding, get ready! Remember the real battle will not be fought in Fellowship House. The real battle will be, first in you—against your own inertia and timidity, then in *your neighborhood*."[15]

Like Bryan and Haynes, Penney believed that the struggle against racism should be waged on an interpersonal level. While Penny and her colleagues did not downplay the importance of legal challenges, they believed success lay in overcoming white prejudices and black suspicion. They argued that positive interracial encounters were more important than policy changes. For this reason, the organization focused on experiments in interracial living.

Fellowship House wanted to experiment with interracial housing on many levels. In a sense, Fellowship House and Fellowship Farm were both experiments in interracial housing. The house at 1431 Brown Street sheltered Penney and the Kanedas, a family of relocated Japanese-Americans, and at various times, a racially mixed group of students, visitors, and members. A more extensive experiment was undertaken in 1951 with the opening of Fellowship Farm in rural Montgomery County. The living accommodations at the farm resembled those of an Israeli kibbutz: single men and women were housed in separate dormitories while families stayed in a converted chicken coop.

Larger experiments than these, however, were imagined. In the late 1940s some members of Fellowship House wanted to take interracial living to another level and establish an integrated housing development. Unfortunately, logistical and financial concerns limited the its capabilities, and the organization was unable to initiate such a project. Still, it gave extensive support to individuals and other organizations engaged in developing integrated housing.[16]

Experiments in planned interracial residential communities in the Philadelphia area date back to 1939, when an independent cooperative, Bryn Gweled, was founded in suburban Southampton, Bucks County. Although organized as an interracial development, the first black family did not join until 1949. By the late 1940s new integrated developments were being planned. In 1952 Morris Milgram, a New Jersey–based builder, began to raise money for an open-occupancy project in the Philadelphia area.[17]

Milgram, a former organizer for the Workers Defense League, a small New York–based leftist organization, had been involved in civil rights issues since the 1930s. After receiving substantial support from the Friends Social Order Committee, he gained the financial backing of Gray and several other black clergymen to purchase two sites: the Concord Park tract in Trevose, Bucks County, and the Greenbelt Knoll tract in Northeast Philadelphia.[18]

Within two years, Concord Park opened for occupancy. Its three- and four-bedroom homes sold for $12,000 to $13,600. Concord Park attracted attention from many black families excluded from the dozens of new developments sprouting up across the Philadelphia area. Milgram became concerned that if the project was overwhelmingly black, whites would not move in. The board voted to establish a quota or "controlled occupancy pattern." In 1955 Gray proposed that the quota be set at 55 percent white and 45 percent black. Despite the quota, white sales lagged until Stuart Wallace, a white real estate salesman from Syracuse, New York, moved into Concord Park. Wallace successfully promoted the development, and by 1958 all houses were sold—55 percent to white buyers and 45 percent to black buyers.[19]

Some Fellowshippers were attracted to the concept of planned integrated housing. Roosevelt and Virginia Barlow, who had been members of Fellowship House since its inception, moved into Greenbelt Knoll when it opened in 1957. Barlow, one of the fire department's few black officers, wanted to demonstrate his commitment to the ideals of Fellowship House by living in an integrated community. Although the Barlow family had expressed interest in Concord Park, employees of the city of Philadelphia were not (and still are not) permitted to live outside city limits. The wooded site contained only nineteen homes, eight of which were sold to blacks. Designed by Robert Bishop, a disciple of Frank Lloyd Wright, Greenbelt Knoll won numerous architectural awards.[20]

In addition to Milgram's developments, Friends Cooperative Housing emerged in 1954. Organized by the AFSC and the Friends Neighborhood

Guild, the Co-op was located at Fairmount Avenue and Eighth Street in North Philadelphia. When it opened, the Co-Op was one-third black, but gradually the population stabilized at 50 percent black and 50 percent white. Also designed by Oscar Stonorov, the Co-Op received support and praise from Fellowship House and the Fellowship Commission.[21]

Although these experiments reaffirmed the beliefs of Fellowshippers and swayed the opinions of some skeptics in favor of integrated housing, they represented only a small fraction of the new housing in the Philadelphia area. These few new developments could not possibly absorb the thousands of black families who wanted to purchase homes. Therefore, the main focus of the civil rights movement would not be the creation of newly constructed integrated communities but the desegregation of existing and future housing.

Shaping a Housing Agenda

ON MAY 9, 1951, THE FELLOWSHIP COMMISSION SPONSORED THE "CONFERence of Organizations on Human Rights." The evening conference featured seven panel sessions, two of which were devoted to housing matters. Scores of diverse organizations—unions, churches, synagogues, government agencies, and professional associations—participated in the conference.[22] The conference participants called for the Housing Authority to declare its opposition to discrimination and the establishment of community-based programs in "shifting" neighborhoods. One organization was noticeable in its absence: the Philadelphia Housing Association dispatched no representatives. While some members of the PHA wanted to address race, others continued to feel that this was beyond their original mission. Despite its absence, the PHA continued its cooperation with the Fellowship Commission by sharing research reports and other data.[23]

In addition to the absence of the Housing Association, there were no left-leaning organizations in attendance. In contrast to the late 1930s, the growing Red Scare had effectively silenced many of Philadelphia's more radical voices. The conference, however, addressed the increasingly repressive climate by hosting a panel on "Loyalty Oaths and Democratic Freedoms." The panel featured representatives of the National Labor Relations Board, the University of Pennsylvania, the Legal Committee of the NAACP and the Citizens Council on Democratic Rights. The panel participants concluded that loyalty oaths were too vague and should be opposed. They also criticized restrictions on speech and action, especially those endured by members of the educational community.[24]

While free speech issues are not normally associated with housing issues, these concerns were raised by activists. Although politically moderate, the Housing Association criticized the Housing Authority for implementing restrictions based on political thought.

> For example, we are distressed to learn that the Regional Director of the Public Housing Administration has taken the position that the Pennypack Woods Mutual Home Ownership Association may purchase the Pennypack Woods Project only if they dismiss two employees who have been alleged by a local newspaper of having previously been members of left-wing organizations.[25]

In addition, the PHA castigated the Housing Authority for firing an employee who had been a conscientious objector during World War II. The Housing Association, the Fellowship Commission, and Fellowship House steered a precarious middle course during this tense period. In contrast to some civil rights organizations who wholly embraced anti-communism, they criticized the persecution of individuals and organizations. The three organizations, however, did maintain that communism was a threat to liberty and that the best defense against this was an integrated society where all were treated equally.[26]

In an effort to reaffirm the belief that open housing was a cornerstone of a democratic society, the CDH addressed discrimination in suburban housing. In late 1951 it hosted a meeting of organizations concerned with the construction of a development in Morrisville, Bucks County, planned by William Levitt, the nation's largest suburban developer.[27] Although Levitt claimed to be liberal on issues of race, this was not reflected in his business philosophy. Levitt argued that he would be committing economic suicide if he changed his segregation policy: "Most whites prefer not to live in mixed communities. The responsibility [for this] is society's. It is not reasonable to expect that any one builder could or should undertake to absorb the entire risk and burden of conducting such a vast social experiment."[28] The CDH and others in the civil rights agencies were concerned that, like Levittown, Long Island, the new development would be segregated. The CDH pledged its assistance and cooperation, yet indicated that civil rights groups in Bucks County should assume leadership and call upon national organizations, such as the NAACP, for support.[29]

The Levittown situation illustrated the growing complexity of the housing issue. If the CDH wanted to fight against segregated housing developments, would it have to confront one builder at a time? Such a course of action would be time-consuming and expensive. Moreover, the majority of these developments were located in nearby suburbs, and Gray believed that segregation in the city presented the CDH with sufficient challenge. The CDH maintained that housing was the most explosive issue in race relations. The Fellowship Commission agreed that the integration of private housing was the "number one problem."[30] The fight to integrate private housing needed to be fought on many fronts: it required activists to confront the increasingly powerful real estate industry and countless white homeowners. The fight to integrate public housing, in contrast, was more focused: activists only needed to confront a much smaller group of public housing officials. Furthermore, while defenders of segregated private housing argued that no government should be allowed to dictate to whom private individuals could sell or rent their property, public housing represented another complexity. Housing projects were built and maintained by tax dollars, yet not all of them were open to black taxpayers.

In May 1952 the CDH reported that it was asked by the Housing Authority to find white residents for the Arch Homes located at 56th and Arch Streets in increasingly black West Philadelphia. The search was unsuccessful. Few white families wanted to live in a black neighborhood, and most of the city's available public housing was located in black neighborhoods.[31] Although projects also existed in white communities, black applicants faced hostility and violence from white tenants and white residents of the immediate environs. Integrating public housing would be no easy task.

In an attempt to address the looming crisis in public housing, housing activists, social workers, and government officials formed the Committee on Public Housing Policy (CPHP). This committee, which Montgomery joined, focused on the structural aspects of housing in Philadelphia. For example, the CPHP debated and resolved the high-rise vs. low-rise question in Philadelphia, and recommended that public housing projects should consist of small, low-rise units that could "facilitate harmonious race relations."[32] The location for the new projects, however, remained in question for some time because white communities opposed the construction of integrated public housing in their neighborhoods. Armed with maps, graphs, and statistics, the CPHP struggled to find an acceptable plan for the placement of new housing projects.

Although supporters of integrated public housing faced hurdles, they nevertheless remained hopeful that every project would be open to all tenants, regardless of race. The Housing Authority's support of segregation had begun to wane. While opposition from white homeowners and tenants remained an obstacle, some officials within the Housing Authority now supported integration. In spite of this progress, city neighborhoods continued to grow more segregated while activists continued to fight segregation.

In 1952, in the midst of this increasing segregation, a new social action director, Rev. Walter Wynn, arrived. Fagan designated Wynn to work with the CEHO and to coordinate housing activism with various governmental organizations. Wynn, responsible for coordinating some of the commission's fair education efforts, wanted to examine the interconnection between segregated housing and segregated education. Simultaneous with Wynn's efforts with the CDH, the Fellowship Commission formed the Committee on Community Tensions (CCT) to handle racial and ethnic tension in the neighborhoods. Since some of the tension was directly related to housing, the CCT's work could augment that of the CDH. In addition, the Fellowship Commission co-sponsored a seven-week seminar that examined blockbusting in a West Philadelphia neighborhood.[33]

As momentum steadily built, the CDH, under Gray's direction, began to draft an integrated housing statement. The activists hoped that the statement would synthesize the beliefs of the civil rights community and provide the ideological grounding for any future legislation. Gray and other members of CDH saw the statement as a clarion call to civil rights activists and the first major opening salvo in a long and bitter battle.[34]

As Gray and his colleagues drafted the housing credo, Montgomery and her colleagues began work on a new housing code. The Philadelphia Housing Association had sponsored the city's first housing code back in 1915. Many housing activists believed that code was outdated and that the city needed a more relevant one. Drafted by housing reformers and supported by the Fellowship Commission, the new code focused on improving the physical condition of the city's housing. The new housing code, passed by city council in July 1954, established higher standards for infrastructural aspects of housing, such as plumbing and electrical wiring, and mandated more housing inspectors.[35]

Shortly after the passage of the new housing code, the CDH unveiled its "Housing Credo." Like many of its wartime statements, the Housing Credo appealed to its reader's sense of patriotism and belief in the American way:

> We believe that America needs citizens who seek constantly to raise their standard of living. We believe that good family life is among the most valuable safeguards of social peace, progress and democracy in America. We therefore seek to safeguard the right of every American to rent or purchase a house which he can afford and adequately maintain in any street or neighborhood that he believes will afford him the best opportunity to raise his family safely and happily.[36]

The credo also called on the real-estate industry to employ fair practices and castigated the print media for publishing discriminatory advertisements. Concerned about the spread of urban blight, the CDH issued a challenge in its credo to new residents and long-term neighbors:

> We call upon all persons to maintain the highest possible standards in their apartment, house, street and neighborhood. We urge them to insist upon the highest standards of inspection and service from the city government.[37]
>
> We urge them to welcome as a neighbor any person who wishes to improve his housing and home life and to invite such new neighbors to join with them in maintaining high neighborhood standards.[38]

In an attempt to spur action on democratic housing, the credo was supplemented by a Code of Ethics that outlined specific malpractices and suggestions for action. The CDH recommended that neighbors support interracial community associations, protest discriminatory practices by real estate agents, and lobby elected officials for legislative change. Endorsed by each of the nine constituent agencies of the Fellowship Commission, both the Credo and the Code of Ethics encouraged Philadelphians to support the newly approved Philadelphia Housing Code.[39]

The Fellowship Commission reaffirmed its support of integrated housing by hosting a conference on the issue in the fall of 1954. While the Fellowship Commission supported integrated housing, it had provided little support for black families who desired to move into white neighborhoods.[40]

In the early 1950s Philadelphia experienced several minor sporadic incidents of racial violence, some of them around housing. By mid-decade the number of violent interracial clashes was steadily increasing. Civil rights activists feared that one of these minor conflicts could escalate into a major one. Therefore, in late summer 1955, the activists mobilized when racial tension over housing in Juniata Park, a predominantly white working-class community in the Lower Northeast, threatened to explode.

The tension began to mount in Juniata Park when Wiley Clark, a black car wash worker, purchased a decrepit house at Judson and Cambria Streets. While working on his house, Clark was approached by his white neighbors who inquired who he was working for. After discovering that Clark was the owner, a steady pattern of violence and intimidation began. Mobs of whites, mainly youths, began to congregate outside the house on a regular basis. The Commission on Human Relations dispatched personnel to the scene, including CDH member Anna McGarry, the CHR's chief troubleshooter. Forces on both sides of the conflict began to mobilize. Local whites, some of whom claimed that Clark was sponsored by Communists and Father Divine's Peace Mission, formed the North Penn Civic Improvement Association to persuade the Clark family to move and to block any future black residents. Other whites put their homes up for sale. The Clarks felt besieged. In an effort to calm the family, Penney spent several nights in their home. A small group of activists within the African American community formed the Citizen's Committee for Wiley Clark and raised substantial financial support for the Clark family.[41]

Many civil rights activists were concerned that Clark was not a good ambassador for integrated housing. Wiley Clark's low-paying job at a car wash indicated that he lacked the resources to complete renovating the house. In addition, Clark admitted that he consumed alcohol, sometimes while working on the house. Although concerned about Clark's economic position and character, civil rights activists vowed to support the family's right to remain in the neighborhood.[42] On September 14 the Citizens Committee for Wiley Clark and the North Penn Civic Improvement Association met in the CHR offices. In that meeting, members of the neighborhood association decried violent methods, even as they endorsed the goal of that violence, the preservation of an all-white neighborhood. Clark's supporters replied that he would remain. The Citizens Committee, along with Fellowship House, raised several thousand dollars in cash and provided two thousand more in housing supplies. In addition to helping the Clark family complete house repairs, Roosevelt Barlow directed a group of volunteers from Fellowship House who brought the house up to city standards. By early November, Clark, with the help of the Citizens Committee, had found a better-paying job and the house was finished.[43]

In the months that followed, there was no violence and no panic selling. The CHR believed that the Clark affair was successfully resolved. Violence and white flight had been halted, and the Clarks were ensconced in their home.[44] Although Fellowship House was instrumental in providing moral, financial, and other means of support for the Clark family, they did not consider it a major victory. The Clarks were merely tolerated by the neighbors, not accepted. For Fellowship House, real triumph would be achieved only when the hardened attitudes of Clark's neighbors changed. Juniata Park was physically integrated, but the races remained segregated in their hearts. For Fellowshippers, it was the heart that mattered. The Clark incident reminded them how difficult it would be the build the Beloved Community.

The Struggle for Public Housing

RIOTING BROKE OUT IN 1953 AT THE TRUMBULL PARK HOMES, A HOUSING project in South Deering, a white working-class neighborhood located in Chicago. The goal of the rioters was to keep several black families from moving into Trumbull Park. Despite the violence, blacks continued to move into the public housing development.[45]

Philadelphia's political leaders and civil rights activists wanted to avoid a Trumbull Park in their city. As South Deering exploded, housing reformers, civil rights activists, and public officials struggled to find solutions to the city's public housing crisis. Walter Phillips, Housing Association board member and leader of the Democratic reform movement, had been appointed director of the Philadelphia Housing Authority in 1951. Phillips attempted to transform the Authority from a bastion of political patronage to an instrument of social change. His vision broadened the racial perspectives of many in public housing, including Montgomery and Housing Association official Elriede Hoeber. After Phillips's appointment to the Housing Authority, Montgomery began to call for the integration of public housing as a means to integrate surrounding communities: "it is hoped that new housing will be an integral part of its larger neighborhood."[46]

The construction of new integrated units and the integration of existing public housing hit a political roadblock. Black leaders maintained that all-black projects perpetuated segregation, while white homeowners associations vowed resistance to black tenants. In 1954 an Intragency Committee on Public Housing and a subcommittee devised criteria for selecting new sites. They listed costs, relation to community services, and contribution to urban renewal as determinants, yet neighborhood acceptance of tenants remained the major issue.[47]

In the summer of 1955, the Philadelphia Housing Authority convened a series of hearings on site selection. Fagan and Cunningham rallied support among civil rights agencies, while Schermer appealed to community organizations. Although the hearings were not well publicized, many of the attendees were white homeowners who opposed construction of integrated public housing in their neighborhoods. After several stormy sessions, the Housing Authority put plans for any new projects on hold. Both Fagan and Montgomery maintained that the Intragency Committee had failed to communicate the idea of "democratic housing" to frightened whites. William Rafsky, chair of the committee, complained that poor scheduling, excessive regulations, and staffing problems doomed the project. In contrast to Rafsky, Gray charged that the plan had failed because of an organized racist offensive against integration; he argued that politicians and small businessmen had manipulated the fears of white homeowners and prompted their resistance.[48]

This manipulation is evidenced in the pose white homeowners struck in arguing their case. Without direct reference to race, white homeowners argued they were protecting their neighborhoods from "undesirables" and preserving them for "people like us." One example of this position is manifested in a letter to Gray from Mrs. Jane Thorp, spokesperson for Northeast United Services, a civic association of far Northeast Philadelphia. In her letter she complained that the process was dominated by "social planners, industrialists, real estate operators and others," and that "[b]y its very nature, a Center City Committee is disqualified to tell neighborhoods how they would or should feel." According to Thorp, many white residents believed the NAACP was recruiting public housing tenants from the South and that the Dilworth administration planned to place projects in strategic wards to fill them with black Democrats. She concluded that "a certain amount of prejudice is to be expected and to be 'accepted' sympathetically, while quietly working toward its elimination." Her letter illustrated the deep-seated opposition among many working- and middle-class whites to integrated public housing.[49]

The struggle over site selection once more highlighted differences between the Housing Association and the Fellowship Commission.

Montgomery and her organization supported placing sites on isolated Redevelopment Authority property.⁵⁰ In contrast, Fagan and the Fellowship Commission knew that proposals to build integrated projects far from businesses and mass transit would not be popular with constituent agencies. Fellowship House would reject the proposal, but the NAACP, who had been critical of the commission's unfocused approach to housing, would be especially displeased. To the NAACP and Fellowship House, public housing represented an opportunity to show that integrated living could work. The conflict over sites ended in stalemate: no new public housing was built. This stalemate ensured that segregation in public housing would continue and that public housing would increasingly be concentrated in in black communities. By the mid-1950s public housing in Philadelphia had emerged as a refuge for the city's growing black underclass.

Montgomery remained hopeful that a solution to the public housing site crisis could be found. In 1957 she allied the Housing Association with the CCCP's Committee on Public Housing to study possible alternatives to the public housing roadblock. They agreed that an updated version of the OHA's approach to housing should be utilized. Montgomery proposed that the Housing Authority purchase and rehabilitate existing houses and then lease them to tenants. Evidence suggested that the scattered site program would be less expensive than new construction and would also place public housing tenants among neighborhood residents, thus integrating them in community life. In 1958 the Housing Authority received permission to develop a program known as subsidized tenancy or "turnkey" housing. Despite its success in cutting costs, there is no evidence to suggest that turnkey housing encouraged or contributed to the growth of integrated neighborhoods.⁵¹

The Fight for Fair Housing

IN HIS ANNUAL REPORT DELIVERED TO THE BOARD OF FELLOWSHIP COMmission on January 21, 1957, Fagan declared, "Housing is by far the most urgent and most important problem we face." Wynn reported to that same body that the Social Action Committee had convinced a small, yet growing number of realtors to abandon discriminatory practices. Several members proposed that a housing corporation, similar to Milgram's, should be developed by Fellowship Commission. Recognizing that segregated housing would not be ended either through appeals to realtors or housing officials, the Board of Commissioners decided that legislation was needed to break down the walls of segregation in housing.[52]

Like the community college issue and the fight for a state fair employment practices law, the Fellowship Commission would have to cultivate legislative support for passage of a fair housing ordinance. By the late 1950s the coalition had become increasingly confident in its role as an organization that formulated policy and attempted to transform it into law. Within the Fellowship Commission, there was considerable debate about the character of fair housing legislation. Should the bill cover all housing, including apartments in private homes, or should it be more limited? Should fair housing legislation be enacted at the state and/or the city level?[53]

Given Governor George Leader's support for civil rights, many activists believed that passage of a statewide bill would be feasible. Moreover, statewide legislation would also demonstrate to whites who departed the city for the suburbs that they could not escape integration. The need for a state law was underscored by racial tension in Levittown, Bucks County.

In late 1957 William Myers, a black technician, and his family moved into all-white Levittown, Bucks County. They were greeted by harassment and violence. Governor Leader, a former neighbor of the Myers family in York County, called out the state police. Fagan and others traveled to Levittown to advise a small group of interracial activists. Although this incident highlighted the need for legislation from Harrisburg, Philadelphia activists agreed that a state law would not be as well enforced in the city as a Philadelphia statute would. The CHR supported a fair housing ordinance in Philadelphia, and many activists hoped that the CHR, or a new agency, would guarantee compliance of a fair housing law. By the late 1950s, CHR was often criticized by activists for not enforcing legislation.[54]

The Fellowship Commission gave first priority to the passage of a state bill. The commission counted on the support of civil rights activists in the Pennsylvania Equal Rights Council, who had been lobbying for a fair employment bill since the late 1940s, in their struggle for fair housing legislation. And indeed, the Equal Rights Council expanded its focus to include fair housing. The Fellowship Commission stressed the link between employment and housing. An increasing number of black workers were forced to commute long distances because they could not find housing near their places of employment. Although black wages had risen in the 1950s, they were still considerably lower than white wages.[55] Thus, black housing choices were limited by both racial and economic factors.

Introduced in late 1958, State Bill 333 mandated the limited integration of private housing. Although the bill was not as broad as many in the civil rights community had envisioned, it ran into fierce opposition from Republicans. In spite of Leader's support, the bill died in late 1959. The Fellowship Commission, which had assisted in drafting the bill and had lobbied local legislators, was not deterred. It now turned its full attention to Philadelphia and prepared to draft a fair housing ordinance.[56]

The campaign for fair housing legislation in Philadelphia exposed deep divisions within the city's civil rights movement. Fagan solicited opinions from constituent members of Fellowship House and the Housing Association. There was considerable disagreement over what the proposed ordinance should cover. The NAACP wanted a comprehensive law that would cover all housing; Penney stated that Fellowship House supported legislation but was unsure of what sorts of housing it should cover. Montgomery, like Penney, expressed reservations about the extent of the bill. The majority of CEHO favored exemptions for apartments in owner-occupied single homes and duplexes. The majority of agencies supported limited legislation. They believed that the most important objective was the passage of basic fair housing legislation; comprehensive amendments could be added at a later date. Nevertheless, some members of the Board of Commissioners and Montgomery expressed concern that support for a city ordinance could undermine state legislation. Some activists voiced concern that the NAACP would sponsor its own ordinance.[57]

Despite opposition within its ranks, the Fellowship Commission supported the passage of the bill. The ordinance had the support of most council members, Mayor Richardson Dilworth, and an increasing segment of the public. The Fair Housing Ordinance became law in early 1961. The ordinance banned most forms of housing discrimination yet excluded apartments in owner-occupied buildings. It also created the Fair Housing Commission (FHC). Like the CHR, the FHC was given powers to investigate housing complaints and to enforce the recently passed legislation.[58]

Although there had been vociferous opposition to the law from realtors and some homeowners, the timing of the campaign was crucial. In contrast to the mid-1950s, the passage of national civil rights legislation and the emergence of a civil rights movement helped to influence the outcome of the campaign. In addition, the Fair Housing Ordinance did not arouse as much white outrage as public housing had. The ordinance removed some legal barriers to segregated housing, but massive social walls remained.

Even if laws were changed, blacks could expect at best ostracism and at worst violence in many white communities.

Despite encouraging political and legal developments, the 1960 census presented a view of an increasingly segregated metropolitan area. Half of the city's black population lived in census tracts that were over 80 percent black, and two-thirds of the substandard dwellings in Philadelphia were occupied by blacks. Although the city's housing supply had increased, fewer than 3 percent of homes were black-owned. Worse, urban renewal was contributing to the growing segregation. As a result of new commercial and residential developments, the Center City black families were displaced; some moved to the expanding ghetto, thus increasing segregation.[59] In the suburbs, the black population actually decreased. Suburban discrimination renewed calls for state legislation, but a fair housing law could not address the financial restraints faced by black families. For most black families, suburban housing was simply too expensive.

Integrating Housing in Philadelphia

IN A 1961 REPORT, THE CHR MAINTAINED THAT "THE CORE OF THE PROBlem and the measure of success lie in residential desegregation," and recommended that "[t]here will have to be a popular sentiment and organized civic movements reaching the proportions of a sustained crusade."[60] Although it could hardly be termed a crusade, new actors appeared in the fight for integrated housing. In 1957 the Yearly Meeting of the Society of Friends founded Friends Suburban Housing (FSH) to help black families purchase homes in the suburbs. FSH functioned as a real estate agency, carefully selecting houses in neighborhoods where opposition to black neighbors was not high. By the early 1960s, FSH had settled over a dozen families. Although the organization reached only a few families, the FSH served as a model for other organizations that wanted to crack the wall of segregation. The FSH, however, did not agitate for changes in housing policy.

In 1962 the Fair Housing Council of the Delaware Valley (FHCDV) was organized by a small group of Quaker activists. The FHCDV attempted to craft a regional approach to housing discrimination.[61] As new organizations emerged, electoral developments would adversely affect the struggle for integrated housing. In 1963 Democrat James Tate, the city's first Irish Catholic mayor, was elected with the strong support of white ethnic working-class voters. The greater part of his constituency was bitterly opposed to open housing. Compared to Clark and Dilworth, Tate's views on race were conservative. Although he enjoyed black electoral support, the hopeful mood that ushered in the reformers was over.

The city's major civil rights organization also witnessed a significant change. The election of Cecil B. Moore as president of the Philadelphia branch of the NAACP represented a break with the past. He emphasized the importance of economic issues in the civil rights movement. He declared: "We intend to picket banks that refuse to lend our people to purchase a modest house in a white neighborhood but will finance a Cadillac."[62] Moreover, Moore signaled his unwillingness to be part of any coalition, black or white. He called for independent leadership in the black community and was critical of black leaders who accepted patronage from Tate. Although Moore was criticized for withdrawing the NAACP from alliances, he merely articulated the concerns of many members of his organization. As early as the late 1940s, many NAACP members complained that the Fellowship Commission had attempted to establish the agenda for the black community.[63]

In the aftermath of the passage of fair housing legislation, the role of the CDR decreased. The small committee had successfully lobbied for legislation and established standards and guidelines for integrated housing, but Fagan believed that a more comprehensive approach to housing was needed. CEHO seemed the logical vehicle to assume this responsibility. By the early 1960s the CEHO included representatives from several dozen civil rights and housing agencies. The Board of Commissioners urged the CEHO to become more aggressive in its new role as the new housing arm of the Fellowship Commission.[64]

Inspired by the work of the FSH, Wynn proposed that the Fellowship Commission collect information on "friendly areas." Anxious to counter criticism that the commission was duplicating the FSH, Wynn maintained that the CEHO was only interested in educating black families about housing choices; they were not establishing a rival real estate venture. Both Fagan and Montgomery supported the creation of housing information centers that would educate potential black homebuyers about the most receptive neighborhoods. In addition, the housing information centers would direct them to sympathetic agents and mortgage institutions.[65]

The need for open housing was underscored by the North Philadelphia uprising of August 1964. Although the violence erupted after a confrontation with police, social conditions were the root cause of the uprising.

Several days after the violence, the Citizens Emergency Committee (CEC), led by Rev. Joshua Licorsish of Zoar Methodist Church, formulated a poverty program to address the area's problems. They ranked the problems in order of their magnitude as housing, education, and employment. The CEC pressed Tate for immediate changes such as job-training and family counseling. In addition, they demanded that the city launch a housing rehabilitation program and proposed the expansion of subsidized tenancy programs. Moreover, they argued that a North Philadelphia community organization should have a major role in policy-making.[66]

The August uprising would also have a wide-ranging impact on the struggle for integrated housing. Although the Fellowship Commission and its constituent agencies were quick to criticize the violence, they argued that society's neglect of racial discrimination had created explosive conditions. The Housing Association, however, refrained from comment for six months. In the annual policy statement on housing, board member George Schermer stressed the need for "penalties" to encourage "racial inclusiveness . . . in the planning of all new city and suburban housing." Concerned that his statement might offend allies, Montgomery's assistant, Cushing Dolbeare, condensed his remarks into a brief, yet direct statement: "We want to end segregation and will deal later with the means of doing so."[67]

In 1965, Montgomery retired from the Housing Association and was succeeded by Dolbeare. She had increased the Housing Association's influence on public policy in her two decades as executive director. Most importantly, through her cooperation with the Fellowship Commission, the Housing Association had contributed its resources in the fight for integrated housing. Montgomery brought the association from under the shadow of Newman but, because she had had to contend with members and board members reluctant to embrace the struggle against racism in housing, her tenure was not all those in the civil rights movement might have wished.

Cushing Dolbeare, her successor, was more progressive on issues of race. A graduate of Swarthmore College, Dolbeare had directed the Citizens Planning and Housing Association (Metropolitan Housing Association) in her native Baltimore before joining the Philadelphia Housing Association in 1956. A Quaker, she described herself as a "militant liberal," but unlike Montgomery, she held a strong commitment to civil rights. During her short tenure, she shepherded the Housing Association through the most profound and radical transformation in its long history.[68]

Dolbeare wanted to strengthen the Housing Association's cooperation with the Fellowship Commission and planned a multifaceted and comprehensive approach to racial discrimination. Shortly after becoming executive director, the Housing Association united with the Urban League to form the Joint Committee on Minority Housing (JCMH). This new committee employed a regional approach toward housing and in some cases duplicated the work of the FHCDV.[69]

Under Montgomery, the number of black members grew, yet the number remained relatively small. In contrast, Dolbeare encouraged black participation by shifting the focus of the organization. She renewed the fight for public housing, pushing for subsidized tenancy and community renewal, while maintaining that black tenants and homeowners should have major roles in directing government policy.[70] Her grass-roots perspective represented an about face from the Housing Association's previous approaches to race and housing.

In response to the Housing Association's new focus, some funding sources withdrew their contributions. Increasingly critical of Mayor Tate and the CHR, Dolbeare argued that city authorities were not doing enough to alleviate the abysmal housing conditions of the city's black underclass. In an effort to bypass the city, the Housing Association turned to the federal government.[71]

President Lyndon Johnson's War on Poverty brought millions of federal dollars into Philadelphia. The heart of the federal antipoverty program was the Community Action Program (CAP), which funded numerous projects in the city. The architects of the War on Poverty believed that the involvement of the poor was crucial, but many local politicians did not want to yield power and money to ghetto residents. The federal legislation called for "maximum feasible participation" of the residents of the target neighborhood, but as Michael Gillette argues, there was no consensus on what "participation" meant. Dolbeare and her colleagues hoped CAP could energize and empower impoverished residents, but others in the city wanted to limit their involvement.[72]

Across the United States, antipoverty activists challenged local politicians for control of Community Action boards. In order to deter such community challenges, Tate skillfully placed his allies in firm control of federal programs and limited input from activists. The mayor's political manipulation of federal programs stifled the growth of community-based initiatives and furthered alienated him from the interracial civil rights movement.[73]

Undeterred by mayoral inaction, the Housing Association and CEHO continued to press their demands. In addition to demanding more rehabilitated housing, they also focused on the link between employment and housing. Dolbeare maintained that suburban housing for blacks was meaningless until blacks could find jobs in the suburbs. As early as 1964, Dolbeare argued that the employment organization, CEJO, and the housing organization, CEHO, should merge.[74] Although CEJO was technically a constituent member of the Fellowship Commission, it received its entire budget from the Board of Commissioners. Formed in 1943, CEJO had successfully led the struggle for fair employment legislation in the 1950s. In the 1960s the organization attempted, among other activities, to integrate unions and businesses. In 1966 members of CEJO began attending meetings of the Housing Association, CEHO, and the JCMH. In early 1967 CEJO and CEHO established a joint subcommittee chaired by a young black community activist from Southwest Philadelphia, W. Wilson Goode. The subcommittee outlined problems faced by black workers, such as suburban mass transit and the shortage of low-income housing in the region. Although their research demonstrated the need for new initiatives involving race, housing, and employment, response from city government and the business community was tepid.[75]

The joint subcommittee criticized barriers faced by blacks in acquiring homes in the suburbs, but resistance to integration in Philadelphia remained strong. Dolbeare argued that there was a "Maginot Line" preventing black settlement in the city's semi-suburban Northeast.[76] Black buyers were routinely discouraged from seeking homes there, a clear violation of the Fair Housing Ordinance. The threat of violence continued to limit black housing choices.

In October 1966 the Wrights, an African American family, moved into the predominantly white working-class neighborhood of Kensington. Several nights of rioting broke out as hundreds of whites attacked police with bricks and bottles. Shortly after the violence erupted, Penney and other members of Fellowship House began staying with the family to encourage them, as they had with the Clarks. Although Tate deployed a large number of police, civil rights activists claimed that he had acted too late. They pointed out that he had not openly condemned the rioters. Penney, Victor Paschkis (Penney's recent husband and a founder of Concerned Scientists), and fifteen members of the FHCDV were arrested after staging a sit-in at Tate's offices. With the moral and political support of the CHR, the Wright family stayed for several months in Kensington. But by early 1967, exhausted and frightened, the Wright family had moved out of the neighborhood.[77]

Tate's indifference to the plight of blacks and his tacit support for segregated housing created tension between him and the interracial civil rights community. Since the early 1940s, relations between the civil rights movement and City Hall had ranged from fair to excellent. Clark and Dilworth had been very supportive of the work of the interracial civil rights organizations. In contrast, Tate's attitude represented a disregard that bordered on hostility toward their agenda. On June 6, 1967, CEHO announced the mass resignation of its members: the city no longer had an official committee on minority housing. CEHO chairman Nathan Edelstein stated that Tate had failed to meet with them to discuss the implementation of fair housing. Since federal regulations required the city to include a citizens committee, Tate scrambled to locate a more amenable committee.[78]

The rift with City Hall did not discourage the CEHO. The organization launched a six-point attack on housing inequities. Its proposals included support for low-income families and rigorous code enforcement, but the cornerstone of its attack was a campaign for a comprehensive statewide bill, one that would cover all housing except rooms in owner-occupied homes. The Housing Association and the FHCDV joined the CEHO's lobbying efforts for the passage of strong, statewide housing legislation.[79]

As the CEHO worked on a comprehensive approach to open housing, Dolbeare refocused the Housing Association on community-based action. In 1967 the association launched a series of educational programs designed to empower lower-income, mainly black residents. These courses covered the housing code, techniques of buying and renting, and building neighborhood organizations. The programs, attracting hundreds of community activists, social workers, and public housing tenants, demonstrated a shift in policy for the Housing Association. Dolbeare and her colleagues believed that hierarchical approaches to the city's housing crisis were no longer viable. They believed that black community organizations, not government or private agencies, would be the primary forces for change. Dolbeare, however, was eager to involve the Housing Association as advocates for the city's poor. The Association joined with the North City Congress (NCC), a black North Philadelphia organization, to fight attempts of a group of middle-class white residents of the Fairmount (Art Museum) section of the city to block the Housing Authority's conversion of several triplexes into homes for public housing tenants. Through the Housing Association, a compromise was reached. The Housing Authority agreed to scatter a limited number of tenants in the area.[80]

The struggle in the Art Museum area was one of an increasing number of protests over city housing conditions in the late 1960s. Yet, the suburbs and large sections of the city remained bastions of segregation. In an effort to widen its geographical reach and strengthen its advocacy role, the Housing Association joined forces with the FHCDV, becoming a single organization called the Housing Association of the Delaware Valley (HADV).

By the late 1960s the 600 members of the Housing Association were increasingly black activists or white liberals. This shift in attitude was facilitated by the resignation of veteran board members, like Henry Beeritz, and the inclusion of new members, like Rose Wylie of the Richard Allen Homes Tenant Council. With this realignment of the Housing Association came increased support for joining the Fellowship Commission. In some ways pressure to join the coalition had been building since the 1940s. In 1968, the Housing Association finally became one of the commission's constituent members.[81]

As a result of the Housing Association's affiliation, CEHO was dissolved and the commission's housing budget was allocated to the Housing Association, which became the Fellowship Commission's official housing arm. Both Fagan and Dolbeare maintained that the union strengthened the battle for integrated housing by coordinating both financial and human resources. Although the interracial civil rights organizations had been successful in securing the passage of legislation, they had not overcome the solid wall of white resistance to integrated housing. By the late 1960s Philadelphia's neighborhoods were becoming increasingly segregated as whites departed for the suburbs and the Northeast. Many black families who wanted homes avoided white neighborhoods, opting instead for increasingly black suburbs such as Yeadon and Cheltenham. In addition to a lack of integrated neighborhoods, opposition to public housing in white communities remained strong.[82]

White resistance contributed to the emergence of a radical shift within the struggle for democracy in housing. The Housing Association increasingly linked its efforts to other struggles for social change. In 1969 Dolbeare declared that the Housing Association was willing to support causes not normally associated with housing, such as police brutality and nuclear disarmament. In October the Housing Association affirmed its new direction by calling for an end to the Vietnam War. Although the working relationship with the Fellowship Commission continued, the support for the Vietnam moratorium caused a rift within the civil rights community.[83]

Support for other struggles did not indicate a retreat from housing; it served to enhance the program. Assistant Director Anne Turner stated that her objective for 1969 was "devising a strategy of action for a citizen housing organization that is truly anti-racist and anti-colonialist."[84] Following

Turner's directive, the Housing Association helped community activists create Redevelopment Action Groups (RAGs) to press the Redevelopment Authority to concentrate on neighborhood development.[85]

While the Housing Association helped to give neighborhood activists a sense of empowerment, it could not overcome opposition to public housing. In 1968 the Department of Housing and Urban Development mandated that local authorities disperse public housing sites in areas with no public housing. The Housing Authority earmarked sites in white neighborhoods like Manayunk and Roxborough. These sites, however, were isolated and located near incinerators. Housing Association members argued that Housing Authority officials wanted to segregate tenants in the least desirable sections of every community and rejected the proposals.[86]

Although disappointed by the proposals, the Housing Association was successful in removing Frank Steinberg as chairman of the Philadelphia Housing Authority. Steinberg had vehemently opposed placing public housing units in white areas, claiming: "Color likes to live with color. If you can put colored people in the Northwest, colored wouldn't be happy and white people wouldn't be happy." However, the resignation of Steinberg in 1969 did not signal a change in Housing Authority. In 1971 former Police Commissioner Frank Rizzo was elected mayor. Rizzo's primary supporters were working-class whites, and he vowed to defend their neighborhoods against public housing. For nearly a decade, he blocked construction of the Whitman Park housing project in South Philadelphia.[87]

As the 1970s dawned, segregation was increasing in both public and private housing. Although the interracial civil rights movement had contributed to the passage of legislation, resistance remained. The struggle for democracy in housing had influenced the peaceful integration of University City, West Mount Airy, and a few other communities, but vast areas of the city remained hostile to black residents.

The struggle, however, had transformed the Philadelphia Housing Association. Within two decades the organization changed from a reform agency hesitant to address race to a grass-roots organization that championed radical change in housing affairs. Stymied by resistance to integration and influenced by the Black Power movement, the Housing Association of the late 1960s shifted its focus to ghetto residents and encouraged them to be catalysts of change in their communities.

CHAPTER 6

Labor in the Vineyard

The Interracial Civil Rights Movement and the Struggle for Equality in Employment

IN THE EARLY NINETEENTH CENTURY PHILADELPHIA BOASTED ONE OF the wealthiest free black communities in the country. Blacks held real estate valued at $327,000 and were represented in over 130 skilled occupations. By the Civil War, however, black footholds in skilled jobs began to decline. Economic competition contributed to a rise in racial tension as blacks and whites, especially immigrants, fought for jobs in an increasingly tight labor market. Antebellum Philadelphia witnessed eight major race riots. Competition over scarce jobs contributed to the endemic pattern of racial violence in the City of Brotherly Love.[1] This final chapter examines the interracial civil rights movement's attempt to address racial discrimination in labor. While their work yielded several important policy victories, changing economic conditions tempered any success.

In the wake of the Civil War, blacks became increasingly restricted from traditional occupations such as barbering and waiting tables. Du Bois found that black men were concentrated in manual labor, and the majority of black women were in domestic service. Black workers, in addition to facing discrimination from white-owned businesses, were also excluded or restricted from labor unions. The main trade union confederation, the American Federation of Labor (AFL), called for the organization of all workers regardless of creed, race, or nationality. However, the AFL represented craft unions and was not interested in representing unskilled workers of any race. Since the overwhelming majority of black workers were unskilled, they were largely ignored by AFL organizers.[2]

Both labor and capital conspired to restrict black economic aspirations. In 1898 white employees of the Philadelphia and Western Streetcar Company walked out after two blacks were hired as motormen. Many blacks also distrusted business owners, many of whom hired blacks as strikebreakers and cynically fired them after a labor settlement. As World War I progressed, American manufacturers needed a new labor force. The skyrocketing demand for American war materiel coupled with a rapid decline in European immigration created a dilemma for industrial corporations. Anxious to fill orders, they sent labor agents to the South to recruit black workers. Aware of new opportunities in industry, many blacks in the North also advised their southern brethren to escape racial oppression and come to the "Land of Hope."[3]

Philadelphia, one of the world's largest manufacturing centers, became one of the principal meccas for black job-seekers. The city's heavy industries, such as Baldwin Locomotives, Midvale Steel, and Cramp Shipbuilding, shifted production to war-related products. The city's thriving textile industry also retooled for the war. The migration profoundly changed the dynamic of the black worker in Philadelphia. Although some African Americans advanced into skilled positions, the overwhelming majority were concentrated in unskilled, dirty, and dangerous job classifications.[4] Despite harsh conditions, hostility from white co-workers, and indifference from employers, most migrants believed that better days were coming.

For many black workers, the Marine Transport Workers represented progress in the employment sector. Although most labor unions excluded blacks, the Industrial Workers of the World (IWW) made an earnest attempt to organize blacks. By the early 1920s some 10 percent of the "Wobblies'" million members were African American. The Wobblies maintained that race was one of the weapons used by industry owners to keep the working class divided. In addition to supporting racial unity in the workplace, the Wobblies also condemned segregation and lynching.[5]

In 1913 black longshoremen in Philadelphia affiliated with the IWW and established the Marine Transport Workers (MTW). Backed by the AME Church, the new union struck for recognition. Subsequent strikes in 1915 and 1916 won the union control of the docks and increased daily wages from $1.25 to $4.00. Although the majority of the MTW were black, many whites joined the union. Under the leadership of Benjamin Harrison Fletcher, a black Philadelphian, the local became the most successful IWW unit in the nation. Moreover, in a period marked by racial tension, the MTW demonstrated that whites and blacks could find common cause in the workplace.[6]

By 1920, however, the combined assaults of business, the federal government, and the AFL had weakened the MTW. Fletcher, who had extended his influence in other Atlantic ports, became a victim of the nation's first Red Scare and spent time at the federal prison in Leavenworth, Kansas. An unsuccessful strike in 1920 and the subsequent efforts of the International

Longshoremen's Association ended this radical experiment in interracial labor organizing.[7]

The collapse of the MTW signified a transformation for the local black workforce. As the migration continued into the 1920s, wartime hopes were dashed by economic changes and a return to racial exclusion. Thousands of black women working in textiles, government facilities, and other industries were fired shortly after the end of the war. Technological advances in industry and the decline in postwar factory orders contributed to an increase in black layoffs. By the mid-1920s the local economy had fallen into a recession. The worst, however, was yet to come. In 1929, the stock market crash delivered a knockout punch to the city's already struggling black workforce. Since black unemployment prior to the crash was 75 per cent higher than the rate for whites, black workers did not realize the immediate impact of the Depression.[8]

Interracial Activism and Labor

AS THE DEPRESSION WORSENED, THE COMMITTEE ON THE INTERESTS OF the Colored Race and the Committee on Race Relations united to form the joint Committee on Race Relations. Both committees had been in existence since the early 1920s and had struggled to define and articulate their missions. Although established primarily as advisory bodies, a small yet increasing number of members believed they should build a movement.

Meier and Rudwick maintained that the founders of the NAACP stressed constitutional rights rather than economic justice. They argued that the founders' middle-class background limited their understanding of the average black worker. Furthermore, the NAACP believed that without the franchise, black economic justice would be impossible to achieve.[9] Although the Quakers did not have to address constitutional issues, labor discrimination constituted a major problem in Philadelphia. Like the NAACP founders, the elite class backgrounds of the two committees shaped their response to black economic problems. The two committees focused on black-owned businesses such as Frederick Massiah's construction firm, John Drew's suburban bus company, and Raymond Alexander's law firm. These businesses were touted as examples of black achievement that could inspire other black entrepreneurs and demonstrate to whites the potential for black economic independence. In an effort to bolster their pro-business stance, they invited representatives of the National Negro Business League to speak about the growth of black enterprises.[10]

Not all members of the two committees believed that an emphasis on black entrepreneurial spirit was the right course. The growing influence of Helen Bryan steered the committees toward a more systematic understanding of the black economic crisis. Bryan highlighted the need for more attention to employment discrimination. In an effort to reach out to black workers, she organized a support committee for a group of Center City black elevator operators who had struck over money and benefits.[11] Bryan, however, realized that her work was limited by the conservatism of the committee members. The establishment of the YPIF in 1931 represented an opportunity to confront racism in employment. Bryan hoped that the YPIF would develop into an organization that would engage in direct action against segregation. In a summary of the opening conference, the YPIF assessed the economic situation faced by blacks:

> Fear of competition excludes Negroes from political and economic opportunities and tends to force the colored groups as a whole to live on lower economic levels than white groups.
>
> The policy of the American Federation of Labor is supposedly impartial, but there is constant and intensive discrimination in the Philadelphia Trade Unions. Numerous Unions exclude the Negro altogether.[12]

Although the YPIF's observation was accurate, it did not grasp the catastrophic effect of the Depression on the city's black workforce. In 1932, 56 percent of the city's black workforce was unemployed. One-third of the black population received public relief, the fourth highest percentage in the nation.[13] To ameliorate the crisis, black organizations and newspapers mobilized. In 1930 E. Washington Rhodes, editor of the *Philadelphia Tribune*, and Wayne Hopkins, director of the Armstrong Association, formed a committee to launch a "Crusade for Jobs." The committee had limited results: it managed to get a black gas-station attendant and a black film projectionist hired. Their short-lived campaign did not benefit the majority of unemployed blacks.[14] Both Rhodes and Hopkins lacked a realistic approach to the problem of black unemployment. As supporters of the local Republican machine, they continued to believe that patronage jobs could rescue the black community. Rhodes and Hopkins, however, represented only one segment of the city's black elite. Emerging leaders such as Arthur

Huff Fauset, Crystal Bird Fauset, Rev. Marshal I. Shepard Sr., and newspaper editor J. Max Barber of the *Philadelphia Independent*, supported the New Deal. Although officially non-partisan, Bryan and Wentzel backed the New Deal.[15]

As relative newcomers to the world of race relations, the YPIF advanced no definitive plan to address black unemployment and discrimination. Instead, the activists supported the work of black organizations and raised awareness of the crisis through its public programs. By the mid-1930s, however, the YPIF began to critically examine economic issues. Increasingly, Bryan believed that racism and capitalism were inexorably linked. Although she supported the New Deal, she became critical of government programs that reinforced segregation.[16]

The emergence of the National Negro Congress (NNC) in 1936 served as a catalyst for Bryan and her allies. The NNC maintained that the inequities suffered by black workers stemmed primarily from economic causes and claimed that the New Deal was too limited. The NNC's goal was the creation of a mass struggle that encompassed the "broadest numbers of Negro organizations that are willing to join in the fight for the rights of Negroes."[17] Bryan expressed interest in cooperating with the NNC, but left the YPIF before the two groups could embark on any meaningful joint activities. The philosophy of the NNC affected the YPIF, some of whom participated in NNC-backed "Don't Buy Where You Can't Work" protests on Lancaster Avenue in West Philadelphia.[18]

As Penney and Cunningham steered the YPIF toward a path independent of the Committee on Race Relations, they envisioned educational programs that would include labor discrimination. They were uncertain about what role activism would play in determining the future of their proposed Fellowship House. Although many members of the Committee on Race Relations, the parent body of the YPIF, doubted that such a center could survive, Penney and Cunningham gradually found supporters. One committee member, Joseph Platt, believed that the proposed center should focus primarily on the needs of unemployed youths, both black and white.

> Seeds of radicalism find fertile soil when boys and girls become imbued with a feeling of failure, frustration and hopeless discouragement at an age when they should be forging ahead with the enthusiasm and optimism which are the heritage of youth. As members of a privileged group, we need to break down the walls that separate most of us from the problem of unemployment and relief.[19]

Like many social activists of the 1930s, Platt was concerned that social unrest could erupt among the disadvantaged. Both Penney and Cunningham also understood the potential danger, yet they viewed racial conflict as more problematic than an upsurge of radicalism. As they continued to negotiate for a center where the YPIF could launch educational programs, global forces began to shape Philadelphia's demographic profile.

By early 1940 a national defense mobilization had started. In response to the growing threat in Asia and Europe, the federal government began to rebuild the nation's flagging armed forces. The city's employment situation was significantly altered as government contracts rejuvenated many industries, especially shipbuilding and other heavy industries. In August 1938, 32.4 percent of the city's workforce was idle; but by the attack on Pearl Harbor in December 1941, only 6 percent of Philadelphia's workers were unemployed. Despite the improvement in the city's economic fortunes, blacks continued to be excluded. According to the 1940 census, nearly 30 percent of the city's black workers remained unemployed compared to 15 percent of white workers. Moreover, the majority of employed blacks were concentrated in the low-paid fields of factory operatives and personal and domestic service. Unions and businesses continued to limit black advancement into skilled fields.[20]

Across the nation, black workers faced exclusion from the profitable and rapidly expanding defense sector. In response to the continuing discrimination, A. Phillip Randolph, leader of the nation's largest black labor union, the Brotherhood of Sleeping Car Porters, planned a march of thousands of African Americans on Washington. The purpose of the proposed march was to secure opportunities for blacks in the defense sector and the armed forces. Randolph hoped that the march would foster a full-scale civil rights movement, challenging segregation in all aspects of American life. Anxious to forestall the march, Roosevelt met with Randolph and NAACP secretary Walter White. On June 19, 1941, Roosevelt issued the famous Executive Order No. 8802 that established the Fair Employment Practice Commission (FEPC) within the Office of Production to eliminate discrimination in employment. The CFEP was granted the authority to investigate complaints and redress valid grievances. Satisfied with Roosevelt's efforts, Randolph and his colleague postponed the march indefinitely.[21]

The publication of a federal edict guaranteeing equality in employment could be described as nothing less than as inspirational to Philadelphia's interracial activists. They quickly enshrined E.O. 8802 as one of the most progressive civil rights documents in American history. For the first time since Reconstruction, a federal agency was devoted to race relations. E.O. 8802 became a rallying point for civil rights activists. Moreover, Charles Hamilton Houston, a strong supporter of Fellowship House and dean of the Howard University School of Law, became an FEPC commissioner.[22] Although the executive order had been passed, it would be the responsibility of the activists to realize the potential.

Both the Fellowship Commission and Fellowship House devoted considerable attention to labor issues. Fellowship House invited G. James Fleming, director of the local FEPC board, to speak about government efforts to battle discrimination. The Fellowship Commission struggled with methods to increase public support for the FEPC. Like most civil rights organizations, they linked the struggle for equal employment with the battle against the Axis.[23] Despite the presence of a small labor committee within the Fellowship Commission, Fagan believed that labor discrimination needed an agency specifically geared to addressing the complexities of race and economics.

In 1943 several interracial activists led by Fellowship House member Frederick Brill founded the Council on Equal Job Opportunity (CEJO). The purpose of this new agency was to "establish and protect the right and opportunity of all persons to seek, obtain and hold gainful employment without discrimination on account of race, creed, color, national origin or ancestry. To achieve this end, the Council engages in educational work and supports adoption of appropriate legislation."[24] Through its membership, CEJO affiliated with over a dozen organizations, ranging from labor unions to churches.

With dozens of Philadelphia employers and labor unions continuing to exclude blacks, CEJO faced a daunting challenge. Shortly after the establishment of CEJO, the Philadelphia Transit Company (PTC) became the focus of protest by the Fellowship Commission, the NAACP, and the United People's Action Committee, a small black protest organization directed by former NNC leader Arthur Huff Fauset. The city's leading transportation company refused to upgrade black workers to motormen and engineers. Although transit companies across the North were removing the color bar, the PTC remained firm. In addition to opposition from management, the company union, the Philadelphia Rapid Transit Employees Union (PRTEU), threatened "chaos and confusion" if black employees were upgraded.[25]

Civil rights activists and CIO-affiliated activists claimed that PRTEU was a tool of the company and supported a bid by the Transport Workers

Union (TWU) to represent the workers. In the spring of 1944, the War Manpower Commission issued new guidelines for the PTC. Eight black employees were trained to be trolley operators. On August 1, PRTEU walked out. The strike disrupted the production of critical war materiel. Workers at the Philadelphia Navy Yard, the Frankford Arsenal, and countless other defense-related companies experienced difficulty getting to and from work. A sustained work stoppage would affect the flow of supplies to combat theatres in Europe and the Pacific. Military and civilian officials urged the strikers to return to work.[26]

The labor dispute also held the potential for massive racial violence. Racial tension ran high and many Philadelphians feared that the violence that exploded in Detroit and other cities would erupt here. On the evening of August 1, the five agencies of the Fellowship Commission convened an emergency meeting to handle the crisis. Their broad-based approach included appeals to Roosevelt, Mayor Bernard Samuel, media outlets, and PTC management. In addition, the commission urged its constituent agencies and supporters to protest the strike and to report all incidents of racial tension.[27]

As tension grew and a heat wave developed, thousands of flyers were distributed by Arrow children throughout black neighborhoods urging citizens to "SIT TIGHT, Keep Your Heads and Your Tempers." Civil rights agencies were concerned that blacks would attack white strikers. For several years, there had been animosity between white PTC workers and black passengers. In 1942, a black youth was severely beaten by white PTC employees after an altercation on a trolley. Blacks retaliated by attacking the car barn housing the white workers. The strike could re-ignite black anger.[28]

On August 3 representatives of thirty civil rights and social organizations met at the behest of the CEJO and the NAACP. They decided to ask Attorney General Francis Biddle to conduct a grand jury investigation of the strike. As the meeting proceeded, the army announced that if the strikers did not return, troops would operate and guard the mass transit system. Strikers ignored the ultimatum, and on August 5 five thousand army personnel moved into the city. Four strike leaders were arrested and strikers were informed that they would be fired and lose their draft deferments. The strikers returned, the black trainees resumed their training, and by August 17 the military returned control to the PTC. Later that year, the TWU replaced PRTEU as the bargaining unit for PTC workers.

Interracial organizations hailed the resolution of the strike as a victory in the struggle against racism. The strikers realized that a hate strike could not garner widespread support in Philadelphia. The peaceful resolution of the strike also demonstrated that large-scale racial violence could be averted. Although there were isolated incidents of racial violence, the situation did not deteriorate into a major race riot. The Fellowship Commission, CEJO, Fellowship House, the NAACP, and other agencies had effectively placed pressure on law enforcement, City Hall, and the media. Their timely efforts were crucial in preventing an explosion of violence. It was one of the interracial civil rights movement's greatest victories.[29]

Fagan invited the CEJO to join the Fellowship Commission; the CEJO accepted the invitation in 1945. As the war ended, the interracial organizations faced a new challenge: Could they maintain fair employment legislation in the postwar world? For many Americans, the FEPC was a wartime emergency measure. On the other hand, Philadelphia's interracial activists envisioned it as a cornerstone of a new paradigm in race relations. Although there was an FEPC bill in Congress and several states had passed comprehensive fair employment legislation, Pennsylvania's bill remained stalled in committee. Brill maintained that the CEJO's major objective should be the passage of fair employment laws.[30]

The Fellowship Commission also focused on job discrimination. Fagan believed that the coalition should fight for federal, state, and local legislation. In an effort to bring public attention to the need for fair employment laws, the Fellowship Commission launched "FEPC Emergency Week" in May 1946. It circulated hundreds of thousands of leaflets and placed advertisements in major newspapers. During the war, it had maintained that the FEPC was essential to the war effort. In addition, Fellowship House and the Fellowship Commission also pledged to integrate Center City businesses.[31]

Cracks in the united front began to emerge when the NAACP withdrew from the CEJO. One of the NAACP's officers, Goldie Watson, wanted to revive the branch's FEPC Action Committee with the provision that it operate independent of any other organization. The local branch withdrew its affiliation with CEJO. Concerned that such a move would affect its standing in the black community and thus undermine its effectiveness, CEJO made several overtures to the NAACP to rejoin, but to no avail. In addition to Watson's independent stance, the NAACP elected Charles Shorter as executive secretary. In contrast to previous NAACP leaders, Shorter had vast experience in labor issues. Shorter had worked for the Armstrong Association and during the war was employed by Sun Shipbuilding as a specialist in race relations. The NAACP seemed poised to embark upon its own approach to racial discrimination in the workplace.[32]

The Struggle for a Permanent FEPC

THE IMMEDIATE POSTWAR PERIOD WITNESSED AN INCREASE IN FAIR EMployment activism. By 1947 Chicago, Milwaukee, and Minneapolis had established fair practices ordinances.[33] These laws covered only municipal employees, yet were viewed by many civil rights activists as stepping stones to more comprehensive legislation. In Philadelphia the struggle for the FEPC was aided by an ascendant Democratic Party. Dilworth, Clark, and Phillips linked the need for a city FEPC with their attempt to reform Philadelphia's "corrupt and contented" city government. Civil service reform coupled with a city FEPC would free the city's black community from the grip of Republican patronage. Although officially non-partisan, the interracial organizations championed the work of the reformers. Aware that a city ordinance would encounter some opposition from businesses and labor unions, the Fellowship Commission launched a series of educational seminars in 1947.[34]

As the unofficial labor arm of the Fellowship Commission, the CEJO was responsible for much of the activity around the city ordinance. By the late 1940s the CEJO included many of the city's prominent activists. Raymond Pace Alexander and Anna McGarry served as first vice chairs, while Cunningham and Morris Milgram were on the executive committee. Their lobbying and public campaign bore fruit in 1948 when the City Council approved fair employment legislation.[35]

One of the most comprehensive laws of its kind in the United States, the Philadelphia Fair Employment Practice Ordinance banned discrimination by employers, labor unions, and employment agencies. The law, however, excluded fraternal, sectarian, charitable, and religious organizations. In addition, the ordinance also established a five-member unpaid commission. The principal duties of this Fair Employment Practices Commission were to formulate and execute a "comprehensive educational program designed to eliminate and prevent prejudice and discrimination," and to investigate and adjudicate unfair labor practices.[36]

In 1951 Philadelphia's FEPC became the Commission on Human Relations (CHR). The CHR oversaw complaints of discrimination in education, housing, and public accommodations. In its short lifespan, the FEPC successfully adjudicated hundreds of cases. In addition, it launched an educational program that reached hundreds of thousands. Influenced by the tactics of Fellowship House and the Fellowship Commission, the Philadelphia FEPC sponsored hundreds of lectures, established a FEPC sabbath in churches and synagogues, and sponsored sixteen radio programs. The Philadelphia FEPC also utilized direct-mail advertising to reach thousands of businessmen, printed posters that were placed on mass transit vehicles, and distributed thousands of stickers that carried messages such as, "Americans Ask: Is He a Good Worker? Not What Is He, a Good Worker?" Although the FEPC knew that it had scarcely cracked the wall of labor discrimination, a November 1950 memorandum praised its efforts.[37]

The coupling of the regulatory and educational provisions of the Philadelphia Fair Employment Practices Ordinance has been a strong factor in arresting job discrimination based on race, color, religion, or ancestry. It has been a link in developing community attitudes favorable to providing equal opportunity for all.[38]

The Struggle for a State FEPC

THE ESTABLISHMENT AND RELATIVE SUCCESS OF THE PHILADELPHIA FEPC encouraged the interracial organizations. None were more pleased than the members of the CEJO, who hailed the creation of the commission as a major victory. Their triumph, however, was clouded by increasing financial difficulties. Brill wondered how the committee would survive in the future. In an effort to preserve the organization, the CEJO and the Board of Commissioners agreed to change CEJO's affiliation with the Fellowship Commission in 1950. In contrast to other constituent agencies responsible for raising their operating budgets, the CEJO would receive most of its funding from the Fellowship Commission. Although CEJO was free to raise funds and retain its autonomy, it would constitute the official labor policy arm of the Fellowship Commission. The other constituent agencies supported the change since the CEJO was the only such agency with a narrowly defined mission, namely labor issues. With its foundation secured, the CEJO established a threefold agenda: 1) the passage of statewide legislation; 2) the investigation of specific industries; and 3) providing African Americans with information about employment opportunities. In the early 1950s the struggle for a statewide fair employment law would consume most of CEJO's resources.[39]

In an effort to strengthen its financial coffers, the CEJO initiated an ongoing fundraising campaign. Focusing on sympathetic unions and religious organizations, the campaign also aimed at raising the need for a statewide bill. As the activists organized their campaign, an important institutional change occurred within the CEJO. The new official post of executive director was created with the strong backing of Fagan. The role of chair, which had been held by Fred Brill and his successor Reverend Harry Schofield, evolved into a more ceremonial post. The first executive director, Reverend Walter Wynn, was also the social action director of the Fellowship Commission. Although the change brought the CEJO ideologically closer to the Fellowship Commission, it also helped streamline the daily operation of the CEJO by concentrating management responsibilities in the hands of the executive director.

The struggle for a Pennsylvania FEPC was aided by the support of Governor John S. Fine. In May 1952 Fine established the Governor's Industrial Race Relations Commission and charged it with the responsibility of studying the extent of discrimination in Pennsylvania. Reverend William Gray Jr., chair of the Fellowship Commission's Committee on Democracy in Housing (CDH), was chosen to lead the new commission. Gray argued that a two-tiered labor system had evolved in the Keystone State; there was little discrimination in low-paid unskilled labor but major barriers remained in the semi-skilled and skilled fields. The report provided the intellectual justification for an FEPC.[40]

The report also energized the State Council for an FEPC. Chaired by former Fellowship Commission president, Clarence Pickett, the State Council included dozens of labor unions, religious organizations, civil rights agencies, and ad hoc committees. The CEJO served as the Fellowship Commission's representative on the council.[41] The passage of an FEPC was opposed by Republican state senators, who had managed to halt the bill in committee. The State Council planned to place pressure on legislators while at the same time appealing to the public for support. These efforts included several rallies in Harrisburg and numerous petitions across the state. Although not a member of the State Council, Fellowship House organized petitions in support of the law and prioritized it in its educational programs. In 1954 George Leader, Democratic candidate for governor, rekindled hope when he vowed that if elected he would push for the passage of an FEPC. On the other hand, Lloyd Wood, the Republican nominee, refused to commit to fair employment. After Leader's victory in November, he began to place increased pressure on reluctant legislators.[42] After months of hesitation, the proposed fair employment law, House Bill 229, advanced to the Senate floor. The CEJO, however, refused to back the bill because it was amended to include age as well as race, religion, and national identity. The CEJO argued that an FEPC bill ought to prevent discrimination based only on factors that do not affect workplace performance. Furthermore, CEJO activists worried that the age provision would complicate the administration of the law and could expose it to constitutional challenges.[43]

In spite of the opposition from the CEJO and several other groups in the State Council, the language on age was included. Ultimately, the CEJO realized that a compromise would have to be reached if the bill was to pass. In November 1955 the bill was signed into law by Governor Leader. Modeled on the Philadelphia law, the Pennsylvania statute banned discrimination by labor unions, employers, and employment agencies and established a commission responsible for enforcing the law and administering an educational program to support the law.[44] With the passage of the legislation, the CEJO turned its focus to the workplace. Although both Philadelphia and Pennsylvania had fair employment laws, activists attempted to discover what legislation meant to black workers who still felt the sting of discrimination. Wynn resolved to make the law's promise a reality.

Work for All

IN THEIR ATTEMPT TO BRING RACIAL JUSTICE TO THE LABOR FIELD, INterracial activists faced an increasingly complex situation. Although Philadelphia's manufacturing sector had grown during the war, by the mid-1950s the city's traditional source of economic strength had started to decline. Between 1951 and 1956, the city lost seventy-four industrial firms and over 9,000 jobs; remaining companies slashed 40,000 workers from their payrolls. Since one-third of the city's working population was employed in manufacturing, these cuts were especially painful.[45] In contrast to the heavy industry of Pittsburgh and Detroit, Philadelphia's manufacturing sector was concentrated in non-durable goods such as clothing and household products. In 1947 textiles accounted for 25 percent of the city's manufacturing output. By the mid-1950s, however, the textile industry was moving to the South to avoid high labor costs. In addition, structural changes in the economy also prompted relocation. Many of the city's aging plants had been built in the nineteenth century and were located in neighborhoods and utilized rail spurs. In the postwar era, businesses were increasingly reliant on tractor-trailers to transport their goods, and Philadelphia's narrow streets placed these manufacturers at a disadvantage.[46]

Changing demographics also complicated the picture. The industrial sector had provided a level of economic security for generations of

European immigrants and their children. By the postwar era, the percentage of black workers in industry was increasing, yet at the same time many of these manufacturers were either closing or shifting operations elsewhere. Opportunities for blacks in industry were opening, yet industry's importance was declining. Could the interracial organizations adapt their approach to a changing economy?

In the late 1940s a quiet yet steady campaign was undertaken to upgrade black employees in Philadelphia's downtown department stores. The principal goal of this campaign was to encourage the stores to hire black sales clerks, mainly women. In 1946 Shorter of the NAACP petitioned and conducted negotiations with officials of Gimbel Brothers to upgrade black women to sales positions. Once Gimbels integrated, the Fellowship Commission through its contacts appealed to Wanamakers, Lit Brothers, and Snellenbergs to follow Gimbels' lead. By 1950 a small number of black sales clerks were working behind the counters of Philadelphia's department stores.[47]

The relative success of the short-lived campaign could be attributed to several factors. By the late 1940s the Fellowship Commission included among its board several of the city's leading businessmen. Without these contacts, the effort would have been more difficult. Black shopping patterns also contributed to the resolution of this issue. By the 1940s many black small businesses had closed, and many black shoppers, aided by improved mass transit, headed to Center City to shop. The stores wanted to increase the patronage of black shoppers; therefore, hiring some black workers in public positions was good public relations. Although these black workers represented the vanguard of an emerging service sector, the campaign had negligible effects on the majority of the black workforce.[48]

In the early 1950s the CEJO was preoccupied with garnering public support for passage of a state FEPC. In its effort to increase support for the FEPC, the CEJO members had contacted dozens of businesses and unions. This campaign introduced them to a wide range of workplace and discrimination issues.

As the FEPC neared passage in 1955, the CEJO launched a study of Philadelphia's laundry industry, the first in a series of industry surveys. These surveys investigated the status of African Americans in specific industries and proposed remedies. Wynn believed that before the movement could assist black workers, they needed to understand the complexities of each major industry. Although he proposed a comprehensive study of the region's black workforce, others in the CEJO deemed this too expensive, and the CEJO decided instead to focus on specific industries. The members of the CEJO hoped that through these case studies they could determine the needs of black workers.[49] Although these studies covered traditional areas of black employment, such as petroleum refineries, they also examined fields that had been closed to black workers.

One of these areas was the food service industry, in which firms since the late nineteenth century had systematically excluded blacks from Center City hotels and restaurants. In 1957, as the study proceeded, Clarence Pickett declared that the Fellowship Commission would only meet at restaurants and hotels where the wait staff was integrated. Pickett's decision forced Fellowship commissioner Gustave Amsterdam, president of the Bellevue Stratford Hotel, to alter his company's policies.[50] The integration of Center City hotels and restaurant staffs was increasingly linked to downtown prosperity. If the hospitality industry appeared to be a bastion of segregation, many tourists and business travelers might decide to visit another city.

As historian Dennis Clark has noted, support for integration was often driven by economic determinants. Clark argues that most major political or business leaders did not want their cities perceived as centers of racial intolerance or segregation.[51] Although there was resistance to integration by some Philadelphia businessmen, many more thought it good public relations. Despite general support for integration in hospitality, governmental pressure needed to be applied to some businesses. In 1959 Wynn and others from the CEJO appeared before the CHR to testify about the resistance to integration in the hospitality industry.[52] By the late 1950s, the CEJO was increasingly focused on discrimination in the steadily expanding service sector. The increasing responsibilities of the CEJO, coupled with stagnant funding, prompted the members to reevaluate their mission. Prior to 1955 its work had focused almost solely on the passage of fair employment legislation. These activists struggled to define their mission amidst a changing economy and a rising civil rights movement.

As the CEJO attempted to synthesize its goals and objectives, other voices emerged to address job discrimination. In 1959 four hundred of the city's black clergy formed an organization that placed economic justice at the forefront of its agenda. Lead by Rev. Lorenzo Shepard Jr. of Mt. Olivet Baptist Church and Rev. Leon Sullivan of Zion Baptist Church, the ministers decided to link black employment with black consumer spending. Adapting the "Don't Buy Where You Can't Work" tactics to the late 1950s, they embarked on a campaign of "selective patronage." The goal of this campaign was to encourage black shoppers to boycott the products and services of businesses that refused to hire blacks at every level. They planned to select one firm at a time and issue a set of reasonable demands.[53]

In addition to the emergence of this new force in civil rights, the late 1950s witnessed more labor-oriented activism on the part of Fellowship House. Fellowship House had provided extensive support for the CEJO through its educational forums and other activities, but had not launched any programs clearly directed at job discrimination. Fellowship House's strength lay in its grass-roots approach, and Penney began to reach out to sympathetic labor unions and businesses. In the mid-1950s small numbers of labor activists began to attend weekends at Fellowship Farm. In an effort to attract union members, Penney brought internationally known labor activists such as Tom Mboya of Kenya to the farm. Increasingly, union members and officials began to participate in the organization's educational programs. For example, from October to December 1958 over ninety labor activists affiliated with Local 190 of the Knit Goods Workers attended a seven-session Leadership Training Program at Fellowship House. In addition to learning about organizing and negotiating, the union activists were urged to incorporate civil rights within the labor movement. Fellowship House, however, was unsuccessful at reaching some craft and industrial unions that continued to discriminate. Although its work in this field was limited, Fellowship House addressed a need that the CEJO had ignored. Like other issues, Penney believed that "hearts and minds" had to be changed for any new legal or social policy to be effective.[54]

Influenced by the rising calls in the black community for economic justice, the CEJO began to stress a more comprehensive approach to job discrimination. In a February 19, 1960, memorandum, C. W. Maxwell, the new president of CEJO, maintained that integration had to occur at the highest level. Maxwell argued that corporations must hire African Americans as managers and appoint them to their boards.[55] Like the effort to integrate department stores, high-level pressure could lead to integration in local corporations. Many Fellowship commissioners, like Gustave Amsterdam, were affiliated with major local corporations and were well positioned to apply pressure to their colleagues.

Although the CEJO was assuming a more proactive posture, the organization faced serious internal problems. In addition to its endemic budget problems, the CEJO suffered from a lack of direction. A June 29, 1961, memo detailed the issues facing the organization: "Despite the devotion and efforts of a handful of persons and the agencies they represent its lay leadership has been unable to provide the sustained creative attention and program called for since the passage of the Philadelphia and Pennsylvania FEPC laws."⁵⁶ The joint committee also proposed remedies for the problems of the agency. It recommended hiring a full-time executive director. Although Wynn technically served the CEJO in that capacity, he remained responsible for several other major programs as the Fellowship Commission's social action director and thus could not devote all of his energies to labor issues.⁵⁷

In addition, the committee recommended that the CEJO focus on two issues: 1) the problem of unskilled black workers in an increasingly changing economy and 2) the upgrading of black employees. Although the committee's report was well received by the CEJO, members disagreed over the future direction of the organization. Terry Chisholm argued that the organization should focus on fighting discrimination, while Ben Stahl maintained that the CEJO should assume a leadership position in the civil rights struggle and "be the linchpin in the fight against other forms of discrimination."⁵⁸

Despite substantial disagreement over the future, most members of the CEJO supported the joint committee's recommendations. In an effort to broaden its influence in the corporate world, it reached out to the region's business community. Wynn and Fellowship Commission president Thomas McBride believed that pressure could be placed on corporate heads to provide more training programs for unskilled, mainly African American workers. As the CEJO's focus began to shift, there was concern that they were neglecting the prevalence of job discrimination. Wynn maintained that voices in the black community were highlighting inequality and calling for sustained protest while CEJO remained silent.⁵⁹

Racial discrimination by the Greyhound bus company was one of the areas Wynn mentioned. Although black ridership had increased, there were few black drivers and even fewer managers. The Four Hundred Ministers Organization, however, targeted a local company that was dependent on black consumers. The Tastykake Baking Company had a liberal record toward black hiring, and the ministers believed that affecting change would not be difficult. After a short, yet solid boycott of Tastykake products, the company hired more blacks as drivers and managers. The numbers were small, yet many in the black community viewed this as an important symbolic victory. The selective patronage program would serve as a model for future protests.⁶⁰

In the 1950s the Philadelphia branch of the NAACP had successfully secured employment for African Americans at the Philadelphia Gas Works and the Delaware River Port Authority. The NAACP had pursued an independent approach to labor discrimination since the 1940s. In 1962 the election of Cecil B. Moore as branch president represented a change in both tactics and objectives. In contrast to earlier NAACP leaders, Moore placed economic concerns at the top of his agenda. He also advocated the use of direct-action tactics to achieve integration. In May 1963 he led a group of pickets at a construction site in North Philadelphia. Violence erupted, but Moore had made his stand and black workers were eventually hired. Although Moore's confrontational manner alienated many in the interracial movement, he attracted large segments of the city's growing black underclass to the NAACP. His subsequent protests led to an increase in black hiring at the city's main post office and at Greyhound.[61]

As the NAACP and the Four Hundred Ministers became the vanguard in the struggle for racial equality in employment, the interracial civil rights movement attempted to define itself in this increasingly dynamic period. The CEJO did not attempt to compete with either the NAACP or the Four Hundred Ministers. Instead, they concentrated on their role as watchdogs of fair employment practices. In early 1964 the CEJO cited six unions, including the Motion Picture Operators, for discriminating against blacks. In addition, it completed a major investigation of small businesses and documented a steady pattern of discrimination.[62]

The CEJO also began to cultivate closer relations with major corporations. Although the CEJO had been closely connected with progressive elements of the labor movement since the 1940s, it had only tentative contacts with the business community. The purpose of this rapprochement with local corporations was twofold: to increase the percentage of black hiring, and to upgrade black employees into skilled and managerial positions.[63] In contrast to the direct-action protests of Moore's NAACP, the CEJO adopted an approach that resembled that of the Urban League and the pre-Moore NAACP. Although it would cautiously support protests, the CEJO would endeavor to open doors by creating an ongoing dialogue with local corporations.

Along with its new relationship with corporations, the CEJO increasingly functioned as a job service agency. By the mid-1960s a growing number of African Americans turned to the CEJO for discrimination complaints or assistance in finding work. The CEJO reviewed complaints but, since it lacked any power of enforcement, referred them to the CHR. Job placement, however, received more attention. Wynn was especially enthusiastic about assisting job-seekers. Traditionally, African Americans had utilized the black clergy for advice on finding work. Although this declined after the Great Migration, black jobs seekers continued to contact black ministers. Wynn had brought a number of black ministers into the CEJO and attempted to fashion a comprehensive employment program.[64]

As the CEJO attempted to craft a jobs program, the executive committee of the Fellowship Commission launched its own effort. In June 1965 the Job Opportunities for Youth (JOY) program was initiated. JOY paired unemployed black youths with employers. In addition to introducing young people to the world of work, JOY also served to lessen tension among an increasingly angry young black male population. In the wake of the devastating August 1964 North Philadelphia uprising, redirecting inner-city black rage became a major priority for civil rights agencies.[65]

Undeterred by the executive committee's efforts, the CEJO continued to seek closer ties with the area's business community. Although corporations such as DuPont, Prudential Insurance, and the Pennsylvania Railroad company claimed to support a more integrated workforce, like businesses in the 1940s they argued that they could not locate qualified black applicants. In an effort to alleviate this situation, Wynn attempted to revive a vocational training plan co-sponsored with the school district, but he could not elicit sufficient support from the membership.[66] By the mid-1960s the impact of Great Society programs were affecting Philadelphia, and many members wanted to avoid any duplication of federal government programs.

Despite the War on Poverty, black unemployment remained high. In an effort to address this endemic crisis, the CEJO sought alliances with other organizations interested in the area's economic development. In late 1966 the CEJO began to cooperate with the Junior Chamber of Commerce to encourage college graduates to remain in the Philadelphia area. Although the project was not aimed at minority job seekers, James E. Williams, the CEJO's new director, stressed that the effort must include an attempt to reach black college graduates. The project, dubbed Operation Native Son, began in 1967 and continues to this day to be one of the region's most important job fairs.[67] Perhaps the most important collaborative project involved the CEJO contribution to the establishment of the first Philadelphia Plan in 1967. Aimed at battling discrimination in the construction trades, the plan required that businesses and unions who were working on federally funded sites hire specific numbers of African American workers.[68]

In addition to working with business and government organizations, the CEJO also strengthened its role with the black community. In late 1966 the CEJO began to collaborate with the Opportunities Industrialization

Centers (OIC). Formed by Reverend Louis Sullivan of North Philadelphia's Zion Baptist Church, the OIC established job-training centers across the nation. In addition to training black and Hispanic workers, the OIC also attempted to bolster economic independence among people of color by bankrolling projects like Progress Plaza, a North Philadelphia shopping center. An employment and training center opened in North Philadelphia in the summer of 1967. Operated by Sun Oil and co-sponsored by OIC, North City Congress, the Urban League, and the Fellowship Commission, the facility trained hundreds of hard-core unemployed in service station operation.[69]

The CEJO's increasing commitment to job placement was demonstrated by the opening of a job-referral center in Center City. The CEJO Referral Center focused on the needs of unemployed and underemployed blacks. The new facility was staffed by volunteers from businesses, which represented the CEJO's continuing ties to the business community.[70]

By the late 1960s the CEJO's role as a watchdog agency had been eclipsed by the CHR. In addition, civil rights agencies, Black Power organizations, and black nationalists began to propose more radical solutions for economic inequality. Despite calls for a more radical approach, the CEJO continued to pursue a moderate agenda. On the other hand, members of Fellowship House began to search for more direct solutions to racism. In contrast to the CEJO, Fellowship House was much closer to the deteriorating economic conditions of the inner city. Through its black history programs, Fellowship House attracted unemployed youths, many of them former gang members. Penney became increasingly concerned about the future of this rapidly growing lost generation.[71]

National mainstream civil rights leaders shared many of Penney's concerns. In 1967 Dr. Martin Luther King Jr. began to shift his focus toward economic issues. Although he received little encouragement from the civil rights community, his Poor People's Campaign represented an attempt to introduce class issues into the civil rights movement. In late 1967 Bayard Rustin and A. Phillip Randolph proposed the "Freedom Budget," a six-point plan to address critical issues. They ranked economic issues at the forefront of the agenda. Early in 1968 Fellowship House declared its support for Dr. King's campaign. Following his assassination, however, black youths at Fellowship Farm criticized the tactics and objectives of the interracial civil rights movement.[72] For these dissenters, a Beloved Community could not be built in an atmosphere of grinding poverty, police repression, and assassination.

Like Fellowship House, the Fellowship Commission faced criticism from more radical voices. Fagan attempted to ameliorate some of these protests by adopting a more militant tone, but the commission's detractors remained unconvinced. In contrast to the 1940s and the 1950s, the interracial civil rights organizations were viewed as relics. Although agencies such as the Philadelphia Housing Association had undergone radical transformation, some of the constituent agencies remained moderate.

By 1969 the CEJO, the movement's labor activist arm, had changed from an organization primarily concerned with the passage of civil rights legislation and employment discrimination to one focused on job placement. The departure of Wynn, the increasing role of the CHR, and the upheavals of the late 1960s contributed to this shift in direction. It was symbolic of what would soon happen to the interracial civil rights movement.

Children from Fellowship House support the Freedom Crusade, City Hall, Sept. 1950. Evening Bulletin Collection. Special Collections Research Center, Paley Library, Temple University.

Joseph Clark, Democratic candidate for mayor, speaks to a meeting of the Fellowship Commission, fall 1951. Maurice Fagan, one of the founders of the PFC, is seated far right.

Richard Allen Homes. The integration and location of public housing projects became a major challenge for the movement in September 1943. Philadelphia Housing Association (Housing Association of the Delaware Valley), Special Collections Research Center, Paley Library, Temple University.

Frank Sinatra's visit to Fellowship House, spring 1945. Jewish Community Relations Council Collection, Special Collections Research Center, Paley Library, Temple University.

The opening of the Fellowship Commission building on October 15, 1946. Marjorie Penney, one of the founders of Fellowship House and a driving force in the establishment of the Fellowship Commission, addresses the audience. Philadelphia Fellowship Commission Collection, Special Collections Research Center, Paley Library, Temple University.

Schoolchildren from the Fellowship Club at Philadelphia's Stoddard Junior High arrive at the Fellowship Commission, 1947. Philadelphia Fellowship Commission Collection, Special Collections Research Center, Paley Library, Temple University.

The Philadelphia Housing Association also reached out to schools. Here students from Gratz High visit the association's headquarters. n.d. Records of the Philadelphia Housing Association (Housing Association of the Delaware Valley), Special Collections Research Center, Paley Library, Temple University.

At City Hall, passersby support the passage of the Taft-Wagner-Ellender housing bill, 1948. Philadelphia Housing Association Collection (Housing Association of the Delaware Valley), Special Collections Research Center, Paley Library, Temple University.

Fellowship House Commission Dinner, 1950s. E. Luther Cunningham, Fellowship House founder, at far left; Maurice Fagan, Executive Director Fellowship Commission, second from right. Philadelphia Fellowship Commission Collection, Special Collections Research Center, Paley Library, Temple University.

Epilogue

Every Man 'neath His Vine and Fig Tree Shall Live in Peace and Unafraid

IT IS DIFFICULT TO PINPOINT WHEN A MOVEMENT ENDS. RATHER, THE late 1960s and early 1970s represent a watershed for the movement. While the focus on race remained important, Philadelphia's activists expanded into new and unfamiliar areas.

Fellowship House, the anchor of the movement, underwent sweeping changes in the late 1960s. Black youth whose parents had participated in Arrow programs challenged the tactics and goals of Fellowship House. For an increasing number of African Americans, interracial activists living in a poor and increasingly volatile black community represented a naive anachronism. Their words turned to deeds when Little Fellowship House was briefly occupied by a group of militants in 1970. In an effort to respond to these changes, Penney stepped down and was replaced by an African American, Amos Johnson.

Many members believed that race issues were being sufficiently addressed by public agencies and that Fellowship House should redirect its energies toward other issues. In the early 1970s the House began to focus on prisoners' rights, Native American issues, sexism, the Middle East crisis, age discrimination, and environmental issues. An innovative youth counseling program, Woodrock was initiated by Mal Benjamin and Val Udell. Today, Fellowship Farm continues to fight against intolerance; however, the organization focuses on preventing youth violence.

Like Fellowship House, the Fellowship Commission shifted its direction in the early 1970s. Although the Fellowship Commission continued to work on issues such as school and job discrimination, new issues such as gay rights, consumer affairs, and health care received increasing attention. New committees were created and the annual budget, raised by members and contributions, reached over $200,000 in the early 1980s. By 1980 Fagan had resigned as director and the CEJO had been dissolved. During that decade the Fellowship Commission aided Southeast Asian refugees to establish

Mutual Assistance Associations. As the functions of the Fellowship Commission were replaced by the CHR, membership began to level off. Foundation support also began to dry up. By late 1994 the Fellowship Commission was bankrupt and effectively defunct.

In contrast to the other two organizations, the evolution of the Housing Association in the post–civil rights era was less painful. By the late 1960s, it had successfully shifted into its new role as a tenant action agency. In 1971 Cushing Dolbeare resigned as managing director and was replaced by Shirley Dennis, a young African American real estate dealer and community activist. Throughout the 1970s, it championed the right of the poor, aged, and disabled to safe and affordable housing. The Housing Association became the city's leading proponent of the Section 8 program, which had its roots in the "used house" program of the late 1950s. In addition, the organization continued to build on the foundation of 1960s activism by fighting for the participation of inner-city residents in policy decisions. Today, the Housing Association of the Delaware Valley remains one of the nation's premier housing advocacy groups.

The Housing Association successfully adjusted to the changing social atmosphere by transforming its organizational structure. Under Dolbeare the Housing Association became a more democratic organization. She actively encouraged members to become more involved in policy articulation. In contrast, both the Fellowship Commission and Fellowship House remained hierarchical. Both Fagan and Penney directed their respective organizations for decades and were reluctant to allow others to share in decision-making. Their effective yet highly centralized method of leadership was criticized by some members in the late 1960s.

How can we gauge the effectiveness of these organizations? In terms of policy-oriented work, it is relatively easy to measure. The interracial civil rights movement directed a series of successful campaigns. Their achievements include the passage of fair housing and employment legislation and the establishment of the Community College of Philadelphia. These activists also agitated for the creation of the CHR, which ultimately assumed some of the activities of the interracial organizations. Ironically, however, the growth of the CHR would diminish the power and influence of these organizations.

The impact of the movement must also be measured by its contribution to national developments. The Federation of Fellowship included over a dozen organizations and reached thousands of people. Members of

Fellowship House served as missionaries of tolerance influencing activists across the nation. In 1941 several Fellowship House members spoke to the Cuyahoga County (Ohio) Christian Youth Council. Within months this Cleveland-based group created an organization, the Fellowship, and sponsored an interracial summer camp and launched a study of consumer cooperatives. In 1943 Samuel Amos Brackeen, minister of the Bethany Baptist Church of Elyria, Ohio, reported on the progress of the Fellowship: "This group in Cleveland has been in operation about two years. During that period of time The Fellowship has attempted to enhance the social, economic, and spiritual life of the community. There have been attempts to test the civil rights laws of Ohio to see that all people, regardless of color, get equal treatment without discrimination."[1]

In addition to influencing the development of similar groups, these organizations also contributed directly to the civil rights movement. The Childhood Education Project, co-sponsored by the Fellowship Commission, the Philadelphia School District, the Massachusetts Institute of Technology, and the National Bureau of Intercultural Education, was cited by the United States Supreme Court in its historic *Brown v. Topeka Board of Education* decision. In addition, Fellowship House provided crucial support to southern civil rights activists from the 1930s through the 1960s.

One of their principal goals was to create an atmosphere of tolerance, what they and others termed the Beloved Community. While the goal of a multiracial utopia remains a dream, it is important to recognize that these organizations contributed to a lessening of racial tension. In a series of editorials in 1966, journalists at the *Philadelphia Bulletin* praised the interracial civil rights movement. Reflecting on a quarter century of activism, the editorial board argued that without the work of Fellowship Commission and Fellowship House, race relations in Philadelphia could have deteriorated into a "bloody mess."[2] Thus, their goal of halting widespread violence had been achieved.

The lives of the activists themselves were changed by their involvement. Board member Randolph Walker, an African American firefighter who had been with Fellowship House since 1941, recalled that his involvement in Fellowship taught him to accept people regardless of race or creed. A generation later, Susan Rosenbloom, an ambitious college student, came to Fellowship House as an intern in the turbulent 1960s. Rosenbloom worked in the organization during its most difficult period when some activists questioned its validity. She believes that she and others grew because of their involvement in projects, but also in the often harsh debates of the late 1960s. Rosenbloom became a leader in community organizing in the Washington, D.C. area.

But what of the tens of thousands who visited Fellowship House, listened to the Fellowship Commission's radio programs, or attended an open housing forum sponsored by the Housing Association? We cannot know all of their stories. We cannot know whether their views on race changed. We do, however, know some of their stories and it is our duty to uncover more. One of the most profound statements came from Elaine Herman, a librarian for the Philadelphia school district. In the 1940s, Herman was a student at predominantly white Olney High. She was also a member of Olney's High School Fellowship and organized events at the school and at 1431 Brown Street. At Fellowship House she met and worked with black Fellowshippers, an experience that she credited with broadening her vision and challenging her narrow perception of race.

This movement constitutes an important, yet neglected chapter in twentieth-century urban race relations. It is hoped that scholars will continue to study these organizations and their impact on public policy and the lives of individuals such as Randolph Walker and Elaine Herman.

Notes

INTRODUCTION

1. The four original constituent agencies of the Fellowship Commission were the Jewish Community Relations Council, the Committee on Race Relations (Society of Friends), the Philadelphia Council of Churches, and the Fellowship House. In 1945 four new member agencies had joined: the NAACP (Philadelphia branch), the National Conference of Christians and Jews, the Nationalities Services Center, and the Council for Equal Job Opportunity.

CHAPTER 1

1. Julie Winch, *Philadelphia's Black Elite: Activism, Accommodation, and the Struggle for Autonomy, 1787–1848* (Philadelphia: Temple University Press, 1988), 80–83.
2. *Ibid.*, 83.
3. Charles Blockson, *The Underground Railroad* (New York: Prentice Hall, 1987), 235.
4. Louis Gerteis, "Morality and Utility in the Abolition Movement," in *The Abolitionists: Means, Ends, and Motivations*, ed. Lawrence Goodheart and Hugh Hawkins (Lexington, MA: D.C. Heath, 1995), 124. For a comprehensive examination of Philadelphia's abolitionist heritage, see Richard Newman and James Mueller, eds., *Antislavery and Abolition in Philadelphia: Emancipation and the Long Struggle for Racial Justice in the City of Brotherly Love* (Baton Rouge: Louisiana State University Press, 2011).
5. Roger Lane, *Thomas Dorsey's Philadelphia and Ours: On the Past and Future of the Black City in America* (New York: Oxford University Press, 1991), 240.
6. Lane, 241–49, and Harry C. Silcox, "Nineteenth Century Philadelphia Black Militant: Octavis V. Catto (1839–1871)," *Pennsylvania History* 44, no. 1 (January 1977): 52–76.
7. Lane, 251, and Ida Wells Barnett, *Crusade for Justice: The Autobiography of Ida Wells Barnett* (Chicago: University of Chicago Press), 221–23.
8. William Edward Burghardt Du Bois, *The Philadelphia Negro* (Philadelphia: University of Pennsylvania Press, 1899), 1–9.
9. *Ibid.*; U.S. Department of Commerce, Bureau of the Census, *Negro Population, 1790–1915* (Washington: GPO, 1918), Table 10, 93.
10. John Dittmer, *Black Georgia in the Progressive Era, 1900–1920* (Urbana: University of Illinois Press, 1977), 124–31; Ralph Luker, *The Social Gospel in Black and White: American Racial Reform* (Chapel Hill: University of North Carolina Press, 1991), 185–86; Morton Sosna, *In Search of the Silent South* (New York: Columbia University Press, 1977), 15.
11. John Hope Franklin, *From Slavery to Freedom: A History of African Americans* (New York: McGraw Hill, 1994), 317–19; Roberta Senechal, *The Sociogenesis of a Race Riot: Springfield, Illinois, in 1908* (Chicago: University of Illinois Press, 1990), 29–46; Charles Flint Kellogg, *NAACP: A History of the National Association for the Advancement*

of Colored People, vol. I: 1909–1920 (Baltimore: Johns Hopkins University Press, 1967), 34–54.

12. Jesse Thomas Moore Jr., *A Search for Equality: The National Urban League 1910–1961* (University Park: Pennsylvania State University Press, 1981), 47–48; Vincent P. Franklin, *The Education of Black Philadelphia* (Philadelphia: University of Pennsylvania Press, 1979), 21; Ida Wells Barnett, *Crusade for Justice: The Autobiography of Ida Wells Barnett* (Chicago: University of Chicago Press, 1970), 372–73; Dorothy Salem, *To Better Our World: Black Women in Organized Reform, 1890–1920* (New York: Carlson, 1990), 45–46; Nancy Weiss, *Farewell to the Party of Lincoln: Black Politics in the Age of FDR* (Princeton: Princeton University Press), 5–22.

13. "Armstrong Association: Fifty Years of Community Service," 1957, MS., Urban League–Armstrong Association Collection, Urban Archives, Paley Library, Temple University, Philadelphia.

14. John Bauman, "The Philadelphia Housing Association," in . Jean Barth Toll and Mildred Gillam, eds., *Invisible Philadelphia: Community Through Voluntary Organizations* (Philadelphia: Atwater Kent Museum, 1995), 420–21.

15. Donald K. Gorrell, *The Age of Social Responsibility: The Social Gospel in the Progressive Era, 1900–1920* (Macon, GA: Mercer University Press, 1988), 27–34.

16. Luker, *Social Gospel in Black and White*, 268.

17. Samuel Kelton Roberts, "Crucible for a Vision: The Work of George Edmund Haynes and the Commission on Race Relations, 1922–1947" (diss., Columbia University, 1974), 18.

18. James McPherson, *The Abolitionist Legacy: From Reconstruction to the NAACP* (Princeton: Princeton University Press, 1975), 154–55; Kellogg, *NAACP: A History of the National Association for the Advancement of Colored People*, 125–26.

19. Mary Hoxie Jones, *Swords into Plowshares: An Account of the American Friends Service Committee, 1917–1937* (New York: Macmillan Press, 1937, 328.

20. James R. Grossman, *Land of Hope: Chicago, Black Southerners, and the Great Migration* (Chicago: University of Chicago Press, 1989), 14–21; Neil Fligstein, *Going North: Migration of Blacks and Whites from the South 1900–1950* (New York: Academic Press, 1981), 8–16.

21. Roberts, "Crucible for a Vision," 76.

22. Sosna, *In Search of the Silent South*, 21–24.

23. William Tuttle, *Race Riot: Chicago in the Red Summer of 1919* (New York: Atheneum, 1970), 237–41.

24. Sosna, *In Search of the Silent South*, 21–24.

25. Jacquelyn Dowd Hall, *Revolt Against Chivalry: Jesse Daniel Ames and the Women's Campaign Against Lynching* (New York: Columbia University Press, 1979), 62–64.

26. *Ibid.*, 63.

27. Roberts," Crucible for a Vision," 100.

28. *Ibid.*, 66.

29. *Ibid.*, 81.

30. *Ibid.*, 100.

31. *Ibid.*, 107–8.

32. James F. Findlay Jr., *Church People in the Struggle: The National Council of Churches and the Black Freedom Struggle, 1950-1970* (New York: Oxford University Press, 1993), 18-19.

33. William D. Fuller, "The Negro Migrant in Philadelphia," report, Records of the Philadelphia Housing Association, 1-20.

34. Vincent P. Franklin, "The Philadelphia Race Riot of 1918," *Pennsylvania Magazine of History and Biography* 99 (1975): 339-45.

35. Minutes of November 21, 1923 Meeting, Records of the Committee on Race Relations, Philadelphia Yearly Meeting Collection, Record Group 2, Series 2-3, Quaker Collection, Swarthmore College.

36. "Inter-Racial Committee," pamphlet, 1922, Records of the Philadelphia Housing Association, Urban Archives, Paley Library, Temple University.

37. Minutes of April 26, 1926 Meeting, Records of the Committee on Race Relations.

38. Minutes of November 14, 1927 Meeting, Records of the Committee on Race Relations.

39. Minutes of September 11, 1928 Meeting, Records of the Committee on Race Relations; John Moore, ed., *Friends in the Delaware Valley: Philadelphia Yearly Meeting, 1681-1981* (Haverford, PA: Friends Historical Association, 1981), 241.

40. Robert L. Zangrando, *The NAACP Crusade Against Lynching, 1909-1950* (Philadelphia: Temple University Press, 1980), 104-5; Paul E. Baker, *Negro-White Adjustment: An Investigation and Analysis of Methods in the Interracial Movement in the United States* (New York: Association Press, 1934), 37; *Philadelphia Tribune*, May 1 and May 15, 1930.

41. Minutes of June 3, 1930 Meeting, Records of Committee on Race Relations.

42. Jones, *Swords into Ploughshares*, 328; Minutes of April 15, 1930 Meeting, Records of Committee on Race Relations.

43. Zangrando, *The NAACP Crusade Against Lynching*, 93-94.

44. Marjorie Penney Paschkis, interview by Rosa King Zimmerman, July 20, 1976; transcript, West Chester Oral History Program, (History) Records of Fellowship House, Urban Archives, Paley Library, Temple University.

45. "A Summary of Fellowship's Projects Since May, 1931," 1940 (Steering Committee); Fred Wentzel, "Together: The Story of the Philadelphia Young People's Interracial Fellowship," published radio address, n.d., (History) Records of Fellowship House.

46. Fred D. Wentzel, "Together," and "Dear Friend," letter June 4, 1931, (Steering Committee) Records of Fellowship House.

47. Minutes of June 30 and September 18, 1931 Meetings, Continuation Committee of the Pendle Hill Interracial Conference, (Steering Committee) Records of Fellowship House; and Anna McGarry article.

48. Charles Pete Banner-Haley, *To Do Good and to Do Well: Middle Class Blacks During the Depression in Philadelphia, 1929-1941* (New York: Garland, 1993), 148-49; "A Summary of Fellowship's Projects Since May, 1931," 1940, (Steering Committee) Records of Fellowship House.

49. Minutes of September 19, 1933 Meeting, Records of the Committee on Race Relations; "A Summary of Fellowship's Projects Since May, 1931," 1940 (Steering Committee) Records of Fellowship House.

50. *Ibid.*, "A Summary."

51. Gladys Rawlins, interview by author, April 1995, Gwynedd Valley, Pennsylvania.

52. Robin D. G. Kelley, *Hammer and Hoe: Alabama Communists During the Great Depression* (Chapel Hill: University of North Carolina Press, 1990), 169–70; Patricia Sullivan, *Days of Hope: Race and Democracy in the New Deal Era* (Chapel Hill: University of North Carolina Press, 1996), 57–58; Minutes of January 8, 1938 Meeting, Records of the Committee on Race Relations.

53. Announcement of Mordecai Johnson's Sermon 1935, n.d., (Steering Committee) Records of Fellowship House.

54. Fred D. Wentzel, "Together."

55. *Ibid.*; letter from Rev. Marshal Shepard to Charles Hamilton Houston, March 20, 1935, (Steering Committee) Records of Fellowship House.

56. Banner-Haley, *To Do Good and to Do Well*, 129–30.

57. Franklin, *The Education of Black Philadelphia*, 166; Viscount Nelson, "Race and Class Consciousness of Philadelphia Negroes with Special Emphasis on the Years Between 1927 and 1940" (diss., University of Pennsylvania, 1969), 391–95.

58. *Fellowship Call* I, no. 1 (October 24, 1936), (History) Records of Fellowship House.

59. "A Summary of Fellowship's Activities Since May, 1931," 1940, (Steering Committee) Records of Fellowship House.

60. *Ibid.*

61. Minutes of November 17, 1936 Meeting, Records of the Committee on Race Relations.

62. Minutes of October 19, 1937 and October 21, 1938 Meetings, Records of the Committee on Race Relations.

63. "The Steel Wire of Sanity," *Medford Leas Life* (April 1976): 4.

64. *Ibid.*

65. "Hate Takes a Holiday," *Young People* 16 (April 21, 1940), 128; Philip Jenkins, *Hoods and Shirts: The Extreme Right in Pennsylvania, 1925–1950* (Chapel Hill: University of North Carolina Press, 1997), 10–11.

66. "Hate Takes a Holiday," 129; and Penney, "A Little Dove of Peace," *Journal of Human Relations* 5, no. 3 (1957): 40.

67. Press release, October 1939, (Steering Committee) Records of Fellowship House; funeral program for Edwin Luther Cunningham, November 6, 1964, St. Paul's Baptist Church, Philadelphia.

CHAPTER 2

1. "He Came, He Saw, He Conquered," announcement 1945, (Publications) Records of Fellowship House; *Freedom Flyer* (Stoddard Junior High School Fellowship Club newspaper), vol. 1, no. 1 (May 18, 1945); and letter to Frank Sinatra from Marjorie Penney, April 5, 1945, (Correspondence) Records of Fellowship House.

2. Vincent Franklin, *The Education of Black Philadelphia: The Social and Educational History of a Minority Community, 1900–1950* (Philadelphia: University of Pennsylvania

Press, 1979), 4–7; Margaret Hope Bacon, "The Pennsylvania Abolition Society's Mission for Black Education," *Pennsylvania Legacies* (November 2005): 21–24.

3. Shirley Turpin Parham, "A History of Black Public Education in Philadelphia, Pennsylvania 1864 to 1914" (diss., Temple University, 1986), 35.

4. *Ibid.*, 44.

5. *Ibid.*, 54; and David Canton, *Raymond Pace Alexander: A New Negro Lawyer Fights for Civil Rights in Philadelphia* (Jackson: University of Mississippi Press, 2009), 4–26.

6. Franklin, *The Education of Black Philadelphia*, 71–79. For an excellent examination of this issue, see Davison Douglas, *Jim Crow Moves North: The Battle over Northern School Segregation, 1865–1954* (New York: Cambridge University Press, 2005).

7. Banner-Haley, *To Do Good and to Do Well*, 48–49; Minutes of February 14, 1928 Meeting, Records of the Committee on Race Relations Peace Collection, Swarthmore College.

8. Minutes of January 18, 1929 Meeting, Records of the Committee on Race Relations Peace Collection, Swarthmore College; Barbara Savage, *Broadcasting Freedom: Radio, War, and the Politics of Race, 1938–1948* (Chapel Hill: University of North Carolina Press, 1999), 22–24.

9. *Philadelphia Tribune*, September 17, 1931.

10. Minutes of February 14, 1932 Meeting, Records of the Committee on Race Relations Peace Collection, Swarthmore College.

11. Fred D. Wentzel, "Together."

12. *Philadelphia Tribune*, September 17, 1931; Canton, *Raymond Pace Alexander*, 27–41.

13. Lee Baker, "The Role of Anthropology in the Social Construction of Race, 1896–1954" (diss., Temple University, 1994), 89; John B. Kirby, *Black Americans in the Roosevelt Era: Liberalism and Race* (Knoxville: University of Tennessee Press, 1980), 205–6.

14. "Guidelines for Speakers," 1938, (Steering Committee) Records of Fellowship House.

15. "Tolerance Trio: Report of Questions Asked at the Various Camps," 1939, (Speakers Bureau) Records of Fellowship House.

16. Minutes of June 18, 1940 and October 24, 1939 Meetings, Records of the Committee on Race Relations Peace Collection, Swarthmore College.

17. Minutes of December 17, 1940 Meeting, Records of the Committee on Race Relations Peace Collection, Swarthmore College; Minutes of October 22, 1940 Meeting, (Steering Committee) Records of Fellowship House.

18. Marjorie Penney, "A Little Dove of Peace," *Journal of Human Relations* 5, no. 3 (1957): 35.

19. Roosevelt and Virginia Barlow and Randolph Walker, interview by author, October 1995, Philadelphia; "Fellowship House Makes Bow As All Races Work Together," *Philadelphia Tribune*, April 17, 1941; "Inside Fellowship House," booklet, 1948, Records of Fellowship House.

20. Rawlins interview by author, April 1995.

21. Penney, "A Little Dove of Peace," 36; "Arrows Handbook," 1950, (Programs) Records of Fellowship House.

22. Minutes of May 20, 1941 Meeting, Records of the Committee on Race Relations; Vacation School Report, July 1941, (Education) Records of Fellowship House.

23. Rawlins interview by author, April 1995; Vacation School Report, July 1941.

24. Fredric Miller, "A History of the Fellowship Commission," in *Invisible Philadelphia*, 610.

25. "Maurice Fagan, 82, A Sparkplug in Founding of Anti-Bias Groups," obituary, *Philadelphia Inquirer*, August 20, 1992.

26. Avis Carlson, "Philadelphia's Stitch in Time," *Survey Graphic* 33, no. 7 (July 1944): 324–25.

27. *Ibid.*

28. "The Fellowship Commission," brochure, 1941, (History) Records of the Philadelphia Fellowship Commission.

29. Carlson, "Philadelphia's Stitch in Time," 324–25.

30. Stanley Arnold, "The Philadelphia NAACP," in *Invisible Philadelphia*, 47; "Philadelphia Fellowship Commission," press release, 1943, (History) Records of the Fellowship Commission.

31. "The Fellowship Commission," pamphlet, 1941, (History) Records of the Fellowship Commission.

32. *Ibid.*

33. "The Negro and Defense," pamphlet (New York: Council for Democracy, 1941), 1-20; Kirby, *Black Americans in the Roosevelt Era*, 208–25.

34. Sponsors List, October 1941, (Board of Directors) Records of Fellowship House.

35. By-Laws of Fellowship House, 1942, (Board of Directors) Records of Fellowship House.

36. "Dear Friend," letter, 1942, (Programs) Records of Fellowship House.

37. Units for Unity brochure, 1942, (Programs) Records of Fellowship House.

38. Franklin, *The Education of Black Philadelphia*, 158; Minutes of September 14, 1943 Meeting, (Board of Commissioners) Records of the Fellowship Commission.

39. Dominic Capeci Jr., *Race Relations in Wartime Detroit: The Sojourner Truth Housing Controversy of 1942* (Ann Arbor: University of Michigan Press, 1989), 1. Also see Thomas Sugrue, *The Origins of the Urban Crisis: Race and Inequality in Postwar Detroit* (Princeton: Princeton University Press, 1996).

40. Fellowship House News Letter, July 20, 1943 (Publications), and the Citywide Interracial Committee, Membership list, 1943 (Educational Programs), Records of Fellowship House; Franklin, *The Education of Black Philadelphia*, 159.

41. *Philadelphia Tribune* April 3, 1941, and Raymond Schmandt, "Catholic Organizations in Philadelphia," in *Invisible Philadelphia*, 230; High School Fellowship Announcement, October 12, 1943, (Educational Programs) Records of Fellowship House; David W. Southern, *John LaFarge and the Limits of Catholic Interracialism, 1911–1963* (Baton Rouge: Louisiana State University Press, 1996), 203–5. For an excellent account of Philadelphia's Catholic Interracial Council, see Edward Schmidt, "A Vocation for Neighborliness: Anna McGarry's Quest for Community in Philadelphia," *U.S. Catholic Historian* 22, no. 2 (Spring 2004): 81–97.

42. Handbook, 1948–49, (Board of Directors) Records of Fellowship House.

43. Letter from Malcolm Johnson to Fellowship House, May 13, 1944, (Education) Records of Fellowship House.

44. Letter from Rita Ferrelli to Fellowship House, May 12, 1944, (Education) Records of Fellowship House.

45. Handbook, 1948–49, (Board of Directors) Records of Fellowship House.

46. "During 1944–1945," pamphlet, (Publications) Records of Fellowship House.

47. House Party Program, August 4, 1943, (Programs) Records of Fellowship House.

48. Franklin, *The Education of Black Philadelphia*, 156–57.

49. "The Fellowship Commission," brochure, 1981 (Board of Commissioners), and *Report to the Community*, Records of the Fellowship Commission.

50. *Philadelphia Tribune*, February 2, 1946.

51. David W. Southern, *Gunnar Myrdal and Black-White Relations: The Use and Abuse of an American Dilemma, 1944–1969* (Baton Rouge: Louisiana State University Press, 1987), xiii; Gunnar Myrdal, *An American Dilemma: The Negro Problem and Modern Democracy* (New York: Harper and Row, 1944), 997–1024.

52. Letter to C. Jared Ingersoll from Maurice Fagan, December 17, 1944, (Correspondence) Records of the Fellowship Commission.

53. Memorandum from Maurice Fagan to Rev. George Trowbridge, May 12, 1945, (Board of Commissioners) Records of the Fellowship Commission.

54. Memorandum from Maurice Fagan to Rev. George Trowbridge October 12, 1946, (Board of Commissioners) Records of the Fellowship Commission.

55. "Great American Teams," 1942, (Publications) Records of the Fellowship Commission.

56. "Valor Knows No Creed," radio script, September 14, 1942, (Programs) Records of the Fellowship Commission.

57. "WIP Fights Race Hatred With New Segment," *Billboard*, November 3, 1945.

58. Ruby Smith, "Lessons in Race Relations Brought Philadelphians Weekly Via Radio," *The Philadelphia Afro-American*, February 14, 1948.

59. *Ibid.*

60. *Ibid.*

61. "WIP Fights Race Hatred With New Segment."

62. Fellowship House News Letter, January 1946, (Publications) Records of Fellowship House.

63. "Report of Crozer Seminary Retreat, Spring 1949" (Board of Directors), Records of Fellowship House; *Philadelphia Tribune*, January 20, 1945; letter from Marjorie Penney to Mrs. Stanley Chambers, November 24, 1944, and letter from Marjorie Penney to Miss Warren, November 16, 1944, Records of Fellowship House.

64. "The Philadelphia Fellowship Commission," pamphlet, 1945 (Special Committees), and Minutes of September 10, 1946 Meeting, Records of the Fellowship Commission.

65. Letter to Florence Kite from Maurice Fagan, November 12, 1945, Records of the Fellowship Commission.

66. James Reichley, *The Art of Government: Reform and Organization in Philadelphia* (New York: Fund for the Republic, 1959), 68–72; Kirk Petshek, *The Challenge of Urban*

Reform: Policies and Programs in Philadelphia (Philadelphia: Temple University Press, 1973), 16–28.

67. Charles A. Ekstrom, "The Electoral Politics of Reform and Machine: The Political Behavior of Philadelphia's 'Black' Wards, 1943-1969," in Miriam Ershkowitz and Roger Zikmund, eds., *Black Politics in Philadelphia* (Philadelphia: Temple University Press, 1973), 91–94; Matthew J. Countryman, *Up South: Civil Rights and Black Power in Philadelphia* (Philadelphia: University of Pennsylvania Press, 2007), 13–42.

68. Ekstrom, 93–94.

CHAPTER 3

1. Southern, *Gunnar Myrdal and Black-White Relations*, 108–9.

2. Peter Kellogg, "Civil Rights Consciousness in the 1940s," *The Historian* 22, no. 1 (November 1979): 18–24.

3. Reichley, *The Art of Government*, 3–13; Lloyd M. Abernethy, "Political Parties in Philadelphia," in *Invisible Philadelphia*, ed. Toll and Gilliam, 58889.

4. Petshek, *The Challenge of Urban Reform*, 50–52; Murray Friedman and Carolyn Beck, "An Ambivalent Alliance," in Murray Friedman, ed., *Jewish Life in Philadelphia, 1945-1985* (Ardmore, PA: Seth Press, 1986), 142–47; letter from Marjorie Penney to Richardson Dilworth, December 22, 1949, and letter from Marjorie Penney to Joseph Clark, December 21, 1949, (Correspondence) Records of Fellowship House.

5. Minutes of March 16 and June 5, 1948 Junior High School Fellowship Teachers' Meetings (Junior High Fellowship), and Minutes of November 8, 1949 High School Fellowship Teachers' Meeting (High School Fellowship), Records of Fellowship House. Also see Lisa Levenstein, *A Movement Without Marches: African American Women and the Politics of Poverty in Postwar Philadelphia* (Chapel Hill: University of North Carolina Press, 2009), 121–44.

6. Helen Stark Tomkins, "Fellowship House Farm," in *Invisible Philadelphia*, 607–8; Minutes of December 9, 1947 Meeting, (Board of Commissioners) Records of the Fellowship Commission.

7. Tomkins, "Fellowship House Farm"; *Philadelphia Tribune*, March 3, 1941.

8. Friedman, ed., *Jewish Life in Philadelphia*, 194–97; interview with Mitzi Jacoby Barnes, Aurora, Colorado, March 18, 1998.

9. Penney "A Little Dove of Peace," 36; Andy Wallace, "Elaine Brown, 87, teacher founded Singing City Choir," *Philadelphia Inquirer*, September 9, 1997, B5.

10. Report of Committee on Fellowship Retreat "Farm Program," letter, May 25, 1948, (Board of Directors) Records of Fellowship House.

11. "Private Opinions: A Fellowship Retreat," 1949, (Board of Directors) Records of Fellowship House.

12. Genna Rae MacNeil, *Groundwork: Charles Hamilton Houston and the Struggle for Civil Rights* (Philadelphia: University of Pennsylvania Press, 1983), 199; letter to Charles Hamilton Houston from Marjorie Penney, October 18, 1944, (Correspondence) Records of Fellowship House.

13. "Crozer – Spring 1949," report, (Board of Directors) Records of Fellowship House.

14. Franklin, *The Education of Black Philadelphia*, 191.

15. *Ibid.*

16. Interview with Mitzi Jacoby Barnes, Aurora, Colorado, April 4, 1996.

17. "Philadelphia's Negro Population: Facts on Housing," Philadelphia Commission on Human Relations, 1953; Theodore Hershberg et al., "A Tale of Three Cities: Blacks, Immigrants, and Opportunity in Philadelphia, 1850–1880, 1930, and 1970," in Hershberg, ed., *Philadelphia: Work, Space, Family, and Group Experience in the Nineteenth Century* (New York: Oxford University Press, 1981), 476–79; letter to Walter C. Wynn from Earl Johnson, August 25, 1953 (Education), and Minutes of January 31, 1951 Meeting (Board of Commissioners), Records of the Fellowship Commission.

18. Minutes of December 8, 1947 Meeting, (Board of Commissioners) Records of the Fellowship Commission.

19. "Should Philadelphia Have a City College?" brochure, July 24, 1946 (Citizens' Committee for a Free College); memo from Maurice Fagan to Judge McDevitt, October 22, 1948, (Education) Records of the Fellowship Commission.

20. Letter from Maurice Fagan to Rev. E. Luther Cunningham, March 11, 1949, (Education) Records of the Fellowship Commission.

21. Public Hearings on Proposed Charter October 11, 1949, Records of the City Charter Commission, Archives of the City of Philadelphia; Public Hearings on Proposed Charter, January 30 and October 31, 1950, Records of the City Charter Commission, Archives of the City of Philadelphia.

22. Dear Speakers' Letter, March 30, 1951, (Speakers' Bureau) Records of Fellowship House.

23. *Ibid.*

24. Petshek, *The Challenge of Urban Reform*, 34, 39; and Abernethy, "Political Parties in Philadelphia," 589.

25. Penney, "A Little Dove of Peace," 40–41.

26. Helen Stark Tomkins, interview by author, September 1996, Kennett Square, Pennsylvania.

27. "Arrows Work For Fellowship," handbook, 1950, (Arrows) Records of Fellowship House.

28. Henry S. Resnik, *Turning on the System: War in the Philadelphia Public Schools* (New York: Random House, 1970), 29–34.

29. *Democracy in Education*, conference report, October 1951, (Publications) Records of the Fellowship Commission.

30. *Report to the Community* 4, no. 5 (February 1953): 4, Records of the Fellowship Commission.

31. *Report to the Community* 4, no. 1 (October 1952): 1, Records of the Fellowship Commission.

32. Franklin, *The Education of Black Philadelphia*, 203.

33. "Statement to City Council Committee on Law and Government on the Admissions Policy of Girard College," 1954, (Education) Records of the Fellowship Commission.

34. Helen Stark Tomkins and Val Udell, interview by author, September 1995, Fellowship Farm, Fagleysville, Pennsylvania; "Together at Fellowship House Farm," brochure, 1956, Records of Fellowship House.

35. Penney, "A Little Dove of Peace," 41.

36. Ira G. Zepp Jr., *The Social Vision of Martin Luther King*, vol. 18 of *Martin Luther King, Jr. and the Civil Rights Movement* (New York: Carlson Publishing, 1989), 12; Martin Luther King Jr., *Stride Toward Freedom: The Montgomery Story* (New York: Harper and Row, 1958), 96.

37. Gerald Horne, *Red and Black: W. E. B. Du Bois and the Afro-American Response to the Cold War, 1944–1963* (Albany: State University of New York Press, 1986), 126, 132.

38. Letter to Dr. C. Leslie Cushman from Marjorie Penney, July 20, 1950, and "Dear High School Fellowshipper" letter, July 1950, (High School Fellowship) Records of Fellowship House.

39. Kenneth O'Reilly, *Racial Matters: The FBI's Secret File on Black America, 1960–1972* (New York: Free Press, 1989), 27, 44–45; "A Steel Wire of Sanity," 4; Gerald Horne, *Benjamin Davis and the Communist Party* (New York: University of Delaware Press, 1994), 172; letter from Elmer McClain, December 2, 1947, Records of the Fellowship Commission.

40. Fredric M. Miller, "Fellowship Commission," in *Invisible Philadelphia*, 610; Arthur C. Willis, *Cecil's City: A History of Blacks in Philadelphia, 1638–1979* (New York: Carlton, 1990), 59–60; Minutes of March 14, 1944, September 18, 1950, and February 6, 1952 Meetings, (Board of Commissioners) Records of the Fellowship Commission.

41. Miller, "Fellowship Commission," in *Invisible Philadelphia*, 611.

42. Memo Regarding Congressional Investigations of Alleged Communists in Philadelphia School System, March 1953, and Minutes of April 6, 1955 Meeting, Records of the Fellowship Commission.

43. O'Reilly, *Racial Matters*, 44–45.

44. "C'mon out to the PEOPLE farm!" brochure, 1958, Records of Fellowship House.

45. "Foreign Visitors at Fellowship Farm," n.d., and Summer Calendar, 1956, (Farm Programs) Records of Fellowship House; interview with Mohammed Latif, Temple University, February 21, 1997.

46. "Together at Fellowship House Farm," brochure, 1956, (Farm Programs) Records of Fellowship House.

47. Interview with Louis Massiah, Philadelphia, December 2, 1996.

48. Finance Report, 1955, (Development) Records of Fellowship House; Carolyn Teich Adams et al., *Philadelphia: Neighborhoods, Division, and Conflict in a Postindustrial City* (Philadelphia: Temple University Press, 1991), 73–79.

49. Landon Y. Jones, *Great Expectations: America and the Baby Boom Generation* (New York: Coward, McCann & Geoghegan, 1980), 11–19; and Paul C. Light, *Baby Boomers* (New York: W. W. Norton, 1988), 19–27.

50. Newsletter, October 1956, Records of Fellowship House.

51. "Together at Fellowship House Farm," brochure, 1956, and School District In-Service Course List, 1965, Records of Fellowship House.

52. Resnik, *Turning on the System*, 30–40.

53. "Review: A Birds Eye View of Fellowship House," unpublished report, March 14, 1959, Records of Fellowship House.

54. *Ibid.*

55. Mitzi Jacoby Barnes, telephone interview by author, April 4, 1996, Aurora, Colorado; October 23, 24 and November 20, 1953, unpublished reports of protests, Records of Fellowship House.

56. William R. Odell, *Educational Survey Report for the Philadelphia Board of Public Education* (Philadelphia: Board of Public Education, School District of Philadelphia, 1965), i–v and 15; Resnik, *Turning on the System*, 41.

57. Miller, "Fellowship Commission," in *Invisible Philadelphia*, 611; Minutes of June 13, 1961 Meeting, (Board of Commissioners) Records of the Fellowship Commission; *Philadelphia Bulletin*, October 26, 1961; "Kingsway," unpublished report, November 1961, Records of Fellowship House.

58. Resnik, *Turning on the System*, 42–45; and Petshek, *The Challenge of Urban Reform*, 40–41.

59. Albert P. Blaustein, *Civil Rights U.S.A. Public Schools, Cities in the North and West, 1962*, United States Commission on Civil Rights (New York: Greenwood Press), 113–20.

60. Miller, "The Fellowship Commission," in *Invisible Philadelphia*, 611.

61. Latif interview by author, February 21, 1997.

62. "History of Fellowship House Farm," 1980, (History) Records of Fellowship House.

63. Willis, *Cecil's City*, 105–14; Paul Lermack, "Cecil Moore and the Philadelphia Branch of the National Association for the Advancement of Colored People: The Politics of Negro Pressure Organization," in Joseph Zikmund and Miriam Ershkowitz, eds., *Black Politics in Philadelphia* (Philadelphia: Temple University Press, 1973), 146–48. For an excellent analysis of the rise of Cecil B. Moore, see Countryman, *Up South*.

64. Lermack, "Cecil Moore and the Philadelphia Branch of the National Association for the Advancement of Colored People," 146–51; Press Release, November 6, 1964, (Education) Records of the Fellowship Commission.

65. *Philadelphia Bulletin*, September 8, 1963; "History of Fellowship House," 1980, Records of Fellowship House.

66. *Community College Act of 1963*: Act 484, Pl 113.

67. "History of Fellowship House," 1980.

68. *Philadelphia Bulletin*, August 29, 1964; Newsletter, September 1964, Records of Fellowship House.

69. Latif, interview by author.

70. Press Release, November 6, 1964, (Memorandums) Records of the Fellowship Commission.

71. Petshek, *The Challenge of Urban Reform*, 43; Resnik, *Turning on the System*, 44.

72. "Commission Criticizes Board of Education," press release, June 20, 1966, Records of the Fellowship Commission.

73. "A Brief Overview of Fellowship House, 1967 Program and Problems," unpublished report, Records of Fellowship House.

74. "An Appeal to Reason," summer 1967, and "Operation Green Grass—Summer 1967," report, Records of Fellowship House.

75. *Philadelphia Bulletin*, August 1 and August 3, 1965, and *Philadelphia Tribune*, August 8, 1965.

76. "I'm the Goddamn Boss," *Time*, vol. 84 (September 11, 1964): 24–25.

77. *Philadelphia Bulletin*, June 28 and September 22, 1967; "Fellowship Commission Denounces Cecil B. Moore's Call For Violence," press release, October 2, 1967, Records of Fellowship Commission.

78. *Philadelphia Bulletin*, November 18, 1967; Newsletter, December 1967, Records of Fellowship House.

79. Minutes of November 29, 1967 Meeting, Records of Fellowship Commission.

80. "Proposal on Educational Parks," April 11, 1967 and Memo from James Nixon, January 1, 1968, (Educational Policy and Planning Committee) Records of the Fellowship Commission. Perhaps the reason there was not widespread violent white opposition to desegregation in Philadelphia is because there was not a concentrated effort by the civil rights community to support busing and similar strategies. For a look at other northern cities, see Ronald Formisano, *Boston Against Busing: Race, Class, and Ethnicity in the 1960s and 1970s* (Chapel Hill: University of North Carolina Press, 1991), and Jonathan Rieder, *Canarsie: The Jews and Italians of Brooklyn Against Liberalism* (Cambridge: Harvard University, 1985).

81. Homer C. Floyd, "School Desegregation Can Succeed: The Pennsylvania Experience," in Murray Friedman, Roger Meltzer, and Charles Miller, eds., *New Perspectives on School Integration* (Philadelphia: Fortress Press, 1979), 32–34.

82. Thomas Sugrue, *Sweet Land of Liberty: The Forgotten Struggle for Civil Rights in the North* (New York: Random House, 2008), 449–60.

CHAPTER 4

1. "10 Most Segregated Urban Areas in America," Salon.com, March 20, 2011.

2. William Edward Burghardt Du Bois, *The Philadelphia Negro* (1899; reprint, Philadelphia: University of Pennsylvania, 1996), 297.

3. John Bauman, *Public Housing, Race, and Renewal* (Philadelphia: Temple University Press, 1987), 19; "History of the Philadelphia Housing Association," (History) Records of the Philadelphia Housing Association (Housing Association of the Delaware Valley) (HADV) Urban Archives, Paley Library, Temple University; John Sutherland, "The Origins of Philadelphia's Octavia Hill Society: Social Reform in the Contented City," *Pennsylvania Magazine of History and Biography* 99, no. 1 (January 1975): 20–44; Julie Johnson, "The Octavia Hill Association," in Toll and Gilliam, eds., *Invisible Philadelphia*, 416–20.

4. "History of the Philadelphia Housing Association," (History) Records of the Housing Association.

5. John Bauman, "The Philadelphia Housing Association," in *Invisible Philadelphia*, 420.

6. "History of the Philadelphia Housing Association," (History) Records of the Philadelphia Housing Association.

7. Charles A. Hardy, "Race and Opportunity: Black Philadelphia During the Era of the Great Migration, 1916–1930" (diss., Temple University, 1989), 162–63.

8. *Ibid.*, 138.

9. *Ibid.*, 142.

10. John F. Bauman, "Disinfecting the Industrial City: The Philadelphia Housing Commission and Scientific Efficiency, 1909–1916," in Michael H. Ebner and Eugene M. Tobin, eds., *The Age of Urban Reform: New Perspectives on the Progressive Era* (Port Washington, NY: Kennikat Press, 1977), 117–27; "Supplementary Study of the Housing of the City Negro" and Guide to the Collection of the Philadelphia Housing Association. Records of the Housing Association; William D. Fuller, "The Negro Migrant in Philadelphia," pamphlet, 1924, Records of the Philadelphia Housing Association; Hardy, "Race and Opportunity," 137; Nelson, "Race and Class Consciousness of Philadelphia Negroes with Special Emphasis on the Years Between 1927 and 1940" (diss., University of Pennsylvania, 1969).

11. Minutes of Housing Sub-Committee, Negro Migration Committee, March 9, 1917.

12. Report to the Board of Directors, 1917, Records of the Philadelphia Housing Association.

13. *Ibid.*

14. A. L. Manly, "Where Negroes Live in Philadelphia," *Opportunity* 1, No. 1–5 (May 1923): 10–15.

15. Vincent Franklin, "The Philadelphia Race Riot of 1918," *Pennsylvania Magazine of History and Biography* 99, no. 1 (1975): 339–44.

16. Memo, June 9, 1920, and letter from John Ihlder to A. L. Manly, October 20, 1920, Records of the Housing Association.

17. Fuller, "The Negro Migrant in Philadelphia."

18. Bauman, "The Philadelphia Housing Association," 420–22; Bauman, "Black Slums/Black Projects: The New Deal and Negro Housing in Philadelphia," *Pennsylvania History* 41 (July 1974): 316.

19. Bauman, "The Philadelphia Housing Association," 421.

20. Minutes of the April 8, 1926 Meeting, Records of the Committee on Race Relations.

21. *Ibid.*

22. Minutes of the June 8, 1926, June 17 and September 13, 1927 Meetings, Records of the Committee on Race Relations; Thomas Woofter Jr., *Negro Housing in Philadelphia* (Philadelphia: Committee on the Interests of the Colored Race, 1927), 3–12.

23. Gwendolyn Wright, *Building the Dream: A Social History of Housing in America* (Cambridge: MIT Press, 1983), 220–21.

24. Nelson, "Race and Class Consciousness of Philadelphia Negroes," 110–17; Banner-Haley, *To Do Good and to Do Well*, 50–51.

25. Nelson, "Race and Class Consciousness of Philadelphia Negroes," 110–17; Bauman, "Black Slums/Black Projects," 317–18.

26. Findings From the Pendle Hill Conference of Young Church People, May 22–25, (Steering Committee), Records of Fellowship House.

27. Bauman," Black Slums/Black Projects," 315; Banner-Haley, *To Do Good and to Do Well*, 58–61; Nelson," Race and Class Consciousness of Philadelphia Negroes," 119–27.

28. Banner-Haley, *To Do Good and to Do Well*, 49.

29. Bauman, "Black Slums/Black Projects," 325-27.

30. *Ibid.*; Nelson, "Race and Class Consciousness of Philadelphia Negroes," 124–27.

31. Letter from J. D. Goodman to Bernard Newman, October 1, 1935, Records of the Philadelphia Housing Association.

32. Banner-Haley, *To Do Good and to Do Well*, 153; Keith Griffler, *What Price Alliance?: Black Radicals Confront White Labor, 1918–1938* (New York: Garland, 1995), 134–35.

33. Nelson, "Race and Class Consciousness,"125-133, and "Mass Action Sought on Local Housing," *Philadelphia Tribune*, December 9, 1937.

34. Nelson, "Race and Class Consciousness of Philadelphia Negroes," 128–35.

35. Mark Naison, "From Eviction Resistance to Rent Control: Tenant Activism in the Great Depression," in ed. Ronald Lawson, ed., *Tenant Movement in New York City, 1904–1984* (New Brunswick: Rutgers University Press, 1986), 100–118.

36. Banner-Haley, *To Do Good and to Do Well*, 136. Although Paul Lyons's work, *Philadelphia Communists* (Philadelphia: Temple University, 1982), provides a general survey of the CPUSA from the late 1930s to the 1950s, he says nothing about liberal activists from interracial organizations.

37. "Communism and the Negro," Symposium of Negro Editors, *Crisis* 34 (April-May 1932): 118.

38. Minutes of October 19, 1937 Meeting, Records of the Committee on Race Relations.

39. Kirby, *Black Americans in the Roosevelt Era*, 23–26.

40. Bauman, "Black Slums/Black Projects," 333–35; Nelson, "Race and Class Consciousness of Philadelphia Negroes," 136–37.

41. Minutes of October 24, 1939 and February 16, 1940 Meetings, Records of the Committee on Race Relations.

42. Nelson," Race and Class Consciousness of Philadelphia Negroes," 143.

43. Arthur Huff Fauset, "I Write As I See," *Philadelphia Tribune*, March 6, 1941; Bauman, "Black Slums/Black Projects," 336; Minutes of April 15 and May 20, 1941 Meetings, Records of the Committee on Race Relations.

44. Fredric Miller, David Clow, and Graham Finney, "Physical Planning in Philadelphia," in *Invisible Philadelphia*, 25; Bauman, "The Philadelphia Housing Association," in *Invisible Philadelphia*, 422.

45. Avis Carlson, "Philadelphia's Stitch in Time," in *Survey Graphic*, July 1944; Charles Johnson, *To Stem This Tide: A Survey of Racial Tension in the United States* (New York: AMS Press, 1943), 49.

46. *Ibid.*

47. "Philadelphia Fellowship Commission," report, 1944, Records of the Fellowship Commission.

48. Letter from Laurence Foster to Edmund Bacon, September 14, 1943, and Minutes of September 18, 1943 Meeting, City-Wide Interracial Committee, Records of the Philadelphia Housing Association and Records of the Fellowship Commission.

49. "Report on Study made of Tacony Incidents and Their Causes," September 1943, and Summary of Minutes of the Housing Committee of the City-Wide Interracial Committee of Philadelphia from September '43 to April '44, Records of the Housing Association. For an excellent analysis of the Detroit situation, see Capeci, *Race Relations in Wartime Detroit*.

50. Johnson, *To Stem This Tide*, 49.

51. Letter from Laurence Foster to Edmund Bacon, September 14, 1943, and minutes of September 18, 1943 Meeting, City-Wide Interracial Committee, Records of the Housing Association and Records of the Fellowship Commission.

52. Willis, *Cecil's City*, 81–82; Minutes of the January 6, 1944 Meeting of the City-Wide Interracial Committee of Philadelphia, Records of the Philadelphia Housing Association.

53. Units for Unity Script, February 1944, (Units for Unity) Records of Fellowship House.

54. "Court Uphold Negro's Right to Property," *Issues* 2, nos. 4–5 (April-May 1944): 3.

55. Minutes of March 14, 1944 Meeting, (Board of Commissioners) Records of the Fellowship Commission; Minutes from Special Meeting Called to Consider Action Relative to Local FEPC, June 25, 1943, Records of NAACP, Philadelphia Branch.

56. Petshek, *The Challenge of Urban Reform*, 136; Minutes of June 12, 1945 Meeting, (Board of Commissioners) Records of the Fellowship Commission.

57. Letter from Maurice Fagan to Florence Kite, November 12, 1945, (Correspondence) Records of the Fellowship Commission.

58. Minutes of June 12, 1945 Meeting, (Board of Commissioners) Records of the Fellowship Commission.

59. "No Homes For Veterans," *Issues* 3, nos. 11–12 (November-December 1945): 1.

60. "Negro Housing Needs," *Issues* 5, nos. 7–8 (July-August 1947): 5.

61. "You Are the Eyes and Ears of the Fellowship Commission," brochure, 1947, Records of the Fellowship Commission.

62. Survey of Racial, Religious and Nationality Designations in the *Philadelphia Evening Bulletin*, June 4 to June 10, 1951, (Media) Records of the Fellowship Commission.

63. Helen Stark Tomkins, "Fellowship House Farm," in *Invisible Philadelphia*, 607; Minutes of High School Fellowship Teachers' Meeting, June 8, 1948, Records of Fellowship House.

64. Carolyn Adams et al., *Philadelphia: Neighborhoods, Division, and Conflict in a Post-Industrial City* (Philadelphia: Temple University Press, 1991), 30–34; Gwendolyn Wright, *Building the Dream: A Social History of Housing in America* (Cambridge: MIT Press, 1983), 244.

CHAPTER 5

1. Fredric Miller, David Clow, and Graham Finney, "Physical Planning in Philadelphia," in *Invisible Philadelphia*, 24–26; Reichley, *The Art of Government*, 9–12; "Good Housing in a Better Philadelphia," *Issues* 5, nos. 9–10 (September-October 1947): 1.

2. *Issues* 5, nos. 11-12 (November-December 1947): 4; Memo to Reverend George Trowbridge, September 9, 1947, (Board of Commissioners) Records of the Fellowship Commission.

3. Minutes of December 9, 1947 Meeting, (Executive Committee); Minutes of July 13, 1948 Meeting; and "The House I Live In" Fellowship Forum series, April 13, 1949, Radio Station WHAT, Philadelphia, Records of the Fellowship Commission.

4. Wright, *Building the Dream*, 244-48; Bauman, "Housing Association of the Delaware Valley," 422.

5. Wright, *Building the Dream*, 245-48.

6. *Ibid*.

7. Letter to John Dolbeare from Edith Hansen, May 5, 1949 and Minutes of June 10, 1947 Meeting, (Committees) Records of the Fellowship Commission.

8. Press Release, March 12, 1951, Records of the Philadelphia Housing Association; Minutes of March 20, 1950 Meeting, (Executive Committee) Records of the Fellowship Commission.

9. "Housing in 1949," *Issues* 8, nos. 1-3 (January-March 1949): 1; "Substandard Housing Still With Us," *Issues* (November 1950): 1-2; G. Gordon Brown, *Law Administration and Negro-White Relations in Philadelphia: A Study in Race Relations* (Philadelphia: Bureau of Municipal Research of Philadelphia, 1947), 32-40.

10. Minutes of October 31, 1950 Hearing, Records of the Charter Commission.

11. Charles Abrams, *Forbidden Neighbors* (New York: Harper and Brothers, 1955), 263-64; Luigi Laurenti, *Property Values and Race: Studies in Seven Cities* (Berkeley: University of California Press, 1960), 9-26.

12. Alfred Hassler, "The Arrows Are Coming," *Fellowship* 19, no. 6 (June 1953): 10-17; Newsletter, February 1953, (Publications) Records of Fellowship House.

13. "Units for Unity" brochure, 1951, (Programs) Records of Fellowship House.

14. "A PRIMER ON HOUSING," 1953, (Programs) Records of Fellowship House.

15. *Ibid*.

16. Letter to Robert Wilson from Marjorie Penney, July 15, 1948, (Board of Directors) Records of Fellowship House; Randolph Walker, interview by author, October 1995, Philadelphia; Helen Stark Tomkins, interview by author, September 1995, Kennett Square, Pennsylvania.

17. Morris Milgram, *Good Neighborhood: The Challenge of Open Housing* (New York: W.W. Norton, 1979), 181.

18. *Ibid*., 55-56.

19. *Ibid*., 57; Hannah Lees, "Making Our Cities Fit to Live In," *The Reporter,* February 21, 1957, 33.

20. Milgram, *Good Neighborhood*, 58; Roosevelt and Virginia Barlow, interview by author, October 1995, Philadelphia.

21. Ruffin, "Friends Neighborhood Guild," in *Invisible Philadelphia*, 449-50.

22. Conference of Organizations on Human Rights, May 9, 1951, program, (Committees) Records of the Fellowship Commission.

23. *Ibid*.; letter from Dorothy S. Montgomery to Maurice Fagan, June 21, 1951, Records of the Philadelphia Housing Association.

24. Conference of Organizations on Human Rights, May 9, 1951, program, (Committees) Records of the Fellowship Commission.

25. Letter from William Jeanes to the Philadelphia Housing Authority, June 27, 1952, Records of the Philadelphia Housing Association.

26. Manning Marable, *Race, Rebellion, and Reform.*

27. Letter from Reverend William Gray Jr., November 23, 1951, Records of the Philadelphia Housing Association.

28. Marvin Bressler, "The Myers Case: An Instance of Successful Racial Invasion," *Social Problems* 8 (Fall 1990): 127.

29. Letter from Reverend William Gray Jr., November 23, 1951, Records of the Philadelphia Housing Association; Minutes of May 6, 1952 Meeting of the Committee on Democracy in Housing, (Committees) Records of the Fellowship Commission.

30. Minutes of the March 17, 1952 Meeting, (Board of Commissioners) Records of the Fellowship Commission.

31. Minutes of May 6, 1952 Meeting of the Committee on Democracy in Housing, (Committees) Records of the Fellowship Commission. Also see Matthew Delmont, *The Nicest Kids in Town: American Bandstand, Rock 'N' Roll, and the Struggle for Civil Rights in 1950s Philadelphia* (Berkeley: University of California Press, 2012).

32. Petshek, *The Challenge of Urban Reform;* Memo to Dorothy Schoell Montgomery, January 14, 1954, Records of the Philadelphia Housing Association.

33. Minutes of the October 2, 1952 Meeting (Executive Committee); Minutes of the November 18, 1957 Meeting, (Board of Commissioners) Records of the Fellowship Commission.

34. Minutes of the February 19, 1953 Meeting, (Executive Committee) Records of the Fellowship Commission.

35. "Amended Code Awaits Passage," *Issues* (June-July 1954): 1.

36. "Housing Credo," September 21, 1954, Committee on Democracy in Housing, (Fellowship Commission) Records of the Philadelphia Housing Association.

37. *Ibid.*

38. *Ibid.*

39. Minutes of October 4, 1954 Meeting, (Executive Committee) Records of the Fellowship Commission.

40. *Ibid.*

41. Willis, *Cecil's City,* 83–84; Marjorie Penney Paschkis, interview by Rosa King Zimmerman, July 20, 1976, transcript, West Chester University Oral History Program, (History) Records of Fellowship House.

42. Hannah Lees, "How Philadelphia Stopped a Race Riot," *Greater Philadelphia Magazine* (November 1955): 21; Willis, *Cecil's City,* 83.

43. Roosevelt and Virginia Barlow, interview by author, October 1995, Philadelphia; Lees, "How Philadelphia Stopped a Race Riot," 21–22.

44. *Ibid.,* 22.

45. Arnold Hirsch, "Massive Resistance in the Urban North: Trumbull Park, Chicago, 1953–1966," *Journal of American History* 82, no. 2 (September 1995): 522–36. For a

more comprehensive perspective of the postwar racial situation in Chicago, see Hirsch, *Making the Second Ghetto*.

46. Petshek, *The Challenge of Urban Reform*, 154–57; Reichley, *The Art of Government*, 17–23; Memo for Dorothy Schoell Montgomery, January 14, 1954, Records of the Philadelphia Housing Association; Countryman, *Up South*, 68–79.

47. Petshek, *The Challenge of Urban Reform*, 89, 142–44; letter from Dorothy Schoell Montgomery to Eustace Gay, February 15, 1954, Records of the Philadelphia Housing Association; "Statement on Public Housing Site Selection," April 1956, (Committees) Records of the Fellowship Commission.

48. Petshek, *The Challenge of Urban Reform*, 156; John Bauman, *Public Housing, Race, and Renewal* (Philadelphia: Temple University Press, 1987), 163–65; Speech by William Rafsky, delivered at the Annual Meeting of the National Association of Inter-Group Relations Officials, November 29, 1956, Records of the Philadelphia Housing Association.

49. Bauman, *Public Housing, Race, and Renewal*, 163; letter from Mrs. Jane Thorp to Reverend William Gray Jr., October 12, 1956, Records of the Philadelphia Housing Association.

50. Minutes of the February 24, 1955 Meeting, (CEHO) Records of the Fellowship Commission.

51. Petshek, *The Challenge of Urban Reform*, 158; Memo from Dorothy Schoell Montgomery, June 17, 1958, and letter from Jefferson Fordham and Richard Brown to Kenneth Smith, Records of the Philadelphia Housing Association.

52. Annual Report, January 21, 1957, (Board of Commissioners) Records of the Fellowship Commission.

53. Memo from Reverend William Gray Jr., February 26, 1958, and letter to Reverend Marshall Shepard Sr. from Charles Shorter, August 25, 1958, Records of the Fellowship Commission.

54. Minutes of September 16, 1957 Meeting (Board of Commissioners), and Memo to Florence Kite and Dudley Pritt, November 23, 1959, Records of the Fellowship Commission.

55. *Bulletin*, March 22, 1959, 4; *Pittsburgh Courier*, August 1, 1959, 12; *Philadelphia Tribune*, October 10, 1959.

56. *Pittsburgh Courier*, September 9, 1959, 5; Memo from CEHO, October 14, 1959, (CEHO) Records of the Fellowship Commission.

57. "A Summary of the Position Taken by Various Agencies on a City Fair Housing Practices Ordinance," March 8, 1960; letter from Charles Shorter to Maurice Fagan, February 9, 1960; letter from Maurice Fagan to Charles Shorter, February 15, 1960, Records of the Fellowship Commission.

58. Memo from CEHO, September 14, 1961, Records of the Fellowship Commission.

59. *Pittsburgh Courier*, August 1, 1959, 12; George Schermer, *Desegregation: A Community Design*, 1961, Report of the Commission on Human Relations, 1; Jeanne R. Lowe, *Cities in a Race with Time: Progress and Poverty in America's Renewing Cities* (New York: Vintage, 1968), 352–55.

60. Schermer, *Desegregation: A Community Design*, 4.

61. Bauman, "The Philadelphia Housing Association," 423; Dennis Clark, *The Ghetto Game: Racial Conflicts in the City* (New York: Sheed and Ward, 1962), 98.

62. Willis, *Cecil's City*, 120.

63. *Ibid.*

64. Memo from CEHO, February 27, 1964, Records of the Philadelphia Housing Association.

65. Memo from CEHO, February 18, 1964, Records of the Philadelphia Housing Association.

66. Bauman, *Public Housing, Race, and Renewal*, 189.

67. *Ibid.*, 198; Press Release, November 9, 1964, Records of the Fellowship Commission.

68. Cushing Dolbeare, telephone interview by author, September 1997, Washington, D.C.

69. Bauman, *Public Housing, Race, and Renewal*; Memo from CEHO, November 18, 1966, Records of the Philadelphia Housing Association.

70. Dolbeare, telephone interview by author.

71. Memo from CEHO, November 18, 1966, and letter to Mayor James Tate from Nathan Edelstein and Albert Letson, December 21, 1966, Records of the Philadelphia Housing Association.

72. Dolbeare, telephone interview by author; Michael Gillette, *Launching the War on Poverty: An Oral History* (New York: Twayne, 1996), xix, 199–200.

73. Gillette, *Launching the War on Poverty*, 199–200; Carolyn Teich Adams, "Philadelphia: The Private City in the Post-Industrial Era," in Richard M. Bernard, ed., *Snowbelt Cities: Metropolitan Politics in the Northeast and Midwest since World War II* (Bloomington: Indiana University Press, 1990), 214–15.

74. Minutes of October 17, 1967 CEHO Meeting, (Committees) Records of the Fellowship Commission; Proceedings from YWCA Housing Forum, March 29, 1967; and Memo from CEHO, February 18, 1964; Records of the Philadelphia Housing Association.

75. *Report to the Community,* September-October 1967, vol. 18, no. 5. Goode became Philadelphia's first black mayor in 1984.

76. Memo from Cushing Dolbeare, January 18, 1966, Records of the Fellowship Commission.

77. *Bulletin*, October 4, 8, 29, 1966; March 29, 1967; and Newsletter, October 1966, Records of Fellowship House.

78. "Fellowship Commission's Council for Equal Housing Opportunities Resigns As City's Advisory Committee on Minority Housing," press release, June 6, 1967, Records of the Fellowship Commission; Memo from CEHO, July 2, 1967, Records of the Philadelphia Housing Association.

79. *Report to the Community,* vol. 18, no. 5 (April-May 1967): 1; *Report to the Community,* vol. 18, no. 5 (September-October 1967): 1, Records of the Fellowship Commission.

80. Dolbeare, telephone interview by author; Bauman, *Public Housing, Race, and Renewal*, 196; *Bulletin*, February 3, April 7, October 10, November 1967.

81. Memo from Cushing Dolbeare and Maurice Fagan, January 1968, Records of the Philadelphia Housing Association.

82. *Ibid.*; W. Dennis Keating, *The Suburban Racial Dilemma: Housing and Neighborhoods* (Philadelphia: Temple University Press, 1994), 8–13.

83. Dolbeare, telephone interview by author; Bauman, *Public Housing, Race, and Renewal*, 199.

84. *Ibid.*

85. *Ibid.*, 206.

86. *Ibid.*, 200; "Statement on Public Housing Sites Presented to the Philadelphia Housing Authority," December 1968, Records of the Philadelphia Housing Association; Minutes of May 13, 1969 Meeting, (Board of Commissioners) Records of the Fellowship Commission.

87. *Ibid.*, 202.

CHAPTER 6

1. Du Bois, *The Philadelphia Negro*, 9–108, 136–46, 179–84; Theodore Hershberg, "Free Blacks in Ante-Bellum Philadelphia," in Allen Davis and Mark Haller, eds., *The Peoples of Philadelphia: A History of Ethnic Groups and Lower Class Life, 1790–1940* (Philadelphia: Temple University Press, 1973), 111–35.

2. Du Bois, *The Philadelphia Negro*, 97–101; Sterling Spero and Abram Harris, *The Black Worker: The Negro and the Labor Movement* (New York: Columbia University Press, 1931), 87–115; Marc Karson and Ronald Radosh, "The American Federation of Labor and the Negro Worker, 1894–1949," in Julius Jacobson, ed., *The Negro and the American Labor Movement* (Garden City, NY: Anchor, 1968), 155–57.

3. Spero and Harris, *The Black Worker*, 149–66; Grossman, *Land of Hope*, 33–37, 41–52; Neil Fligstein, *Going North: Migration of Blacks and Whites from the South, 1900–1950* (New York: Academic Press, 1981), 127–31.

4. Charles H. Wesley, *Negro Labor in the United States 1850–1925: A Study in American Economic History* (1927; reprint, New York: Russell and Russell, 1967), 282–97; Hardy, "Race and Opportunity," 204–7.

5. Banner-Haley, *To Do Good and to Do Well*, 10–11. For an in-depth examination of the role of the IWW on the Philadelphia docks, see Peter Cole, *Wobblies on the Waterfront: Interracial Unionism in Progressive Era Philadelphia* (Champaign: University of Illinois Press, 2007).

6. Banner-Haley, *To Do Good and to Do Well*, 11–12; Spero and Abrams, *The Black Worker*, 333.

7. Banner-Haley, *To Do Good and to Do Well*, 12; Spero and Adams, *The Black Worker*, 334–36.

8. Nelson, "Race and Class Consciousness of Philadelphia Negroes"; Bauman, *Public Housing, Race, and Renewal*, 68.

9. August Meier and Elliott Rudwick, "Attitudes of Negro Leaders Toward the American Labor Movement from the Civil War to World War I," in Jacobson, *The Negro and the American Labor Movement*, 43–46.

10. Minutes of the January 18, 1926 Meeting, Records of the Committee on Race Relations.

11. Minutes of the December 11, 1928 and December 17, 1929 Meetings, Records of the Committee on Race Relations.

12. "Findings From the Pendle Hill Conference of Young Church People," May 22-23, 1931, Records of the Committee on Race Relations.

13. Nelson, "Race and Class Consciousness," 61; also see Roger Biles, *A New Deal for the American People* (DeKalb, IL: Northern Illinois University Press, 1990).

14. *Ibid.*, 97; and Banner-Haley, *To Do Good and to Do Well*, 56.

15. Banner-Haley, *To Do Good and to Do Well*, 56-58. Also see Countryman, *Up South*, 21-28.

16. Minutes of the April 21, 1936 and October 19, 1937 Meetings, Records of the Committee on Race Relations.

17. Keith Griffler, *What Price Alliance?: Black Radicals Confront White Labor, 1918-1938* (New York: Garland, 1995), 139-44; John B. Kirby, *Black Americans in the Roosevelt Era: Liberalism and Race* (Knoxville: University of Tennessee Press, 1980), 164-70.

18. Minutes of the December 2, 1938 and June 20, 1939 Meetings, Records of the Committee on Race Relations.

19. Minutes of the December 19, 1939 Meeting, Records of the Committee on Race Relations.

20. Banner-Haley, *To Do Good and to Do Well*, 169; and Gladys L. Palmer, *Philadelphia Workers in a Changing Economy* (Philadelphia, 1944), Appendix Table 15, 163, and Appendix Table 16, 164.

21. Charles S. Johnson, *To Stem This Tide: A Survey of Racial Tension Areas in the United States* (New York: AMS Press, 1943), 114-16; Adam Garfinkle, *When Negroes March: The March on Washington Movement in the Organizational Policies for FEPC* (Glencoe, IL: Free Press, 1959), 32-50.

22. Genna Rae MacNeil, *Groundwork: Charles Hamilton Houston and the Struggle for Civil Rights* (Philadelphia: University of Pennsylvania, 1983), 163-67; letter from Marjorie Penney to Charles Hamilton Houston, October 18, 1944, (Correspondence) Records of Fellowship House.

23. "Philadelphia Fellowship Commission," report and Minutes of the October 12, 1942 Meeting, (Board of Commissioners) Records of the Fellowship Commission; "Units for Unity," schedule, 1944, (Units for Unity) Records of Fellowship House.

24. Council on Equal Job Opportunity (CEJO), brochure, 1946, (CEJO) Records of the Fellowship Commission.

25. Allen M. Winkler, "The Philadelphia Transit Strike of 1944," *Journal of American History* 59 (1972): 76-77; Philadelphia Report on PTC Strike, August 1-6, 1944, (Board of Commissioners) Records of the Fellowship Commission.

26. *Ibid.*, 80-81; and Fellowship House Newsletter, August 1944, (Publications) Records of Fellowship House.

27. *Ibid.*, 82; and Fellowship House Newsletter, August 1944, (Publications) Records of Fellowship House.

28. Dear Friend Letter, August 15, 1944, (Programs) Records of the Fellowship Commission.

158   Notes

29. Johnson, *To Stem This Tide*, 116–17; Fellowship House Newsletter, August 1944, Records of Fellowship House. For an excellent analysis of the Philadelphia Transit Strike, see James Wolfinger, *Philadelphia Divided: Race and Politics in the City of Brotherly Love* (Chapel Hill: University of North Carolina Press, 2007), 142–73.

30. Winkler, "The Philadelphia Transit Strike," 86–89; Minutes of the August 8, 1944 Meeting, Records of the Fellowship Commission.

31. Minutes of the August 8, 1944 Meeting, Records of Fellowship Commission; interview with Marjorie Penney.

32. Minutes of Meeting, Records of the Fellowship Commission and Records of Fellowship House; Willis, *Cecil's City*, 57–58.

33. W. Brooke Graves, *Fair Employment Practice Legislation in the United States*, Federal-State-Municipal Public Affairs Bulletin No. 93 (Washington: Library of Congress, 1951), 87–98.

34. Reichley, *The Art of Government*, 7–12; Minutes of November 14, 1947 Meeting, (CEJO) Records of the Fellowship Commission.

35. Minutes of October 28, 1948 Meeting, (CEJO) Records of the Fellowship Commission.

36. *Fair Employment Practice Ordinance*, Approved March 12, 1948, Amended March 29, 1950, Philadelphia City Code.

37. Willis, *Cecil's City*, 66; Graves, *Fair Employment Practice Legislation*, 104.

38. Graves, *Fair Employment Practice Legislation*, 104–5.

39. Minutes of April 13, 1950 Meeting, (CEJO) Records of the Fellowship Commission.

40. *Report to the Community*, October 1952, Records of the Fellowship Commission.

41. Minutes of August 21, 1952 Meeting of Executive Committee of State Council for a Pennsylvania FEPC, (CEJO) Records of the Fellowship Commission; Robert J. O'Donnell, "Pennsylvania's Self-Survey," reprinted from April 1953 issue of *Interracial Review*, (CEJO) Records of the Fellowship Commission; *Philadelphia Tribune*, June 3, 1952; Minutes of April 17, 1953 Meeting of Executive Committee of State Council for a Pennsylvania FEPC, (CEJO) Records of the Fellowship Commission.

42. Minutes of December 20, 1954 Meeting, (Board of Commissioners) Records of the Fellowship Commission; and Press Release, October 27, 1954, (CEJO) Records of the Fellowship Commission; telegram from Lloyd H. Wood, 1954, (CEJO) Records of the Fellowship Commission.

43. Minutes of May 16, 1955 Meeting, (Board of Commissioners) Records of the Fellowship Commission; "Big News from CEJO," broadside, July 1955, (CEJO) Records of the Fellowship Commission; *Philadelphia Inquirer*, June 19, 1955.

44. Letter from Governor George M. Leader to Charles Shorter, November 29, 1955; *Fair Employment: An Abstract of the Pennsylvania Fair Employment Practice Law*, Approved October 27, 1955, Amended March 28, 1956.

45. Jeanne R. Lowe, *Cities in a Race with Time: Progress and Poverty in America's Renewing Cities* (New York: Vintage, 1968), 360–61.

46. *Ibid.*; Adams et al., *Philadelphia*, 30–39.

47. Patricia Cooper, "The Limits of Persuasion: Race Reformers and the Department Store Campaign in Philadelphia, 1945–1948," *Pennsylvania Magazine of History and Biography* 126, no. 2, 97–112.

48. Willis, *Cecil's City*, 65–66; letter from Irving Glass to Frank Loescher, October 23, 1948, (CEJO) Records of the Fellowship Commission; Miller, "The Fellowship Commission," 612–14.

49. Minutes of the October 27 and December 20, 1955 Meetings, (CEJO) Records of the Fellowship Commission.

50. Minutes of the March 19, 1957 Meeting, (CEJO) Records of the Fellowship Commission.

51. Clark, *The Ghetto Game*, 230–32.

52. Minutes of the November 30, 1959 Meeting, (CEJO) Records of the Fellowship Commission.

53. *Ibid.*; Willis, *Cecil's City*, 85–88.

54. Announcement of Tom Mboya's Visit 1959; (House Party) and Leadership Training Program, October-December 1958, brochure, (Programs) Records of Fellowship House.

55. Memo from C. W. Maxwell, February 19, 1960, (CEJO) Records of the Fellowship Commission.

56. Memo for William Gray, June 29, 1961, (CEJO) Records of the Fellowship Commission.

57. *Ibid.*

58. Minutes of the December 21, 1961 Meeting, (CEJO) Records of the Fellowship Commission.

59. Minutes of the October 31, 1962 Meeting; and Memos for Thomas McBride, February 19, 1960, May 9 and October 11, 1961, (CEJO) Records of the Fellowship Commission.

60. Willis, *Cecil's City*, 85–88.

61. *Ibid.*, 96; "The Philadelphia Branch in Retrospect for the Past Three and a Half Years," unpublished report, 1956 Records of the NAACP, Philadelphia Branch.

62. Minutes of April 2, 1964 Meeting, (CEJO) Records of the Fellowship Commission.

63. Minutes of October 31, 1962 Meeting, (CEJO) Records of the Fellowship Commission.

64. Minutes of April 13, 1962 Meeting, (CEJO) Records of the Fellowship Commission. For an excellent analysis of the relationship between black clergy and workers, see Robert Gregg, *Sparks from the Anvil of Oppression* (Philadelphia: Temple University Press, 1990).

65. Minutes of June 3, 1965 Meeting, (CEJO) Records of the Fellowship Commission.

66. Minutes of September 9, 1965 Meeting, (CEJO) Records of the Fellowship Commission.

67. Memo from Thacher Longstreth and Samuel Weinberg, November 28, 1966, (CEJO) Records of the Fellowship Commission.

68. For a thorough discussion of the Philadelphia Plan, see David Hamilton Golland, *Constructing Affirmative Action* (Lexington: University of Kentucky Press, 2011).

69. *Report to the Community*, vol. 19, no. 1, September-October 1967, Records of the Fellowship Commission; Guian McKee, *The Problem of Jobs: Liberalism, Race, and Deindustrialization in Philadelphia* (Chicago: University of Chicago Press, 2008), 113–81.

70. *Report to the Community,* vol. 19, no. 1, September-October 1967, Records of the Fellowship Commission.

71. Aura Yores, interview by author, September 1997, Philadelphia.

72. Marjorie Penney, "The Freedom Budget: A Remedy for Hopelessness," *Friends Journal,* March 1968; and Susan Rosenbloom, interview by author, September 1997, Philadelphia.

EPILOGUE

1. Letter from Samuel Amos Brackeen to Gladys Rawlins, September 6, 1943, (House Party) Records of Fellowship House.

2. "Fellowship Commission Salute," editorial, *Philadelphia Bulletin,* October 3, 1966.

Bibliography

BOOKS

Abrams, Charles. *Forbidden Neighbors*. New York: Harper Brothers, 1955.
Adams, Carolyn, et al., eds. *Philadelphia: Neighborhoods, Division, and Conflict in a Post-Industrial City*. Philadelphia: Temple University Press, 1991.
Baker, Paul E. *Negro-White Adjustment: An Investigation and Analysis of Methods in the Interracial Movement in the United States*. New York: Association Press, 1932.
Banner-Haley, Charles Pete. *To Do Good and to Do Well: Middle Class Blacks During the Depression in Philadelphia, 1929-1941*. New York: Garland, 1993.
Barnett, Ida Wells. *Crusade for Justice: The Autobiography of Ida Wells Barnett*. Chicago: University of Chicago, 1973.
Bauman, John. *Public Housing, Race, and Renewal: Urban Planning in Philadelphia, 1920-1974*. Philadelphia: Temple University, 1987.
Bernstein, Shana. *Bridges of Reform: Interracial Civil Rights Activism in Twentieth-Century Los Angeles*. Oxford: Oxford University Press, 2011.
Blaustein, Albert P. *Civil Rights U.S.A.: Public Schools, Cities in the North and West, 1962*. United States Commission on Civil Rights. New York: Greenwood Press, 1962.
Blockson, Charles. *The Underground Railroad*. New York: Prentice Hall, 1987.
Brown-Nagin, Tomiko. *Courage to Dissent: Atlanta and the Long History of the Civil Rights Movement*. Oxford: Oxford University Press, 2011.
Bunche, Ralph J. *Selected Speeches and Writings*. Ann Arbor: University of Michigan Press, 1995.
Canton, David. *Raymond Pace Alexander: A New Negro Lawyer Fights for Civil Rights in Philadelphia*. Jackson: University Press of Mississippi, 2010.
Capeci, Dominic. *Race Relations in Wartime Detroit: The Sojourner Truth Housing Controversy of 1942*. Ann Arbor: University of Michigan Press, 1989.
Chen, Anthony S. *The Fifth Freedom: Jobs, Politics, and Civil Rights in the United States*. Princeton: Princeton University Press, 2009.
Clark, Dennis. *The Ghetto Game: Racial Conflicts in the City*. New York: Sheed and Ward, 1962.
Countryman, Matthew. *Up South: Civil Rights and Black Power in Philadelphia*. Philadelphia: University of Pennsylvania, 2006.
Darden, Joe, et al., eds. *Detroit: Race and Uneven Development*. Philadelphia: Temple University Press, 1987.
Delmont, Matthew F. *The Nicest Kids in Town: American Bandstand, Rock 'N' Roll, and the Struggle for Civil Rights in 1950s Philadelphia*. Berkeley: University of California Press, 2012.
Dittmer, John. *Black Georgia in the Progressive Era, 1900-1920*. Urbana: University of Illinois Press, 1977.

Douglas, Davison M. *Jim Crow Moves North: The Battle over Northern School Segregation, 1865–1954*. Cambridge: Cambridge University Press, 2005.

Du Bois, William Edward Burghardt. *The Philadelphia Negro*. 1899; reprint, Philadelphia: University of Pennsylvania, 1996.

Findlay, James F. *Church People in the Struggle: The National Council of Churches and the Black Freedom Struggle, 1950–1970*. Oxford: Oxford University Press, 1993.

Fligstein, Neil. *Going North: Migration of Blacks and Whites from the South, 1900–1950*. New York: Academic Press, 1981.

Franklin, Vincent P. *The Education of Black Philadelphia*. Philadelphia: University of Pennsylvania Press, 1979.

Friedman, Murray. *Jewish Life in Philadelphia, 1830–1940*. Philadelphia: Privately printed, 1983.

Garfinkle, Adam. *When Negroes March: The March on Washington Movement and the Organizational Policies for FEPC*. Glencoe, IL: Free Press, 1959.

Gillette, Michael. *Launching the War on Poverty: An Oral History*. New York: Twayne, 1996.

Gorrell, Donald K. *The Age of Social Responsibility: The Social Gospel in the Progressive Era, 1900–1920*. Macon: Mercer University Press, 1988.

Griffler, Keith. *What Price Alliance? Black Radicals Confront White Labor, 1918–1938*. New York: Garland, 1995.

Grigsby, William, and Chester Rapkin. *The Demand for Housing in Racially Mixed Areas: A Philadelphia Study*. Los Angeles: University of California Press, 1960.

Grossman, James. *Chicago, Black Southerners, and the Great Migration*. Chicago: University of Chicago Press, 1989.

Hall, Jacqueline Dowd. *Revolt Against Chivalry: Jesse Daniel Ames and the Women's Campaign Against Lynching*. New York: Columbia University Press, 1979.

Haynes, George Edmund. *The Trend of the Races*. New York: Council of Women for Home Missions, 1922.

Hecht, James L. *Because It Is Right: Integration in Housing*. Boston: Little, Brown, 1970.

Hershberg, Theodore. *Philadelphia: Work, Space, Family, and Group Experience in the Nineteenth Century*. New York: Oxford University Press, 1981.

Hirsch, Arnold. *Making the Second Ghetto: Race and Housing, 1940–1960*. New York: Cambridge University Press, 1983.

Horne, Gerald. *Benjamin Davis and the Communist Party*. New York: University of Delaware Press, 1994.

———. *Red and Black: W. E. B. Du Bois and the Afro-American Response to the Cold War, 1944–1963*. Albany: State University of New York Press, 1986.

Jenkins, Philip. *Hoods and Shirts: The Extreme Right in Pennsylvania, 1925–1950*. Chapel Hill: University of North Carolina Press, 1997.

Joseph, Peniel E. *Waiting for the Midnight Hour: A Narrative History of Black Power in America*. New York: Henry Holt, 2006.

Johnson, Charles. *To Stem This Tide: A Survey of Racial Tension in the United States*. New York: AMS Press, 1943.

Jones, Mary Hoxie. *Swords into Plowshares: An Account of the American Friends Service Committee, 1917–1937*. New York: Macmillan, 1937.

Keating, W. Dennis. *The Suburban Racial Dilemma: Housing and Neighborhoods*. Philadelphia: Temple University Press, 1994.

Kelley, Robin D. G. *Hammer and Hoe: Alabama Communists During the Great Depression*. Chapel Hill: University of North Carolina Press, 1990.

Kellogg, Charles Flint. *NAACP: A History of the National Association for the Advancement of Colored People. Vol. I: 1909–1920*. Baltimore: Johns Hopkins University Press, 1967.

King, Martin Luther. *Stride Toward Freedom: The Montgomery Story*. New York: Harper and Row, 1958.

Kirby, John B. *Black Americans in the Roosevelt Era: Liberalism and Race*. Knoxville: University of Tennessee Press, 1990.

Lang, Clarence. *Grassroots at the Gateway: Class Politics and Black Freedom Struggle in St. Louis, 1936–1975*. Ann Arbor: University of Michigan Press, 2009.

Lane, Roger. *Thomas Dorsey's Philadelphia and Ours: On the Past And Future of the Black City in America*. New York: Oxford University Press, 1991.

Laurenti, Luigi. *Property Values and Race: Studies in Seven Cities*. Berkeley: University of California Press, 1960.

Levenstein, Lisa. *A Movement Without Marches: African American Women and the Politics of Poverty in Postwar Philadelphia*. Chapel Hill: University of North Carolina Press, 2009.

Light, Paul C. *Baby Boomers*. New York: W. W. Norton, 1988.

Lowe, Jeanne R. *Cities in a Race with Time: Progress and Poverty in America's Renewing Cities*. New York: Vintage, 1968.

Luker, Ralph. *The Social Gospel in Black and White: American Social Reform*. Chapel Hill: University of North Carolina Press, 1991.

MacNeil, Genna Rae. *Groundwork: Charles Hamilton Houston and the Struggle for Civil Rights*. Philadelphia: University of Pennsylvania Press, 1979.

McKee, Guian. *The Problem of Jobs: Liberalism, Race, and Deindustrialization in Philadelphia*. Chicago: University of Chicago Press, 2008.

McPherson, James. *The Abolitionist Legacy: From Reconstruction to the NAACP*. Princeton: Princeton University Press, 1975.

Milgram, Morris. *Good Neighborhood: The Challenge of Open Housing*. New York: W.W. Norton, 1979.

Moore, Jesse Thomas Jr. *A Search for Equality. The National Urban League, 1910–1961*. University Park: The Pennsylvania State University Press, 1981.

Moore, John. *Friends in the Delaware Valley: Philadelphia Yearly Meeting, 1681-1981*. Haverford, Pa: Friends Historical Association, 1981.

Morris, Aldon. *The Origins of the Civil Rights Movement: Black Communities Organizing for Change*. New York: Free Press, 1989.

O'Reilly, Kenneth. *Racial Matters: The FBI's Secret File on Black America, 1960–1972*. New York: Free Press, 1989.

Petshek, Kirk. *The Challenge of Urban Reform: Policies and Programs in Philadelphia*. Philadelphia: University of Pennsylvania Press, 1973.

Ralph, James, Jr. *Northern Protest: Martin Luther King, Chicago, and Civil Rights*. Cambridge: Harvard University Press, 1988.

Reichley, James. *The Art of Government: Reform and Organization Politics in Philadelphia*. New York: Praeger Press, 1965.

Resnik, Henry S. *Turning on the System: War in the Philadelphia Public Schools*. New York: Random House, 1970.

Salem, Dorothy. *To Better Our World: Black Women in Organized Reform, 1890–1920*. New York: Carlson, 1990.

Senechal, Roberta. *Sociogenesis of a Race Riot: Springfield, Illinois in 1908*. Chicago: University of Illinois, 1990.

Sosna, Morton. *In Search of the Silent South*. New York: Columbia University Press, 1977.

Southern, David W. *Gunnar Myrdal and Black-White Relations: The Use and Abuse of an American Dilemma, 1944–1969*. Baton Rouge: Louisiana State University Press, 1987.

Spero, Sterling, and Abram Harris. *The Negro and the Labor Movement*. New York: Columbia University Press, 1931.

Sugrue, Thomas. *The Origins of the Urban Crisis: Race and Inequality in Postwar Detroit*. Princeton: Princeton University Press, 1996.

Sullivan, Patricia. *Days of Hope: Race and Democracy in the New Deal Era*. Chapel Hill: University of North Carolina Press, 1996.

Trotter, Joe, and Jared Day. *Race and Renaissance: African Americans in Pittsburgh since World War II*. Pittsburgh: University of Pittsburgh Press, 2010.

Tuttle, William. *Race Riot: Chicago in the Red Summer of 1919*. New York: Atheneum, 1970.

Weaver, Robert C. *Negro Labor: A National Problem*. New York: Harcourt, Brace, 1946.

Weiss, Nancy. *Farewell to the Party of Lincoln: Black Politics in the Age of FDR*. Princeton: Princeton University Press, 1987.

Wesley, Charles H. *Negro Labor in the United States 1850–1925: A Study in American Economic History*. 1927; reprint, New York: Russell and Russell, 1967.

Wills, Arthur. *Cecil's City: A History of Blacks in Philadelphia, 1683–1979*. New York: Carlton, 1990.

Winch, Julie. *Philadelphia's Black Elite, Activism, Accommodation, and the Struggle for Autonomy, 1787–1848*. Philadelphia: Temple University Press, 1988.

Wolfinger, James. *Philadelphia Divided: Race and Politics in the City of Brotherly Love*. Chapel Hill: University of North Carolina Press, 2007.

Woofter, Thomas J. *Negro Problems in the Cities*. New York: Doubleday, Doran, 1928.

Wright, Gwendolyn. *Building the Dream: A Social History of Housing in America*. Cambridge: MIT Press, 1983.

Zanagrando, Robert L. *The NAACP Crusade Against Lynching, 1909–1950*. Philadelphia: Temple University Press, 1980.

Zepp, Ira G. *The Social Vision of Martin Luther King*. New York: Carlson Publishing, 1989.

OTHER SECONDARY SOURCES (WORKS IN EDITED COLLECTIONS)

Abernethy, Lloyd M. "Political Parties in Philadelphia." In *Invisible Philadelphia: Community through Voluntary Organizations*, ed. Jean Barth Toll and Mildred S. Gillam, 585–90. Philadelphia: Atwater Kent Museum, 1995.

Adams, Carolyn. "Philadelphia: The Private City in the Post-Industrial Era." in *Snowbelt Cities: Metropolitan Politics in the Northeast and Midwest since World War II*, ed. Richard Bernard, 210–20. Bloomington: Indiana University Press, 1990.

Arnold, Stanley. "The National Association for the Advancement of Colored People in Philadelphia." In *Invisible Philadelphia*, 45–50.

Bauman, John. "Disinfecting the Industrial City: The Philadelphia Housing Commission and Scientific Efficiency, 1906–1916." In *The Age of Reform: New Perspectives on the Progressive Era*, ed. Michael H. Ebner and Eugene M. Tobin, 117–35. Port Washington, NY: Kennikat Press, 1977.

———. "Philadelphia Housing Association of the Delaware Valley." In *Invisible Philadelphia*, 420–24.

Ekstrom, Charles A. "The Electoral Politics of Reform and Machine: The Political Behavior of Philadelphia's Black Wards, 1943–1969." In *Black Politics in Philadelphia*, ed. Miriam Ershkowitz and Roger Zikmund, 89–96. Philadelphia: Temple University Press, 1973.

Friedman, Murray, and Carolyn Beck. "An Ambivalent Alliance." In *Jewish Life in Philadelphia, 1945–1985*, ed. Murray Friedman, 50–58. Ardmore, PA: Seth Press, 1986.

Floyd, Homer C. "School Desegregation Can Succeed: The Pennsylvania Experience." In *New Perspectives on School Integration*, ed. Murray Friedman, Roger Meltzer, and Charles Miller, 32–41. Philadelphia: Fortress, 1979.

Gerteis, Louis. "Mortality and Utility in the Abolition Movement." In *Abolition Movement: Means, Ends, and Motivations*, ed. Lawrence Goodheart and Hugh Hawkins, 119–27. Lexington, MA: D. C. Heath, 1995.

Hershberg, Theodore. "Free Blacks in Ante-Bellum Philadelphia." In *The Peoples of Philadelphia: A History of Ethnic Groups and Lower Class Life, 1790–1940*, ed. Allen Davis and Mark Haller, 111–35. Philadelphia: Temple University Press, 1973.

Johnson, Julie. "The Octavia Hill Association." In *Invisible Philadelphia*, 416–20.

Karson, Marc, and Ronald Radosh. "The American Federation of Labor and the Negro Worker, 1894–1949." In *The Negro and the American Labor Movement*, ed. Julius Jacobson, 140–68. Garden City, NY: Anchor, 1968.

Kirby, John. "Race, Class, and Politics: Ralph Bunche and Black Protest." In *Ralph Bunche: The Man and His Times*, ed. Benjamin Rivlin, 28–39. New York: Homes and Meier, 1990.

Kusmer, Kenneth L. "The Black Urban Experience in American History." In *The State of Afro-American History*, ed. Darlene Clark Hine, 104–22. Baton Rouge: Louisiana State University Press, 1989.

Lermack, Paul. "Cecil Moore and the Philadelphia Branch of the National Association for the Advancement of Colored People: The Politics of Negro Pressure Organization." in *Black Politics in Philadelphia*, 151.

Meier, August, and Elliott Rudwick. "Attitudes of Negro Leaders Toward the American Labor Movement from the Civil War to World War I." In *The Negro and the American Labor Movement*, 32–48.

Miller, Fredric. "A History of the Fellowship Commission." In *Invisible Philadelphia*, 610–14.

———. David Clow and Graham Finney. "Physical Planning in Philadelphia." In *Invisible Philadelphia*, 24–27.

Naison, Mark. "From Eviction Resistance to Rent Control: Tenant Activism in the Great Depression." In *Tenant Movements in New York City, 1904–1984*, ed. Ronald Lawson, 94–120. New Brunswick: Rutgers University Press, 1986.

Ruffin, Carole W. "Friends Neighborhood Guild." In *Invisible Philadelphia*, 448–50.

Schmandt, Raymond. "Catholic Organizations in Philadelphia." In *Invisible Philadelphia*, 230–34.

Tomkins, Helen. "History of Fellowship Farm." In *Invisible Philadelphia*, 606–12.

ARTICLES

Bacon, Margaret Hope. "The White Noose of the Suburbs." *Progressive* 24 (October 1960): 37–38.

Bauman, John F. "Black Slums/Black Projects: The New Deal and Negro Housing in Philadelphia." *Pennsylvania History* 41 (1974): 311–38.

Bressler, Marvin. "The Myers Case: An Instance of Successful Racial Invasion." *Social Problems* 8 (1960): 122–30.

Carlson, Avis. "Philadelphia's Stitch in Time." *Survey Graphic* 33, no. 7 (July 1944): 324–25.

Cooper, Patricia. "The Limits of Persuasion: Race Reformers and the Department Store Campaign in Philadelphia, 1945–1948." *Pennsylvania Magazine of History and Biography* 126, no. 2 (2002): 97–112.

Franklin, Vincent P. "The Philadelphia Race Riot of 1918." *Pennsylvania Magazine of History and Biography* 99, no. 1 (1975): 33.

Grier, Eunice, and George Grier. "Market Characteristics in Interracial Communities." *Journal of Social Issues* 13 (Fall 1957): 50–67.

Hirsch, Arnold. "Massive Resistance in the Urban North: Trumbull Park, Chicago, 1953–1966." *Journal of American History* 82, no. 2: 522–36.

"I'm the Goddamn Boss." *Time* 84 (September 11, 1964): 24–25.

Kellogg, Peter. "Civil Rights Consciousness in the 1940s." *The Historian* 22, no. 1 (1979).

Lees, Hannah. "How Philadelphia Stopped a Race Riot." *Greater Philadelphia Magazine* (November 1955).

———. "Making Our Cities Fit to Live In." *Reporter* (February 21, 1957): 31–35.

Manly, A. L. "Where Negroes Live in Philadelphia." *Opportunity* 11, nos. 1–5 (May 1923): 10–16.

Penney, Marjorie. "A Little Dove of Peace." *Journal of Human Relations* 5, no. 3 (1957).

Piggott, W. Benjamin. "The Problem of the Black Middle Class: Morris Milgram's Concord Park and Residential Integration in Philadelphia Postwar Suburbs." *Pennsylvania Magazine of History and Biography* 132, no. 2 (2008): 173–90.

Philips, Anne. "A History of the Struggle for School Desegregation in Philadelphia, 1955–1967." *Pennsylvania History* 42, no. 1 (2005): 49–76.
Schmidt, Edward. "A Vocation for Neighborliness: Anna McGarry's Quest for Community in Philadelphia." *US Catholic Historian* 27, no. 2 (2004): 81–97.
"The Steel Wire of Sanity." *Medford Leas Life*, April 1976.
Sutherland, John. "The Origins of Philadelphia's Octavia Hill Society: Social Reform in the Contented City." *Pennsylvania Magazine of History and Biography* 99, no. 1 (1975): 20–44.
Symposium of Negro Editors. "Communism and the Negro." *Crisis* 34 (April-May 1932): 118.
Winkler, Allen M. "The Philadelphia Transit Strike of 1944." *Journal of American History* 59, no. 1 (1972): 74–84.
"WIP Fights Race Hatred with New Segment." *Billboard*, November 3, 1945.

PUBLISHED REPORTS

Brown, G. Gordon. *Law Administration and Negro-White Relations in Philadelphia: A Study in Race Relations*. Philadelphia: Bureau of Municipal Research of Philadelphia, 1947.
Graves, W. Brooke. *Fair Employment Practice Legislation in the United States, Federal-State-Municipal Public Affairs Bulletin No. 93*. Washington: Library of Congress, 1951.
Odell, William R. *Educational Survey Report for the Philadelphia Board of Public Education*. Philadelphia: Board of Education, School District of Philadelphia, 1956.
Palmer, Gladys. *Philadelphia Workers in a Changing Economy*. Philadelphia: Privately Printed, 1944.
Schermer, George. *Desegregation: A Community Design*. Philadelphia: Report of the Commission on Human Relations, 1961.
U.S. Department of Commerce, Bureau of the Census. *Negro Population, 1790–1915*. Washington: Government Printing Office, 1918.
U.S. Department of Commerce, Bureau of the Census. *Summary of Housing*. Washington: Government Printing Office, 2003.

DISSERTATIONS

Baker, Lee. "The Role of Anthropology in the Social Construction of Race, 1896–1954." Diss., Temple University, 1994.
Droker, Allan. "The Seattle Civic Unity Committee and the Civil Rights Movement, 1944–1964." Diss., University of Washington, 1974.
Fleming, James G. "The Administration of Fair Employment Practices Programs." Diss., University of Pennsylvania, 1948.
Hardy, Charles A. "Race and Opportunity: Black Philadelphia During the Era of the Great Migration, 1916–1930." Diss., Temple University, 1989.
Heumann, Leonard Franklin. "The Definition and Analysis of Stable Racial Integration: The Case of West Mt. Airy, Philadelphia." Diss., University of Pennsylvania, 1973.

168   Bibliography

Kellogg, Peter. "Northern Liberals and Black America, 1936–1952." Diss., Northwestern University, 1970.

Leonard, Kevin Allen. "Years of Hope, Days of Fear: The Impact of World War II on Race Relations in Los Angeles." Diss., University of California, 1992.

Nelson, H. Viscount. "Race and Class Consciousness of Philadelphia Negroes with Special Emphasis on the Years Between 1927 and 1940." Diss., University of Pennsylvania, 1969.

Parham, Shirley Turpin. "A History of Black Public Education in Philadelphia, Pennsylvania, 1864 to 1914." Diss., Temple University, 1986.

Roberts, Samuel Kelton. "Crucible for a Vision: The Work of George Edmund Haynes and the Commission on Race Relations, 1922–1947." Diss., Columbia University, 1974.

LAW CODES

Pennsylvania Statute. *Fair Employment: An Abstract of the Pennsylvania Fair Employment Practice Law*, Approved October 27, 1955, Amended March 28, 1956.

Philadelphia City Statute. *Fair Employment Practice Ordinance*, Approved March 12, 1948, Amended March 29, 1950.

PRIMARY SOURCE COLLECTIONS

Archives of the City of Philadelphia
    Records of the Charter Commission
    Records of the Human Relations Commission
    Records of the Philadelphia Commission on Higher Education

Swarthmore College
    Committee on Race Relations (Philadelphia Yearly Meeting)

Temple University
    Armstrong Association (Urban League)
    Fellowship Commission
        (Includes *Report to the Community*)
    Fellowship House
    National Association for the Advancement of Colored People (Philadelphia Branch)
    Philadelphia Housing Association (Housing Association of the Delaware Valley)
        (Includes *Issues*)

NEWSPAPERS

Philadelphia Afro-American
Philadelphia Bulletin
Philadelphia Inquirer
Philadelphia Tribune
Pittsburgh Courier

AUTHOR INTERVIEWS

Roosevelt and Virginia Barlow
Mitzi Jacoby Barnes
Cushing Dolbeare
Elaine Hermann
Mohammed Latif
Gladys Rawlins
Susan Rosenbloom
Helen Stark Tomkins
Val Udell
Randolph Walker
Aura Yores

Index

abolition, 6, 8–9, 26
AFSC. *See* American Friends Service Committee
Alexander, Raymond Pace, 16–18, 27, 53, 55, 113, 120
Alexander, Sadie, 46, 51, 56
Alexander, Virginia, 18
Alexander, Will, 13, 23
American Civil Liberties Union (ACLU), 56
American Federation of Labor (AFL), 111
American Friends Service Committee (AFSC), 12, 17–18, 21, 91
Amsterdam, Gustave, 125–26
Anderson, Add, 52, 61
Anti-Defamation League, 24, 32–33, 46–47
anti-lynching, 9, 16, 18, 21, 29. *See also* lynching
anti-Semitism, 24, 30, 33, 36, 41, 47
antiwar movement, 67
Arrow program. *See* educational programs

Bacon, Edmund, 79–81
Barber, Max, 70, 115
Barlow, Roosevelt, 31, 48, 91, 97
Barlow, Virginia, 31, 48, 91
Barnes, Mitzi Jacob, 49, 60
Bauer, Catherine, 73, 87
Benedict, Ruth, 5, 36, 45
Benjamin, Mal, 133
"Better Philadelphia Exhibition," 86
Bishop, Robert, 91
black community, 7, 10, 12, 17–18, 21–22, 25, 27, 34, 42–43, 53, 61–63, 69, 72–76, 78–79, 88, 104, 107–8, 114, 119–20, 126–27, 129, 133
black elite, 10, 16, 71, 75, 114
black middle class. *See* middle class

Black Panthers, 66
black power movement, 4, 67, 110, 130
black workers, 62, 101, 107, 111–17, 123–25, 127–28
black working class. *See* working class
B'Nai B'rith, 24, 33, 43
Boas, Franz, 5, 20, 45
Bok, Curtis, 35, 82
Bok, Nellie Lee, 35, 82
Bonds, Adella, 71
Brill, Frederick, 117, 119, 121–22
Brotherhood of Sleeping Car Porters, 116
Brown v. Board of Education, 53, 135
Bryan, Helen, 16–20, 22, 23–24, 28–29, 35, 55, 73–74, 77, 90, 114–15
Bunche, Ralph, 23, 29, 75

CAP. *See* Community Action Program
capitalism, 30, 115
cartoons, 41
Catholics, 9, 19–20, 37, 41, 58, 88, 103
CCCP. *See* Citizens Council on City Planning
CCDR. *See* Citizens Council on Democratic Rights
CCT. *See* Committee on Community Tensions
CDH. *See* Committee on Democracy in Housing
CEC. *See* Citizens Emergency Committee
CEHO. *See* Committee on Equal Housing Opportunities
CEJO. *See* Council on Equal Job Opportunities
Center City. *See* Philadelphia, Pennsylvania
CFCC. *See* Committee for a Free City College
Childhood Education Project, 135

172 Index

Chisholm, Terry, 61, 127
CHR. *See* Committee on Human Relations
Christian, Caye, 42
Christianity, 12, 15, 19–20, 22, 25
CIC. *See* Commission on Interracial Cooperation
Citizens Council on City Planning (CCCP), 82, 100
Citizens Council on Democratic Rights (CCDR), 56
Citizens Emergency Committee (CEC), 105
City Wide Interracial Committee (CWIC), 37, 80–81
civil rights movement, 3–4, 56, 60–61, 63, 92, 102, 104–6, 108, 116, 125, 130, 135
Civil War, 6, 9, 11–12, 26, 111
Clark, Joseph Sill, 46, 51, 61, 104, 108, 120
Clark, Wiley, 97–98
class. *See* middle class; working class
clergymen, 9–11, 20, 22, 37, 71, 91, 125, 129
Cold War, 45, 54–57
Colored Protective Association (CPA), 15
Commission on Interracial Cooperation (CIC), 14–18, 23
Committee for a Free City College (CFCC), 50
Committee on Community Tensions (CCT), 95
Committee on Democracy in Housing (CDH), 7, 88–89, 93–97, 122
Committee on Equal Housing Opportunities (CEHO), 88, 95, 102, 104, 106–9
Committee on Human Relations (CHR), 89, 97–98, 101–3, 106–7, 120, 125, 128, 130–31, 134
Committee on Public Housing Planning (CPHP), 94–95
Committee on Race Relations (CRR), 15, 18–19, 22–23, 28, 32
Committee on School and Community Tensions, 39
communism, 77, 93

Communist Party United States of America (CPUSA), 18
Communists, 51, 55–56, 76, 97
Community Action Program (CAP), 106
Community College of Philadelphia, 6, 63, 67, 134
CommUNITY program. *See* educational programs
Concord Park, 91
"Conference of Organizations on Human Rights," 92
Congress of Industrial Organizations (CIO), 117
Congress of Racial Equality (CORE), 62
Council on Equal Job Opportunities (CEJO), 88, 107, 117–31, 133
CPA. *See* Colored Protective Association
CPHP. *See* Committee on Public Housing Planning
CPUSA. *See* Communist Party United States of America
Crozer Conference, 49
CRR. *See* Committee on Race Relations
Cunningham, E. Luther, 6, 25, 30, 50, 63, 78, 80, 99, 115–16, 120
CWIC. *See* City Wide Interracial Committee

defense industry. *See* industry
Democratic Party, 4, 6–7, 9, 22, 44, 46–47, 50, 56, 80, 92, 98–99, 103, 120, 122
demographic transformation, 58, 123–24
Dennis, Shirley, 134
desegregation: housing, 89, 92, 103; school, 6, 27, 49, 52, 60–61, 64–65, 67
Dilworth, Richardson, 46, 61–62, 64, 99, 102, 104, 108, 120
direct action, 21, 45, 47, 60–62, 114, 128
discrimination: economic, 75; employment, 34, 114, 131; housing, 7, 51, 68, 73, 84, 102–3; job, 119, 121, 125–27, 131; labor, 51, 113, 115, 117, 121, 128; local, 16; racial, 11, 34, 45, 52, 61, 68, 72, 74, 80, 105–6, 111, 127; workforce, 7

Index 173

disenfrachisement, 26
Dolbeare, Cushing, 105-9, 134
Doll Library, 32, 39, 52
"Don't Buy Where You Can't Work" campaign, 75, 115, 125
"Double V" campaign, 34, 41
Drake, St. Claire, 30
Drew, John, 113
Du Bois, Rachel Davis, 28, 72
Du Bois, W. E. B., 5, 10-11, 20, 29, 45, 54, 68-69, 111
Duckrey, Tanner, 36, 39, 50

economic discrimination. *See* discrimination
economic equality. *See* equality
economic justice, 113, 125-26
education, 5-6, 11, 29, 33, 36, 39-40, 44-45, 48-50, 52-53, 58-59, 63, 76, 95, 120, 135; desegregated, 67; higher, 44, 49-50, 62; inequality, 66; integrated, 27, 52, 66; intercultural, 28, 34, 36, 39-40, 49, 53, 62-63, 135; public, 26-28, 34, 49, 59, 64, 67; quality, 66-67; segregated, 26-27, 48, 52-53, 61-62, 64, 66-67, 95
Educational Equality League (EEL), 34, 52-53, 61
educational home rule, 61-64
Educational Policy and Planning Committee (EPPC), 49, 58
educational programs, 6-7, 25, 30, 32, 39, 41, 43-45, 49, 57, 62-63, 69, 84, 89, 108, 115-16, 120, 122-23, 126; Arrow program, 32, 52, 58, 89, 133; CommUNITY program, 42; High School Fellowship program, 37-39, 47-48, 54-55, 58, 60, 84, 136; Units for Unity, 35-39, 42, 81, 85
EEL. *See* Educational Equality League
employment. *See* Fair Employment Practice Commission; Philadelphia Fair Employment Practice Ordinance
employment discrimination. *See* discrimination
employment equality. *See* equality
EPPC. *See* Educational Policy and Planning Committee
equality, 23, 40, 51; economic, 38; employment, 7, 38, 76, 116, 128; gender, 54, 76; racial, 9, 11-12, 14, 22, 75, 128

Fagan, Maurice, 24, 32-33, 39-41, 43-44, 46, 50-52, 63-64, 66, 80-83, 86-88, 95, 99-102, 104, 109, 117, 119, 122, 131, 133-34
Fair Employment Practice Commission, 46, 116
Fair Housing Commission (FHC), 102
fair housing ordinance, 101-2, 107
Families for Fellowship, 57-58
fascism, 24, 34, 40, 76
Fauset, Arthur Huff, 16, 20, 24, 28, 76, 115, 117
Fellowship Commission, 3, 6-7, 33-34, 36-37, 39-47, 49-53, 55-56, 58, 61-66, 79-89, 92-96, 99-102, 104-5, 107, 109, 117-22, 124-27, 129-31, 133-36
"fellowship corners," 41
Fellowship Farm, 52-53, 57, 90, 126, 130, 133
Fellowship House, 3, 6-7, 25-26, 31-32, 34-39, 42-55, 57-66, 79-82, 84-86, 89-93, 97-98, 100, 102, 107, 115, 117, 119-20, 122, 126, 130, 133-36
FHC. *See* Fair Housing Commission
Fine, John S., 122
Fletcher, Benjamin Harrison, 112
food service industry. *See* industry
Four Hundred Ministers, 128
Frazier, E. Franklin, 29
Freedman, Abraham, 50, 83, 86
Friends Cooperative Housing, 91
Friends Suburban Housing (FSH), 103

gender equality. *See* equality
gender-based division of labor, 54
Girard College, 53, 65
Goode, W. Wilson, 107

G.O.P. *See* Republican Party
Gowens, Henry L., 82
GPM. *See* Greater Philadelphia Movement
Gray, William, Jr., 88, 91, 94–95, 99, 122
Grays Ferry, 71
"Great American Teams," 41
Great Depression, 18, 22, 30, 74
Great Migration, 6, 10–11, 13–14, 27, 74, 129
Greater Philadelphia Movement (GPM), 60–62
Greenbelt Knoll, 91
Greenfield, Albert M., 46, 59
Greenfield, Elizabeth "Bunny," 59, 62
Greenfield Report, 59
Gruenberg, Frederick, 86
Gweled, Bryn, 91

Hall, Prathia, 63
Harris, Abram, 29
Harrisburg, Pennsylvania, 63, 67, 69, 71, 101, 122
Hate Incorporated, 42
Haynes, George Edmund, 13–15, 19–20, 40, 90
Hayre, Ruth Wright, 40
Herman, Elaine, 136
High School Fellowship program. *See* educational programs
higher education. *See* education
Hill, Leslie Pinckney, 16
Home and School Association, 58, 65
hospitality industry. *See* industry
housing: black, 71–73, 75–77, 81, 101, 107; city, 72, 108; integrated, 7, 16, 67–68, 71, 75, 79, 81–83, 85, 87–88, 90–92, 94–99, 101–5, 107, 109–10; new, 72, 74–75, 78–81, 83, 92, 95–96, 98, 104; private, 72, 82–85, 87–89, 94, 102, 110; public, 75–79, 81–82, 84, 87–89, 93–95, 98–100, 102, 106, 108–10; segregated, 6, 49, 68, 71–73, 76, 79–80, 84–88, 93–95, 98, 100–103, 105, 107–8, 110, 114
housing code, 69, 72, 76, 89, 95–96, 108

housing conditions, 69, 72–73, 75, 81, 106, 108
housing desegregation. *See* desegregation
housing discrimination. *See* discrimination
housing policy, 88, 94, 103, 105
Houston, Charles Hamilton, 29, 48, 117

ILD. *See* International Labor Defense
industrial sector, 123
Industrial Workers of the World (IWW), 112
industry: defense, 78, 116; food service, 125; hospitality, 125
integrated education. *See* education
integrated housing. *See* housing
integrated neighborhoods. *See* neighborhoods
integrated schools. *See* schools
integration, 12, 67, 125–26, 128
intercultural education. *See* education
International Labor Defense (ILD), 18
interracial civil rights movement, 5–8, 11, 26, 36, 39, 45–46, 57, 62, 64, 67, 72–73, 78, 106, 110–11, 119, 128, 130–31
interracial civil rights organizations, 3, 22, 68, 108–9, 131
interracial movement, 6, 8, 17, 22, 26, 50, 60, 63, 67, 72, 81–82, 128
Irish working class. *See* working class

JADC. *See* Jewish Anti-Defamation Council
James, Dorothy Biddle, 35
James Weldon Johnson Homes, 77
JCMH. *See* Joint Committee on Minority Housing
JCRC. *See* Jewish Community Relations Committee
Jewish Anti-Defamation Council (JADC), 46
Jewish community, 25, 64
Jewish Community Relations Committee (JCRC), 42

Jews, 9, 24–25, 30, 33, 35, 37–38, 41–42, 46–48, 84
Jim Crow, 12
job discrimination. *See* discrimination
Job Opportunities for Youth (JOY), 129
Johnson, Amos, 133
Johnson, Charles S., 21, 40
Johnson, James Weldon, 36, 77
Johnson, Lee, 87
Johnson, Mordecai, 22, 29, 54
Joint Committee on Minority Housing (JCMH), 106–7
JOY. *See* Job Opportunities for Youth
Juanita Park, 97

Kensington, 107
King, Diana, 63
King, Martin Luther, Jr., 3–4, 54, 60, 65, 130

labor, 4–5, 7, 13, 18, 20, 33–34, 51, 64, 76–78, 92, 111–23, 126–27
labor activism, 126, 131
labor discrimination. *See* discrimination
labor dispute, 118
labor market, 5, 7, 111
labor movement, 126, 128
labor unions, 111–12, 116–17, 120, 122–23, 126
Latif, Mohammed, 57, 62, 64
Layten, S. W., 70
Le Boutillier, Sylvia "Boots," 38
Leader, George, 101, 122
Levitt, William, 85, 93
Levittown, 85, 93–94, 101
Licorsish, Joshua, 105
local discrimination. *See* discrimination
Locke, Alain, 28–29, 36
lynching, 9–10, 12–13, 16, 18, 29, 112. *See also* anti-lynching

Mann, Frederic, 59
manufacturing sector, 13, 15, 78, 112, 123
Marine Transport Workers (MTW), 112–13

Martin, Isadore, 16, 70
Massiah, Frederick, 35, 57, 113
Maxwell, C. W., 126
Mboya, Tom, 126
McBride, Thomas, 61, 63, 127
McGarry, Anna, 37, 88, 97, 120
McWilliams, Carey, 40
Meloney, William Brown, 72
middle class: black, 8, 18, 27–28, 43, 62, 77; white, 58, 73, 99, 108
Milgram, Morris, 91, 100, 120
Millen, Herbert, 27
Montgomery, Dorothy Schoell, 81–83, 86–87, 90, 94–95, 98–99, 102, 104–6
Moore, Carolyn Davenport, 34
Moore, Cecil, 62, 65–66, 104, 128
MTW. *See* Marine Transport Workers
multiculturalism, 3, 5–7
Mumford, Lewis, 73
Myers, William, 101
Myrdal, Gunnar, 40

Nation of Islam, 66
National Association for the Advancement of Colored People (NAACP), 3, 11–12, 16–18, 29, 32, 34–35, 48, 52–53, 56, 61–62, 64–66, 70, 74–75, 77, 79, 82, 86, 88, 92, 94, 99–100, 102, 104, 113, 116–19, 124, 127–28
National Association of Colored Women (NACW), 17–18
National Negro Congress (NNC), 23–24, 55, 75–78, 115, 117
Neff, Joseph, 68–69
Negro Migration Committee, 70
neighborhood associations, 97
neighborhood development, 110
Neighborhood Fellowship, 47, 57, 84
neighborhood organizations, 108
neighborhood schools. *See* schools
neighborhoods, 31–32, 35, 47–49, 63, 80, 83–84, 89–90, 92, 94–97, 99–100, 103–4, 106–7, 110, 123; black, 24, 62, 74, 88, 94, 118; city, 73, 95; decrepit, 73;

176   Index

integrated, 100, 109; racially tense, 25, 31, 39, 95; segregated, 109; white, 71, 73–74, 81–82, 96–99, 104, 107, 109–10
Nelson, Alice Dunbar, 28
Newman, Bernard, 69–73, 75, 77, 79, 81, 105
NNC. *See* National Negro Congress
North Philadelphia. *See* Philadelphia, Pennsylvania
Northeast Philadelphia. *See* Philadelphia, Pennsylvania
Northeast United Services, 99
Northwest Philadelphia. *See* Philadelphia, Pennsylvania

Octavia Hall Association (OHA), 68, 100
OIC. *See* Opportunities Industrialization Centers
Operation Green Grass, 65
Operation Native Son, 129
Opportunities Industrialization Centers (OIC), 130

PACH. *See* Philadelphia Advisory Committee on Housing
pacifism, 12, 54
Parker, John J., 17
Parrish, Helen, 68
Paschkis, Victor, 107
PCC. *See* Philadelphia Charter Commission
PCHR. *See* Philadelphia Commission on Human Relations
Peace Corps, 62
Penney, Marjorie, 6, 23–24, 30–33, 35, 37–39, 43, 46, 48, 53–55, 57–58, 60, 66, 78, 80, 84, 90, 97, 102, 107, 115–16, 126, 130, 133–34
Pennsylvania Equal Rights Council, 101
Pennsylvania State Temporary Commission of the Conditions of the Urban Colored Population, 37, 80
PHA. *See* Philadelphia Housing Association

Philadelphia, Pennsylvania: Center City, 21–22, 31, 38, 41, 68, 99, 103, 114, 119, 124–25, 130; North, 25, 31, 47, 53, 57, 59, 62–64, 74–75, 77, 79, 88, 92, 104–5, 108, 128–30; Northeast, 80, 85, 91, 99; Northwest, 71; Seventh Ward, 10, 68–69; South, 31, 38, 70–71, 81, 110; West, 22, 43, 71, 94–95, 107, 115
Philadelphia Advisory Committee on Housing (PACH), 75
Philadelphia Board of Education, 29, 52–53, 59, 66, 135
Philadelphia Charter Commission (PCC), 50
Philadelphia Childhood Project, 39
Philadelphia Commission on Human Relations (PCHR), 51
Philadelphia Fair Employment Practice Ordinance, 120
Philadelphia Housing Association, 3, 6–7, 11, 34, 70–73, 76, 79–83, 85–87, 89, 92–93, 95, 98–100, 102, 105–10, 131, 134, 136
Philadelphia Independent, 114
Philadelphia Rapid Transit Employees Union (PRTEU), 117–18
Philadelphia school district, 6, 26–28, 33–34, 36, 39–40, 42, 49–50, 53–54, 56, 58, 60–61, 65, 129, 135–36
Philadelphia Transit Company (PTC), 117–18
Philadelphia Tribune, 114
Phillips, Walter, 44, 79, 98, 120
Pickett, Clarence, 21, 122, 125
political coalitions, 7
political corruption, 11, 46, 50
Powdermaker, Hortense, 40
prejudice, 8, 19, 23–24, 38–40, 55, 90, 99, 120
private housing. *See* housing
Progressivism, 5–6, 8, 10–11, 25, 68–69, 128
PRTEU. *See* Philadelphia Rapid Transit Employees Union
public housing. *See* housing

Index 177

public policy, 6–7, 29, 87, 105, 136
Public Works Administration (PWA), 75

Quaker activists, 6, 12, 16, 25, 54, 72–73, 103
Quakerism, 5, 8, 12, 17
Quakers, 6, 8, 11–13, 15–17, 19–20, 23, 48, 51, 72–73, 105, 113

race relations, 3–5, 10–22, 24–25, 27–30, 33–36, 39–43, 53, 59–60, 70, 72–74, 76, 78–79, 81, 84–85, 87, 90, 94, 113, 115, 117, 119, 122, 135–36
race riots, 10–13, 36, 71, 111, 119
Race Street Committee, 16
racial conflict, 5, 11, 16, 32, 34, 37, 42, 116
racial discrimination. *See* discrimination
racial equality. *See* equality
racial tension, 3, 13, 25, 31–32, 34–38, 45, 66, 79, 84, 86, 89, 97, 101, 111–12, 118, 135. *See also* neighborhoods
racism, 4, 6, 10–11, 17–19, 23–24, 27, 29, 32, 34–35, 37–38, 40–41, 46–47, 70, 73, 75, 81, 85, 87, 89–90, 103, 105, 114–15, 118, 130
radio, 24, 34, 41–42, 45, 87, 121, 136
Rafsky, William, 99
Randolph, A. Phillip, 116, 130
Rawlins, Gladys, 32
Red Scare, 55–56, 92, 112
Red Summer, 13–15, 42
"red-lining," 88
Reform Democrats, 6. *See also* Democratic Party
Religious Fellowship, 47, 59
rent strikes, 76. *See also* strikes
Republican Party, 4, 9–10, 22, 27, 44, 46, 51, 61, 82, 85–86, 102, 114, 120, 122
restrictive covenants, 72, 82, 84, 87
Rhodes, E. Washington, 27, 76–77, 80, 114
Richard Allen Homes, 79, 84, 109
Rizzo, Frank, 66, 110
Rosenbloom, Susan, 135–36
Rosner, Connie, 38

Samuel, Bernard, 36–37, 44, 46, 86, 118, 135
satyagraha, 54

Schermer, George, 105
Schoell, Dorothy. *See* Montgomery, Dorothy Schoell
school board, 28, 49, 64, 66
school desegregation. *See* desegregation
school district. *See* Philadelphia school district
school reform, 59, 63
school system, 37, 39, 43, 52–53, 58, 61–64
schoolchildren, 6, 28, 35, 37, 52, 59, 67
schools, 6–7, 18, 26–28, 30–31, 39–40, 52–53, 60–65, 67, 73, 133, 136; black, 12, 26–27, 49, 61; elementary, 27–28, 35, 89; high, 28–29, 38, 40, 54–55, 58, 66; integrated, 26, 40, 53, 61–62, 64, 66–67; junior high, 28; neighborhood, 49, 67; parochial, 66; private, 34; professional, 29; public, 26–27, 34, 37, 39, 49, 52–53, 58; segregated, 27, 38, 49; summer, 20–21, 32; white, 26–28, 49, 61. *See also* Committee on School and Community Tensions; desegregation; education; educational programs; Home and School Association; Philadelphia school district
Schrieber, Julius, 42
SCLC. *See* Southern Christian Leadership Conference
segregation, 9–10, 12–14, 16, 18, 22, 26–27, 29, 34, 48–49, 52, 59–61, 112, 114–16, 125; education, 26–27, 48, 52–53, 61–62, 64, 66–67, 95; housing, 6, 49, 68, 71–73, 76, 79–80, 84–88, 93–95, 98, 100–103, 105, 107–8, 110, 114; schools, 27, 38, 39; spatial, 68, 73
Seventh Ward. *See* Philadelphia, Pennsylvania
sharecroppers, 21–22
Shedd, Mark, 65
Shepard, Lorenzo, Jr., 125
Shepard, Marshal, 22, 46, 75, 115
Shorter, Charles, 119, 124
Shubin, Max, 35, 59
Sinatra, Frank, 26

Singing City Choir, 48
SNCC. *See* Student Nonviolent Coordinating Committee
social change, 6, 15, 18–19, 98, 109
Social Gospel movement, 5, 8, 12, 19
South Philadelphia. *See* Philadelphia, Pennsylvania
Southern Christian Leadership Conference (SCLC), 60–61
Southern Tenant Farmers Union (STFU), 22
spatial segregation. *See* segregation
Spaulding, Theodore, 35, 86, 88
Speakers' Bureau, 30, 35, 38–39, 42–43, 78
Stahl, Ben, 127
Steinberg, Frank, 110
Stockholm Peace Petition, 54–55, 57
Stoddard, Alexander, 34, 36, 39–40
Stonorov, Oscar, 86, 92
strikes, 112, 118–19. *See also* rent strikes
Student Nonviolent Coordinating Committee (SNCC), 61
Sullivan, Leon, 125
Sullivan, Louis, 130
Swarthmore College, 5, 12, 19, 21, 105

Tacony Creek, 80–81
Tate, James, 104
Temin, Annette, 59
Tenants League of Philadelphia, 76, 78
Thorp, Jane, 99
Tobias, Channing, 30
"Tolerance Trios," 30
Tomkins, Helen Stark, 51
Trowbridge, George, 49, 88
Turner, Anne, 110

Udell, Val, 133
unions. *See* labor unions
Units for Unity. *See* educational programs
Urban League, 11, 13, 53, 74, 106, 128, 130

Valor Knows No Creed, 41
veterans, 42, 83, 87
Vietnam War, 7, 109

Wagner-Ellender-Taft bill, 87
Wagner-Steagall Act, 77
Walker, Randolph, 31, 48, 135–36
Wall, Lonnie, 43
Wallace, Stuart, 91
War on Poverty, 106
Washington, Booker T., 10
Watson, Goldie, 119
Welsh, William Henry, 33–34
Wentzel, Fred, 19–20, 22, 35, 74, 115
West Philadelphia. *See* Philadelphia, Pennsylvania
WFIL, 42
White, Walter, 17–18, 116
white flight, 71, 89, 98
white middle class. *See* middle class
white schools. *See* schools
white working class. *See* working class
Wilcox, William, 62
Williams, James E., 129
Winnet, Nochem, 86
WIP, 41–42
Within Our Gates, 42
Wobblies. *See* Industrial Workers of the World
Wood, Lloyd, 122
Woofter, Thomas, Jr., 73
workforce discrimination. *See* discrimination
working class: black, 31, 62; Irish, 20; white, 31, 65, 82, 97–99, 103, 107, 110
World War I, 11–15, 71, 79, 111
World War II, 3–5, 34, 36, 40, 42, 45–46, 49, 78, 93
Wright, Anne, 49
Wright, Rev. R. R., 15
Wynn, Walter, 52–53, 95, 100, 104, 122–25, 127–29, 131

Young Peoples Interracial Fellowship (YPIF), 20–25, 28–32, 35, 37, 46, 55, 60, 74, 76–78, 114–16

CPSIA information can be obtained at www.ICGtesting.com
Printed in the USA
BVOW03*2047070514

352475BV00003B/3/P

9 781628 460025